THE LIVING LIGHT DIALOGUE

Volume 19

Reproduction of the cover image of the
1972 edition of *The Living Light*

[*See the appendix for a discussion of the image's symbolism.*]

THE LIVING LIGHT DIALOGUE

Volume 19

Through the mediumship of
Richard P. Goodwin

Living Light Books

The Living Light Dialogue Volume 19
Copyright © 2024 Serenity Association
Through the mediumship of Richard P. Goodwin.

All rights reserved. No portion of this book may be reproduced—electronically, mechanically, or via internet transmission—without advance, express written permission of the publisher except in the case of brief quotations embodied in critical articles and reviews. No derivative work—games, supplemental material, video—may be created without advance, express written permission of the publisher. For information address Living Light Books, P.O. Box 4187, San Rafael, CA 94913-4187.

Cover design copyright © 2024 by Serenity Association
Cover photograph by Serenity Association, 2024; copyright © 2024 by Serenity Association.

www.livinglight.org

Library of Congress Control Number 2007929762
ISBN: 978-1-947199-47-7

FIRST EDITION

This volume of teachings is dedicated to the spirit friends who brought to Earth the Living Light Philosophy. With eternal gratitude, we pray that we may demonstrate these principles and continue to bring to publication these teachings.

CONTENTS

Acknowledgment ix
Preface xi
Introduction xv
Design Class 1 3
Design Class 2 43
Design Class 3 53
Design Class 4 81
The Art of Evolution 105
Special Seminar 1A 125
Class January 15, 1983 139
Class January 17, 1983 141
Class January 19, 1983 149
Class January 21, 1983 155
Class January 23, 1983 163
Class January 26, 1983 179
Class January 27, 1983 183
Class January 28, 1983 185
Class January 29, 1983 207
Class January 30, 1983 209
Class January 31, 1983 219
Class February 1, 1983 221
Class February 2, 1983 237
Class February 4, 1983 249
Class February 5, 1983 263
Class February 6, 1983 267
Class February 7, 1983 289
Class February 8, 1983 297
Class February 9, 1983 301
Class February 11, 1983 307

Class February 13, 1983	319
Class February 14, 1983	331
Class February 15, 1983	333
Class February 16, 1983	347
Class February 17, 1983	351
Class February 18, 1983	361
Class February 20, 1983	371
Class February 21, 1983	383
Class February 22, 1983	385
Class February 23, 1983	393
Class February 24, 1983	399
Class February 25, 1983	401
Class February 26, 1983	411
Class February 27, 1983	413
Class February 28, 1983	425
Class March 1, 1983	429
Class March 2, 1983	435
Class March 3, 1983	461
Class March 4, 1983	465
Class March 6, 1983	473
Class March 7, 1983	483
Addendum	491
Appendix	495
Notes	509

ACKNOWLEDGMENT

Grateful acknowledgment is made to the many friends and associates for invaluable aid in compiling this book, for their helpful suggestions, for their loyal interest and encouragement.

Special acknowledgment is due to those who painstakingly and selflessly transcribed and proofread the text.

PREFACE

It was through the mediumship of the Serenity Association founder, Mr. Richard P. Goodwin, that a philosophy known as the Living Light was given in more than 700 classes over a twenty-five-year period.

To be specific, the philosophy was imparted through Mr. Goodwin by a magistrate who had lived on Earth some 8,000 years ago. The former magistrate is known to Living Light students as "the Wise One," and he narrated the journey of his soul on the other side of life, the experiences—especially the difficulties—he encountered in having to face himself, as well as the teachings he earned to help himself through the realms in which he traveled. It was his decision to share the teachings with souls on both sides of "the curtain."

Prior to the advent of the Wise One, Mr. Goodwin had prayed for a teacher from the realms of light. Mr. Goodwin, since age fourteen, had been the instrument through which spirit was able to communicate with those seeking help. But he saw that his mediumship brought only temporary solace, because the people he was trying to help soon became fascinated with the phenomena and ignored the help that spirit was imparting. He prayed for someone who would bring forth teachings that would benefit any soul seeking a path to a greater awareness of himself and of God.

His prayers were answered in 1964 when the Wise One came through for the first time. Mr. Goodwin, at first apprehensive about what this new teacher would impart, was taken into deep trance and not able to control what was being revealed through him. Upon hearing the recorded classes afterward, however, he became convinced of the goodness of the teacher and of the value of the simple, beautiful teachings. This, then, was the beginning of the Living Light Philosophy given to Earth through the mediumship of Richard P. Goodwin.

In carrying out the request of the Wise One and Mr. Goodwin, students of the Serenity Association transcribed from audiotape the classes that had been brought through. Because most are in the form of teacher-student interaction, the classes became known as *The Living Light Dialogue*; and the students were instructed to publish the classes as a multi-volume set of the Living Light Philosophy. *Volume 1* was published in the autumn of 2007.

The present volume contains forty-seven individual classes, which cover a wide range of topics. The tone of these classes also varies considerably: some are very formal; others, quite informal. All the classes in this volume were given at the Serenity temple and they were given only to students of the philosophy, and some were only given to a very small group of advanced students. Most of the classes have not been available in any form since the day they were given.

One class in this volume is the last wishes of Mr. Goodwin. The prospect of Mr. Goodwin passing on was very real in January of 1983, and a recording was made to guide his students in the event that he did pass on. However, we were indeed fortunate that he remained on Earth and served the Spirit for six more years. On February 24, 1989, he passed on. (*Volume 20* will contain the second recording of his last wishes, which was given on September 21, 1988.)

Many of these classes were recorded on a microcassette recorder, and in many of the recordings, the recorder was frequently stopped and started, often on the guidance of the spirit. That is, a sentence or two would be recorded, and then the recorder was stopped. The discussion would continue without being recorded, and, moments or minutes later, a few more sentences were recorded. The instances when the recorder was stopped are indicated by a line of text with five asterisks. Some classes that originally recorded more extensive interactions between the students and the teacher were edited, at a later date, to remove some of the more personal topics. And in a few classes, the entire discussion was recorded and survives unedited. Due to the editing that occurred, the order of the teachings, as presented in this publication, may not be the order in which they were originally given. In several classes, the personal notes of students who were present in the class were consulted to resolve issues and to complete partial recordings.

Although considerable effort has been made to accurately date these classes, there is the possibility that they may not have been assigned to the correct date. A microcassette tape may have been labelled with one date, but the actual recording may have a different or even multiple dates. In addition, there is no guarantee that all the teachings on a dated tape were actually given on that date: a recording could have been added days or even weeks later, and the tape just happened to be the one that the recording technician picked when he was instructed to begin recording.

The classes are presented in chronological order and range in date from October 10, 1981, to March 7, 1983.

The foundation of the classes—the foundation of the Living Light Philosophy itself—is the Law of Personal Responsibility which states, in part, that we are responsible for all our experiences, and that our experiences are the return of the laws that we have established with our thoughts, acts, and deeds. Through greater awareness of our thoughts and by exercising our divine right of choice, we may choose to establish laws of greater harmony and goodness.

The Living Light Dialogue teaches that we have come to Earth to learn the lessons that are necessary to free us from the dictates and limits of our own thoughts and judgments, which are the mental patterns that we follow through our own lack of awareness and are so very potent, forceful, and limiting. These teachings guide us in making the necessary changes in our thinking in order to free ourselves from those patterns and to express our soul consciousness.

The choice of guiding the direction of our life, as stated by the Wise One when he speaks of being with a person, place, or thing, is, in essence, of being in this world and not a part of this world. He further explains that no matter what experiences we encounter, no matter what we do or do not do, we—our spirit— may view the experience in objectivity from a soul level of consciousness where peace reigns supreme.

The teachings of this volume help us to restore harmony or balance in our life by flooding the consciousness with spiritual affirmations and prayers, a few of which can be found in the appendix. When reason is restored, by balancing our sense functions with our soul faculties, we will consciously experience peace. Without annihilating our ego or our sense functions, we will find a pathway of expression for our soul. Where there was once disturbance, now there is acceptance. Where there was disease, now there is poise. And where there was hopelessness and despair, now there is reason, divine neutrality; and peace shows the way.

If you make the effort to apply these laws, such as, "If man is a law unto himself, what are you doing with the law that you are?", and demonstrate the wisdom of patience, the truth of this philosophy will be your living demonstration.

As the teacher states in CC 130, "My journey of many centuries and much experience has brought me here to Earth to share with you these simple teachings that have come as the effect of a long, long, long journey. Let not *your* journey be so long in the realms of illusion. For it is not necessary for you. For in your evolution, you have earned an awakening. But it is up to you to do something that is constructive and worthwhile."

INTRODUCTION

[This introduction was written by Mr. Goodwin and originally appeared in The Living Light, *which were the first teachings of the Living Light Philosophy published in book form. The entire text of* The Living Light *was republished in* The Living Light Dialogue, Volume 1.*]*

"Think, children. Think more often and think more deeply."

The teachings in this book were given as a progressive series of lessons to a group of four students who were sitting for spiritual unfoldment with me beginning in January of 1964. The communications were regular until October of that year, when nearly a seven-year silence ensued, and resumed in 1971 to the present. They were received in three ways by me as a channel. The main text was taped from a direct control of my voice in deep trance at special sittings of our group, during which I had no experience of the voice or what was being transmitted. A few scattered verses were given independently when I was privileged to see and hear our teacher clairvoyantly. I have also been a channel for this communicant when speaking from the podium at church and in answering difficult questions at our public seminars.

Nearly all we know about our teacher is contained in the lectures. He reports that he had tried for sixteen years to break through an interference barrier that the channel had to deep trance. When our conditions were in resonance with his patient wisdom, he came through ready to teach his understanding. I have seen him as an old man dressed in white with long flowing white hair. He has blue eyes, slightly smiling and deeply compassionate. I have always called him the Old Man. The students liked to call him the Wise One. He is surely one of those often called a Teacher of Light. I do not know his country, although he indicated at one time that he was from 6000 B.C., and a form of a judge in his time.

The text is often difficult, but it is complete, having been transcribed word for word from the original tapes recording the trance voice. It is presented with a minimum of punctuation to be freer for the individual interpretation of each reader. The lessons given before the long silence are phrased with many allegories often paradoxical. There are repetitions and renewals of theme, but it is explained that if an understanding is not perceived, compassion dictates that it be said again. Some of the topics have but a simple mention with little development but all are revealed, we are told, according to merit.

The Old Man is a fine teacher. He has in a hundred ways intertwined his allegory, progressive explanations, unfolding exercises, and timely references to reach a multitude of levels of individual understanding. A notable change is his more direct style of presentation beginning in 1971.

There is an endearing intimacy of person that can be felt through his lectures, a meaningful and loving encounter with a wise friend. Like an old man, he makes a mistake and conscientiously corrects himself a few paragraphs later. He listens often and carefully to our earnest discussions of his words. He consults with a group of experts on evolution and cites their learning in his lesson. His use of the direct address "children" or "my children" is not patronizing but infinitely loving and supportive.

A word must be said about the teachings. The Old Man makes clear that his lessons are not dogma, a creed or a narrow way, but simply his own understanding offered to us as a form of instruction to aid us in our own individual progression. When he speaks of Laws, he does not refer to man-made rules or moral traditions but to the cosmic and atomic way-things-are, the natural world of what-is, the universal laws of life, part of the original creative design and through which creation is fulfilled. These laws are beyond the possibility of being changed, suspended, transcended, or destroyed but they are ever a tool of mankind, not his master. First, through our awareness of the universal laws and then slowly through our developed understanding, the powers of creation are accessible to us. Not power over men's minds or circumstances, but power over whatever is selfish and imperfect in ourselves is the way up the eternal ladder of progression. When the Old Man cautions us concerning the Law of Responsibility or gives us a thinking exercise to explore the Law of Identity in a dynamic manner, he prepares us to take another step. And all move in accordance with the Law of What Can Be Borne.

Our teacher shows us how the two worlds are drawn together. In his realm, he describes, there is a great diversity of thought, many schools of understanding; but the Light is always known by the Light. Because of the interdependence of the two realms, listening to our discussions helped to clarify his teaching to others on his side of the curtain. His love and gratitude he humbly equates with ours.

The lessons to be perceived are not new, they are very old, but they are new to certain levels of our being. I would personally advise the reader, after reading this volume of discourses in full, to make a daily habit (or when there is a feeling or need) to sit quietly with the book. Open it at random and be guided to the Light by the passage that is there for the day. This technique is still used by the original students who were given the lessons and by many students after them who have studied in unfolding classes with me through these teachings.

Go beyond the words into feeling, into the immediate meanings for you. Touch into the inspiration that flows into the form of this book. It is from the Divine.

RICHARD P. GOODWIN
San Geronimo, California
June, 1972

Individual Classes

Design Class 1

Good evening, class.

This evening's class, as you know, is the beginning of understanding the fundamental design of the human body. There is one basic design of the body, male or female. That design is the double triangle, commonly known as the hourglass. There are three distortions of the basic design: the square, the upright tent, and the upside-down tent.

Now we will begin our class this evening, if you will come forward, and I will show you the proper design of the human body. If you'll just face the class, please. Now if you'll put your, if you'll raise your arms high, spread your feet equal. And would you come forward and make a measurement, please? Measure from the left point of the fingers to the tip of the toes. I'll hold that, you measure down there. *[It seems that one student stepped forward as a volunteer to be measured and another student, who was aided by the teacher, made the measurements with a tape measure.]*

Eighty-seven?

No. It's shorter. You're too high here.

Eighty-six.

Eighty-six. Mark down eighty-six, please. Eighty-six. Now this other arm will measure equal, or should. Put the ruler down at the bottom, [Student R]. Get a measure. To the toe.

Eighty-six. [Student R reports.]

Eighty-six. Fine. Now where that point crosses is the center of your body in design. So, mark that point. Did you get that point mark[ed]? Would you come back and get a point marked here, please?

Want to hold that up here? [The student refers to one end of the tape measure.] *OK. Now on the other side. It's clear down here.* [Student R reports.]

That's the point—have you got a cross point?
Yeah.
Are your arms spread equal to your feet?
Back to the other side.
You don't have the measurement.
The cross, the cross is clear down here.

That's right. All right. That is the point which is the center of design for the human body. From that point, everything must flow downwards or upwards.

Now the basic, the most common distortion of the design is the upside-down tent. Now the upside-down tent is simply this: that this portion of the anatomy, you understand, is heavier than this portion of the anatomy. Now that is the basic distortion in design. From the point of where the cross is, everything must flow equally downwards and upwards.

Now the—measurement, please. Now on women especially you measure the hip bone. Come over here and measure the hip bone exact, please. Not the flesh. The bone itself. The hip bone must be measured.

There?

What's your measurement?

Eleven.

One third of that measurement on a woman is proportional bust protrusion.

One third of eleven.

One third of 11 would be 3 3/4, approximately. Now, in reference to the upper part of the anatomy on a woman, she must understand that the measurement from the shoulder—the point of the bust must be dead center between the waist and the tip of the shoulder. In other words, if it's, say, 8 to 9 inches to the point of the bust [from the tip of the shoulder], it must be 8 to 9 inches from the waist to the point of the bust. If not, you are totally out of balance.

Now the number one requirement for women—and I'll save you a lot of time—if you are not willing to have bust support, don't waste your time. Because if your measurement from the top of your shoulder to the point of your breast is not equal from the point of your breast to your waistline, there is no way that you can correct the balance of your anatomy. Now if, for example, you have a bust that are, that extend more than the one third of your actual hip measurement, then you must learn, from design and from color, to correct those changes.

Now every human body has a major beauty asset. Now, for example, would the lady that we are now showing in the design, her most beautiful asset—and surely, she's already aware of it—is her hair. Now we will start with this particular person with the hair. You will notice that the hair is a reddish coloring. You will notice that the forehead is very high. Because the forehead is high, it accentuates the chin, accentuates the nose and gives a lean look. To correct that look, the hair must be brought forward to cover the forehead—do you understand?—and must flow on one side to bring about a fullness to the cheeks and break the sharpness of the chin. That's the first correction. That's the only correction that is needed to correct the facial feature.

The next step is the proportion of the body. Now I'm sure she already knows that the hips have got to be accentuated to balance the shoulders. If you have broad shoulders, then you must accentuate the hipline to bring about the balance for the flow of the entire design of the body.

Thank you very much. You can have a seat now.

Now in reference to how you look and how you want to look, you have to be willing to make various changes in your hair. All coloring must be removed from the hair. There is no coloring that does not harden the hair because it dulls and covers the natural oils of the hair. Consequently, all coloring must be removed from the hair and kept off the hair. Then, hair design is critical, depending on what type of face you have. Now some people—would you come forward? The lady here, please.

Now I spoke to you earlier today.

Uh-huh.

Now there's one thing I do want to mention: if you have passed the age [of] 16, forget about bangs, if you're passed 16. Up until 16, you may wear them. Beyond that point, they're ridiculous. Now, as you know this lady here, basically, had hair down this way and did not show the most beautiful asset that she has: the forehead and the full face. By pulling the hair away from the face and moving—excuse me for messing it up—and moving it around in a swirl and up, that will not only give her height but will accentuate the most beautiful part of her anatomy.

Now each one has a major beauty point. Then, like all of creation, there are what we feel are defects. Now those are the ones that you cover up. Those are the ones that you correct. Now, shoulder-wise, there is not the problem, you see. Her shoulders are not too broad, although in this particular sweater, her shoulders look twice the size. The reason for that [is], though it is a beautiful sweater, the lines are going the wrong way. The lines of the sweater are going outward, which broaden the shoulders. If you have very narrow shoulders, then you can wear lines that go horizontal. If you have broader shoulders and you want lines, they must go vertical. Otherwise, if you will notice here—you'll turn around—the shoulders are much bigger than the hipline; and therefore, it gives a broadening here, which gives to this particular person, at this time, a masculinity that she does not want. Do you understand? The coloring is perfect. The lines are going the wrong way. Had she little, smaller, dinky shoulders, then she would be able to wear lines going horizontal.

Don't take it personal. This is a design class.

Now, first of all, if there was a slight puff, not much, a slight one—do you understand?—this would bring femininity to the shoulder area. You understand? Then, it would balance out with the hips. The only thing, with this sweater, is the lines go the wrong way; the color is perfect. Can you see that?

Uh-huh.

All right. Thank you very much. Now we should start here, let's have you. *[The teacher calls upon a different student.]* I talked to you earlier today.

She did exactly what she needed to do. She put a belt on to accentuate the hips. Now here's one very important note: the wider the belt, the bigger the bust. It's an illusion. If you accentuate the hipline, the waistline, accentuate the hips, you increase the illusion of the size of the bust. So you must always consider that in whatever you wear.

Now you will notice here that she has on a belt. The face shows properly. The drop of the dress is very appropriate. However—turn around—there is one slight thing. What does everyone see? Yes.

Should the points be going down instead of up? Or are you talking about the waistline?

I'm talking about the waistline.

All right. The—

What is wrong with the waistline?

The belt should curve down, maybe, a little bit.

Thank you. Anyone else? What's wrong with the waistline? *[After a pause, the teacher continues.]* Do the hips look rounded or do the hips look square? Do the hips look rounded or do they look boxed?

Square.

Square. [Several students comment.]

They're square. Now her hips are not square. They are very rounded. But because of the design, the illusion is that they're square. One of the things that accentuate the squareness of the hips is the darkness of the belt. Now if that was a white belt, it would help remove the illusion of the square hips. Because white accentuates. So, you see, what this does, it brings a heaviness to the hipline on this particular lined dress. And had the belt been white or of a lighter color or a brighter color, then you would not have the heaviness of the hips; you would not have the box look of the hips. Turn around. Can you see that?

Yes.

Because your hips are not broad.

Uh-huh.

Your hips are not square, but the design—the design of the dress is perfect. The stripes go the wrong way, unless you're willing to put on a white or brighter belt. Now had she put on a V-belt—you see, the lines are Vs?—now had she put on a V-belt of white or light color, picking up the very light bluish-green of the dress, then that would have totally changed the look of the hipline. Thank you very much.

Now let's go ahead, step-by-step, through your whole design. Now you've already seen where the point of your anatomy is. It's much lower than you ever dreamed. That's where it really is. You easily know how to measure [in order] to get an accurate measurement. You know what your bone structure of your hip is. You must have one third of that for your basic bustline; otherwise, you cover it up.

Now, here they have suggested that you make a change in her hairstyle; that she cover the forehead at least down to this point, angling this side to just above the eyebrow, about a half an inch. Pull your hair in the Grecian style, because that's the style in which you look best. Pull it up in the Grecian style.

Now turn around. Not all women can wear the Grecian style. She happens to have the hair and with the styling of the hair around the face, which is beautiful and very simple. Now do you have any questions on your design? And we'll get to the next person.

Not at this time.

Any on your coloring?

OK. I'd like to ask about the color.
The dress is beautiful. It's the wrong color for evening.
Right.
It's a day dress. Should be worn on a bright day. For an evening dress, it needs a different toning. You cannot use yellows for evening. Yellow is an absolute no-no for evening dress, even a street dress. It's a daytime dress. It's a bright dress. It looks very pretty. It's a beautiful design. It's the wrong color for evening. Any other question?
May I ask about accessories? Earrings. What length they should be or size?
That depends—earring length depends on the face of the person. It depends also on the hairstyle.
Uh-huh.
And they change their style; so therefore, the earrings change. The best—now, I'm glad you brought up earrings. Proper dress for a woman should never reveal more that 50 percent of her ear. Evening formal dress or day formal dress should never reveal more than 30 percent maximum of the ear. The ear is not a beauty point. The lobe of the ear—if you must find a beauty point of the ear, it is the lobe of the ear, the lower part of the ear. Now earrings that droop are much more attractive than anything that is bulky, gaudy, that pierces the ear. If you must have an earring that does not droop, then use a pearl or something small of that nature. Don't use those other type of earrings. They're very gaudy. They're very sporty. They're good for twelve- and fifteen-year-olds and that's where it stops. Yes.
I'd also like to know; you mentioned that the bust protrusion should be one third—
One third of the basic hip width.
And is that measured from under the arm or here underneath in the front?
No. It's measured from the bone. You got a bone here.
Right.

The front bone.

OK.

It's measured from here outward.

OK.

And if you don't have one third of your basic hip measurement, then you are not in proportion in the female body. Now if you have more than that, then you dress not to accentuate it. You understand? But you dress, properly, to cover it. Because otherwise, you're out of proportion with your hips. Now is there any other question?

Not right now.

Not right now.

Perhaps some later. Thank you.

Fine. Are there any other questions for the women before we go to the men? We'll go through each one on design. No questions?

Do you want to come up, please, so that they can look at you? *[A male student steps to the front of the class.]*

Now, with a man, it's much more desired—it's much more difficult. It's basically the same design, but they are much more difficult to dress. And it's very simple. The asset on a man is his shoulders. If you don't have the heavy, thick, solid shoulders, then you must dress to accentuate the shoulder. Now to accentuate the shoulder—for he needs to accentuate the shoulder. Turn around and you can see the vest. It's not the droopiest shoulder, but it's not the broad, masculine-look shoulder. To correct that, you either wear epaulettes—you see?—to accentuate it or you wear a design where it has a coloring here to give the shoulder width and strength. Because, you see, if you don't, what happens [is] you have a tent shape. The hips on the man, it comes here as a base shape and goes up to a point. So you don't have a double triangle: two triangles meeting each other. So you must learn to, number one: accentuate the shoulder line on a man. And you do that with dress.

Now one of the things that help, if you don't have solid shoulders on a man, one of the things that help is a turtleneck. But to wear a turtleneck, you must have a long neck, because if you don't have a long neck, you look really like a turtle. *[Several students laugh.]* And the head is just barely sticking out. Thank you very much.

All right. Now who wants to be the first to go through the whole design of their hair, their clothes, their shoes, and down the list? *[After a short pause, the teacher continues.]* [Student S]? It's all right.

Thank you.

You'll be a whole new person when you're through. *[Student S laughs.]* She already knows what to do with her hair. I already talked to her today. She already knows—turn around a moment, please. She already knows that she has broad-looking shoulders. Now because of that, she must not accentuate the shoulders without accentuating the hips. Therefore, by pulling in the waistline, she raises the bust and brings into proportion her shoulders with her hips. So if you have—now she doesn't have real broad shoulders, but they look broad because the hips are not sufficiently accentuated.

Now you'll notice with the dress, though it is very, very pretty, it is open [and] she looks flat-chested. Does anybody agree with that? We won't ask her. Anybody else agree? Not totally flat-chested, but she looks flat-chested. So, if she wants to wear this dress, which is very, very pretty, that means the bustline must increase. Now there's two ways. The bustline increases or she puts some type of a belt to bring it up and accentuate the hipline. Do you see that?

Would the belt be a color? [Student S asks.]

You would have to have a color. You'd have to have a color to accentuate this.

Uh-huh.

You see. Because, surely, you can all see, although she does have a bust, it disappears in the style of the dress and certainly does not match the hips. Yes.

OK. It should, it should be a wide, light-colored belt. Is that correct? [A different student asks.]

No. Because the dress is a total yellow, the best accent she could possibly get with that dress, to really accentuate this and this, is a chocolate brown. You see, then the eye will immediately catch. And by pulling in here with a dark brown, it will accentuate and give her the hourglass shape which is critical to good looks. Without the hourglass shape, you can forget the good looks of the form.

Now is there any other question on that? Did you notice that you looked flatter when you put that dress on?

I wasn't aware so much of that as I was trying to get the waist in by where this fit.

Fine. Now, [did] you have the same look as you had this afternoon in your sweater?

No, I've never found anything that looks . . . I don't know how to describe it.

All right.

Like that sweater.

No. But the only way—that [dress] can look like the sweater.

Uh-huh.

If you have the proper belt and it's pulled in.

Uh-huh.

You see? Then you won't look flat-chested. You're not flat-chested, but she looks flat-chested. And that does not accentuate the hipline and the waist.

She has a brown belt on. [A different student comments.]

Change it. It's reddish, though, but it will give you the idea. Too bad we don't have all of these things here.

It would be great. Thank you. [Student S remarks.]

All right. *[At this point, the volunteer's belt may have been changed.]* It's not too much red. Now does anybody—turn around—now does—turn around—does anybody notice a difference in the hipline?

Uh-huh. [Many students respond.]

Does anyone notice the difference in the bustline?

Yes. Uh-huh. [Again, several students respond]

Turn back around. Do you see the difference? *[The teacher asks Student S.]*

Yes.

You see, you immediately have the illusion that the person is no longer flat-chested. So even with that same dress, all it needs is a dark, deep color to give the division, and so you don't have that just plain, blah look.

I'd like to ask, if, when there's a tie here, is it important not to have so much on the belt, like it—

If you have a tie, you must have an absolute plain belt. If there's any type of tie or design here, then you must have a plain belt. Absolutely plain. If you have no tie or design here, then you can have design in the belt. But be very careful of design in the belt [of] which way the lines are going, because there are lines in all belts.

Now turn around and look in the mirror. How do you like the difference? *[The teacher addresses Student S.]*

It's good. Now would this belt go with this? I mean, is this plain enough in the front?

Let me see the buckle. Yes, that would go. But you should have less red in the brown.

Right.

Deeper on the chocolate side will accentuate more.

And may we ask about sleeve lengths? What it does to us? And the shape of the sleeve?

Absolutely. Short sleeves—now don't forget this—short sleeves, not sleeveless, but short sleeves immediately tend to box you. Immediately. So, if you are slim at the top and you want width, then be sure you check your sleeve length. Because according to shortness of the sleeve is the boxiness of your top part.

Now if you want to slim this down, go to long sleeves or no sleeves. Now the ladies that have small-looking shoulders, you understand, then all they have to do is consider the length of their sleeve and that's how boxy they will get in the illusion. For that's what creation is, is a total illusion.

But that totally changed the dress. Does everybody see that? And it gave her—hold your arms just down to your side, please—it gave her shape that she had lost by the solid color and the drape of the dress.

Now, [are] there any other questions on sleeves or anything else?

Well, if you're trying to minimize your shoulders, but accentuate your bust, would it be long sleeves? [Student S asks.]

Or three quarter [length].

Three quarter.

See, any sleeve that is shorter than the elbow is going to give you the box-look at [the] top. You understand? In other words, it's the upside-down tent look. You see, if it is elbow-length or shorter, you're going to broaden the shoulders. If it is sleeveless or longer than elbow length to the wrist, it's going to slim you in this area: that's the width of your shoulders. So that depends on whether you're making the effort to slim down the width of your shoulders or to broaden the width of your shoulders.

Now we all know that women look more feminine if they don't look like they [have] got the shoulders that a man is supposed to have. Now it depends on how you want to look. If you don't want to be broad up here, you understand, then you must consider that it has to be elbow-length or longer or sleeveless. Turn around—

Thank you.
—so you can see for yourself [in the mirror].
Uh-huh.
If the sleeve came to this point or preferably here—
Uh-huh.
—you would immediately slim the shoulders.
Right.
And not only would you slim the shoulders, you would increase the depth of the bust, for the shorter the sleeve, the broader the shoulder look, the flatter the chest look in the illusion.

Any other questions? *[After a short pause, the teacher continues.]* It's a beautiful dress. And with a belt like that it's really super beautiful.

I'd like to ask about the shape of the skirt, like gathered versus pleats and how big of pleats or A-line.

Short women must be—and short-waisted women—must be extremely careful of gathering because it will make you look fat unless there [are] corrective measures taken with the bustline. Now this is why, if you're not willing to support your bust—you've got to bring it up. If you're not willing to do that, don't waste your time in this class because it's a total waste of energy. It's an absolute total waste. You must bring it up proportionately where, by design, it should be. And that requires, for most all women, support. Does that answer your question, [Student S]?

Well, I'd like to know—
You can look—you look good in a gathered [skirt].
Uh-huh.
Look sideways in the mirror.
Right.
But because you need hips. Now you have hips. They're extremely slim, but you must accentuate them because, you see, if you don't accentuate the hips, your shoulders are too big. There are several things to correct and make your shoulders smaller. One of the indispensable things to do is to broaden the

hips. They must be broadened in order to reduce, along with the length of the sleeve, the style of the dress, in order to reduce the width of the shoulders.

OK.

So, you should do whatever is necessary to broaden the hipline.

OK. Now a straight skirt, if it had a cinched waist, would that still work or would it be—

If it had the proper bodice or belt.

OK.

You see, with her particular shape, she not only needs a wide belt but she preferably needs a bodice that comes up like this. That gives a woman bust, pulls in the waistline, gives the woman hips, and gives her height. That gives height if you are properly dressed. Now if you are very short-waisted, you've got to be very, very careful because instead of giving you the height, it will shorten you. So that's dependent upon the type of bodice that you have; that's dependent upon how the drape of the dress is over your shoulders and the length of the sleeves, and it depends, of course, on your bust being properly supported. Yes.

Now, horizontal lines in the skirt, would that give the illusion of more hip?

It definitely—in this lady it gave the illusion—come here a minute. *[The teacher addresses Student S.]*

Uh-huh.

It gives the total illusion of more width to the hip. The danger is that it gives a square hip. Instead of an hourglass shape, it starts to box the hipline. So, you must be very careful at which way the lines move and you [have] got to be careful of what you put with it.

Stripes are very difficult. Would you come up here, please, with the horizontal sweater lines? *[The teacher asks for another female student to join Student S at the front of the class.]* Both of you turn around that way, please, so I can show them the back of this. Now, pull your hair forward so they can see. Now you notice that lines immediately broaden the shoulders. Immediately broaden the shoulders. So, wearing anything that has lines in it, you've got to be extremely careful, unless you want to have very potent, masculine-looking shoulders.

This is why—see here? Her shoulders are not that wide. They look twice as wide as they actually are simply because the lines are going horizontal. Now women who have very dinky shoulders can broaden their shoulders with this type of design. Women who have shoulders that are sufficient like this, they're over broadened. The lines should come the other way, which would slim the shoulders down immediately. Now [with these] type of lines going here, you've got to do something to break up the square, box-look of the hipline. Thank you very much. Are there any questions on that? *[After a short pause, the teacher continues.]*

Now I would like to say one thing for you. You see this skirt? It's beautiful. To really sharpen that look, a clear white sweater of this style would be perfect. Do you see that? *[The teacher addresses the second volunteer.]*

Uh-huh.

Now you're not to take anything personal if you come to class.

Uh-huh.

But I want you to look in the mirror. Can you see how a white sweater of the identical style would look on her? Are there any questions on that? Can you see that immediately it would have narrowed the shoulders? Hmm?

Uh-huh.

Thank you very much.

May I ask a question?

Certainly. You're up here. You've gone through all that. You ask—yes, you go ahead and ask your questions. *[The teacher addresses the second volunteer.]* You can [be] seated. *[The teacher now addresses Student S.]*

If I wear a light-colored sweater and a dark skirt—
Uh-huh.
—would I need some kind of accent, some kind of color?
You'll need something in the line of a belt or a bodice. *[The teacher pronounces the word* bodice *as bō-dis.]*
Uh-huh.
I think they call them bodice up here. Don't they? *[The teacher pronounces the word* bodice *as bä-dis.]*
That's what I'm familiar with. [A non-volunteer student comments.]
You're familiar with bodice *[bä-dis]*. Well, I'll call them bodice *[bä-dis]* for the Westerners then. Bodice *[bō-dis]* for the Easterners; bodice *[bä-dis]* for the Westerners.[1] You would need an accent at the waist.
At the waist. [The volunteer comments.]
Now if you are wearing white, clear white, with navy blue, the most natural color accent would be bright red. But you are not limited to bright red with navy blue and white. There are other choices. One of the choices—you [have] got to be careful with it—is gray. The right shade of gray. And another of the choices, which is rarely ever seen, is pink. So, with navy blue and white, you can wear certain shades of gray, preferably a pewter gray, or a bright pink. Not an old rose pink, but a bright pink. Either one will accent. You will notice that the gray will not accentuate the hipline nowheres near as [much as] the pink. And the pink will not accentuate the hipline as much as the red. Go ahead with any other questions. *[After a short pause, the teacher continues.]* No questions? You know class doesn't continue [without questions]. Yes.
Could you comment on the pleated skirt and its effect?
The pleated skirt definitely adds weight and heaviness to the body. Therefore, a person, if they want to accentuate the weight here, the lower part, then they can wear a pleated skirt, which is very beautiful. But a pleated skirt should not have a

horizontal striped sweater, unless the person wants to broaden their shoulder line because they have such dinky shoulders.

So, now she would look, as I say, beautiful in an absolute solid white, accentuated with a pink, rather than a red. Because the pink will just give it just enough color contrast to give a hipline, to pull it in and not stand out too much. Can you see that?

Uh-huh. [The volunteer responds.]

I'm not trying to get you to buy a new wardrobe. *[The volunteer laughs.]* You got plenty of clothes. But that particular sweater in pure white in that skirt is beautiful. Does anyone— Yes.

The width of the belt that you recommended, as far as pink, with this particular color contrast, what width would you recommend? [A non-volunteer student asks.]

Not less than two inches and preferably three. Not less than two inches, preferably three.

Thank you.

Because, you see, because of the lines, where's her hips? Where is the waist? You see? The waist has disappeared. The shoulders—turn around just a moment—the shoulders have been accentuated, but where's the waist? There's no waist. Do you understand? It just goes right together. All right? That's what class is all about now.

Now, is there any other question? Earrings. Now, you want height, correct?

Uh-huh. [The volunteer responds.]

Then you cannot wear, unless it's a very small pearl or gold, very dinky in the lobe, you must have something that droops in order to gain height.

Thank you.

These are beautiful earrings. If you want to feel short, they will do the job. This type of earring—can everyone see it?—it shortens. If you're too tall, this is what you wear because it will lower you. If you are short and you want to get tall, then you must have the other type of earring. Now, a drooping earring does not look good on this type of an outfit, even if it's a white sweater. Therefore, a very small pearl or a very small gold that just sits into the lobe will allow the height to remain. Yes.

Richard, what about a loop kind of an earring?

A loop?

Uh-huh.

Well, if you are very—you mean those big loops or any kind of loop?

For example, the kind that that lady's wearing.

If you are tall, *if* you are tall, the loops are fine. Now you [have] got to remember, you are working with your own beauty assets. Now if you are tall, you can wear loops. But if you are short, you must wear anything that gives you height. And a loop, the circle, will not give you height. It will do the direct opposite. So, one quickly learns what makes them look the best. Even though we may like certain things, we consider what makes us look best and we stick with those things. Because you've got loads of choices. But loops, lower, lower the person and not raise them. Therefore, it takes a tall woman, basically a tall woman, to wear loop earrings.

Thank you.

And besides, those kind of earrings, even if you were tall, totally distract from your face, which is your number one asset. Yes.

OK. About the striped sweater, we've been taught that stripes that go horizontally accentuate the bustline and that apparently—

They do.

—is not true.

They—Oh, no. They accentuate the bustline plus the shoulders.

Plus the shoulders. OK.

So, you see, now I want you to take a look. They do accentuate the bustline, but in so doing, they *really* accentuate the shoulder. Do all people see that? See?

Uh-huh. [A few students concur.]

See?

Uh-huh.

Now there has to be other ways—and there are, as all women know—of accentuating the bustline. Because if you want to accentuate the bustline, by design, then you must consider the width of your shoulders. Now to accentuate the bustline by making the shoulders look gigantic, no one really wants to choose, when there are other ways. Is that not true?

That's true.

Now I don't want you to feel bad about your sweater. I happen to like your sweater. But I want you to look in the mirror to see if your shoulder—you feel if your shoulders look broad.

They do. They do and that's why—

And you don't want that to happen.

No.

So you don't need to use horizontal stripes to accentuate the bustline, if you are accentuating shoulders. If you have dinky shoulders—now [if] you have small shoulders—

Uh-huh.

—you can wear something like this: accentuate the bustline and accentuate the shoulders. But this bustline is accentuated at the sacrifice of bigger shoulders.

Uh-huh.

You see? When a white sweater and other corrective measures would do a beautiful job. Go ahead now. Any other questions? Because it's your class. The Spirit works with your questions. Yes.

While you're on the subject, what are the other corrective measures? Considering the recommended attire—

Dimension.

—that was given to her, the white sweater, with this skirt, and a belt or bodice, what would be used to accentuate?

Well, it's very simple. If she doesn't mind being measured, after all we are all adults. Would you come here and measure? Now I can assure you that the measurement of the hip bone and the one third necessary is incorrect. It's too small. That would be the correction that I would make immediately.

Could you please show me exactly? [Student S, who is about to make the measurements of the volunteer, asks.]

Bone to bone, [Student S]. Bone. Feel her bones.

Like here.

The hip bone. Move it from bone to bone. Take one third of the measurement and that's exactly what you should protrude. *[After a short pause, the teacher continues.]*

If anyone's bored, they may be excused.

Bored?

Hmm? Anyone bored?

I think it's great.

It's fourteen, I think. Could you turn, please? [The student measuring the volunteer remarks.]

Sure. [The volunteer remarks.]

You don't quite wrap the tape. You just get the distance between. [A different student instructs.]

Take your fingers and get the distance. Bone to bone. *[After a short pause, the teacher continues.]* The twelve.

OK.

It's eleven—No. It's eleven and one half. I can see it from here. It's eleven and one half.

OK.

You need one third of eleven and one half. Now if you want to go in the library and measure, that's perfectly all right.[2] Go ahead, [Student Z], I know. One third of eleven and one half. Yes.

I was under the impression that horizontal lines, unless it's in a long dress, on a short person foreshortens them more. Is that correct? [A different student asks.]

[The ladies in the library doing the measuring can be heard very quietly discussing the measurements. No attempt was made to transcribe their discussion.]

It does. It gives them shoulders and it shortens them. Uh-huh. Lines are very difficult to wear for anyone. Men or women.

Could you move a bit by the mic, please? [The recording technician asks.]

Lines are very difficult, in apparel, for either men or women. Men can wear lines much better than women. Because they don't have a bust to consider; they don't have hips to consider, like the women have. Lines, especially broad lines, are basically a no-no in good dress. *[After a short pause, the teacher addresses the two ladies in the library.]*

At least two inches short.

We had the wrong bone that we were checking from. [Student S, who is measuring the volunteer, remarks from the library.]

[Student S], this is the bone. Feel my bone. This is the bone. See? You measure from that bone.

[The two students involved in the measuring converse some distance from the microphone, which makes an accurate transcription difficult.]

And then, then it's the flesh. So, you've got to measure out.

Do the Friends say I have the right bone? [Student S asks.]

[Some of the students in the dining room begin to converse. No attempt was made to transcribe those ancillary conversations.]

The front bone. The very front bone. The rest is all flesh. It's the front bone. You got to measure the flesh. That's, yes, that's correct. The front bone. Then that will show her—

[The recording of the class seems to have been stopped at this point. The class continues for a time and then the recording begins again.]

Do you see now, [Student Z]?

Yes, I do.

Yes. And don't worry, you're not going to look like Carol Doda.[3] *[Many students laugh.]*

I'd like to ask you about colors. What would be the best colors for a person of my coloring and my color hair to wear? [Student Z asks.]

All right. Now you have olive skin with a light hair, a sandy-color hair. All right. Therefore, you have to be very careful with color. The navy blue is pretty, but it's not *your* color. Your color is a very light green. Now light green goes with some very dark-haired people or a steel gray, which is also your color. You have to be careful with any earth tones because they darken and do not brighten you, unless you accentuate them with orange or some bright color.

Now the only way you should wear navy blue is when it is brightened with snow white, accented with pink or accented with bright red or even gray. Then you can wear a dark color. Otherwise, it gives too much heaviness to your skin tone, to your coloring. Now there's a lot of colors that you can choose. If you choose the earthy tones, if you are very fond of the earth colors, the browns and the tans, the beiges and things—if you wear beige, accentuate it with a bright green. If you wear an ecru, accentuate it with an orange, and then, you see, you'll give yourself a vibrant [appearance]. Otherwise, it's a deadening color.

Now blues are beautiful colors. They're very heavy and very deadening. This is why they must be accented with a bright color. Browns are heavy colors [and] can be accented with green [or] certain shades of yellow, but basically a green. To lift you up. Otherwise, it's too heavy a coloring. It's far too heavy.

OK. What is a good accent color for rust?

Well, you like rust, and rust, there's several ways you can accent rust. You can accent rust with a very, very light green. [A] very light green. It lightens the heaviness of rust, because rust is a heavy color. If you don't want to accentuate it with green, light green, then you can also accentuate rust with a very brilliant, very, very bright gray. Now it's difficult to find a bright gray, but rust has a beautiful accent with a brilliant, a brilliant gray. You can have green [or] gray. Be very careful about yellow. Very careful about yellow with rust.

OK. That was going to be my next question. Are there any other colors? Are there any colors that I should not wear?

You should wear black.

I should wear black?

For a formal look. For height, if you have black, black [will] look very good on you, as long as you got white with it.

I see.

Navy blue looks very good, if it has white. Colors you shouldn't wear? Yes, you should try to stay away from purple.

Uh-huh.

Because for your coloring, your olive skin—people with olive skin should not wear purple. People with white or bright light skin *should* wear purple. You should stay away from purple. You should stay away from orange, except for an accent. Definitely stay away from orange. It'll make you look like you have yellow jaundice. *[Many students laugh.]* Well, you choose any other colors that you like, I'll tell you whether or not they'll brighten you up.

Like browns and oranges and reds, especially reds. And navys, you told me about that.

Then wear some green with your rust.

Uh-huh.

Brighten up your browns, you see. And then you'll have no problem.

Uh-huh.

But if you wear, for example, an ecru or beige dress—

Uh-huh.

—if you don't accent it with a brilliant orange, a bright, pretty orange, or some bright—even green would brighten it. You have to have something so you're not faded out in it; you don't disappear in it.

Also, what is the best type of a skirt to wear for a short person?

Well, for a short person who truly wants to look like an hourglass, then the best type of skirt depends upon what type of sweater or blouse you're wearing. Now if you're willing to wear a bright or a white sweater, then you can wear a navy blue, pleated skirt beautifully. If you're going to go into any kind of plaids in the skirt, then remember, you must be very careful, for a short person, because it will immediately weight you down and you will look like the tent look instead of the hourglass look.

Now where is—here. I'm glad you're here. Come here. I want to show you. And I'm glad she wore just exactly— *[The teacher asks a different student to step forward.]*

Shall I go? [Student Z asks.]

No, you stay. *[The teacher first addresses Student Z and then addresses the newest volunteer.]* All right. Now, would you mind turning around? Don't take anything personal.

All right. [The new volunteer replies.]

Now we all know that she is not that heavy in the hip or the stomach. The reason that she looks that heavy is the coloring of the skirt and the coloring of the blouse. Now in order to eliminate this heaviness on the hips, she needs a much brighter, very bright blouse. And it needs to be a closed blouse. Because now, remember one thing about your bustline: if you have an open blouse, you have a flatter bustline. If you have a closed blouse, around the neck, or you have ruffled, then you have a fuller bustline as far as look is concerned.

So, women who feel, who are—you see, this is the tent look. Does everybody see the tent look? She's heavier from this point down than she is from this point up. All the weight is down here. Consequently, it gives her a flat-chested look and it also ages her. And I'm glad she's here because she's already been told about her hairstyle and how to cut it and change [it] to give fullness to the face. And because of this, the bone structure— now some women are fleshy here and they look very nice with an open blouse. But she has a chiseled look, which is part of her bone structure. That is not a feminine look; that is not her beauty point. Therefore, this should be covered, you see. If this is covered, then immediately it changes this whole look here and will add more bust feature and put her into shape. You see that, don't you?

Yes, I do.

The reason this makes you look pregnant is because of this color here. This, she could get away with, with this skirt, if she had a very bright, solid color and the neck line was closed. Then there'd be all the difference in the world. Thank you. Do you have any other questions?

Yes. I'd like to know what colors I should be wearing?

Well, you should be wearing light blues. Light blues will lift you up. You don't have to stick to just light blues. You can wear greens. But remember, this coloring adds weight and heaviness. This dark [of] a green. That's more like a forest green. So, whenever you wear it, remember, wherever you put it on your body, that's what you're going to increase weight-wise. Now you will look, in a solid dark color, you [will] look slimmer. But remember this: in a solid, dark color, you will look slimmer and you will look heavier. You'll always look heavier in a solid color. Contrary to popular opinion, a heavy, dark color adds weight to the body. It just adds weight.

How does the neckline . . . besides the one that goes— [A few words are difficult to transcribe.]

A closed neckline? You could wear a little lower neckline, but never an open V-neck like that.

Uh-huh.

And you have to correct the bustline.

And on the length of the skirt, what should that be? From the waist down?

The length of your skirt?

Uh-huh.

Because you have pretty legs, the length of the skirt is fine. It can go a little bit longer, not much shorter. Should not show the knee.

Uh-huh. Should not show the knee.

You see, everyone has their certain points that they should concentrate upon. [Student A] is fortunate. *[The teacher is speaking with Student A.]* [Student S] is fortunate; [Student S] has her beautiful hair.

What's mine? [A different student interjects.]

[Student Z] has—Excuse me. *[The teacher says a few words that are difficult to transcribe.]* She has her beautiful face. You [have] got to take the major asset. Don't you see what I mean?

Uh-huh.

And [Student A] has her legs. So, what you concentrate upon is accentuating your major beauty point. Would you come up here? I want to show—no, this one.

Me?

Yes. Her! No. No. You! *[The teacher calls another volunteer to the front of the class.]* What color is that dress? It's indistinguishable. It's difficult to tell.

Now, I told you all not to get personal about this, didn't I? Very small shoulders. Everyone agree? They look very slim. Right?

Uh-huh. [Multiple students respond.]

Hip-less. Absolutely hip-less. A waist like this, which has got to be corrected.

That's true.

Now what's the problem? It's very simple: there is—if you take the measurement from this point to this point, I guarantee you that it is longer from here to this point than it is to this waistline.

Uh-huh.

Would you mind measuring her? *[The teacher addresses a different female student.]* Because your eye tells you immediately.

[The student asks a question that is difficult to transcribe.]

No, you just put your arms, just let your arms down. Measure from here to the point of the bust.

OK.

Right to the point.

OK. Eight and a half.

Measure from that point to her waist. It's certainly not eight and one half.

About six and one half, maybe six and three quarters.

Now measure down and show them where eight and one half is.

Eight and a half.

Go from the point of the bust.

OK.

Eight and a half inches down.

OK.

I'll show you what you're doing to yourselves.

It would be right about here.

Mark this point. This is where the bust appears to be. Think of that. You're that much out of proportion the way you're dressing and the lack of support. You see? It's sagging to the knee, almost. Now what does that do to a person?—you wanted to come to class, didn't you?

Yeah.

All right. Pull your blouse in. Pull it tight. And pull your bra up. If you don't have one, shame on you; you're in the wrong class.

I do.

Then pull it up. Now, now—[Student Z]. Excuse me. You just hold that. You hold that.

All right. Now you notice what she really has. Has everyone noticed? She has a very long waist. Now with a bodice *[bä-dis]* or bodice *[bō-dis]*, whichever you prefer, this here, she would accentuate and she would gain some hips. You see? You see, right now there's no hips! Look at this! *[Several students laugh.]* You see what I mean? You see? It's way too low. You see, I think they call them snake hips. *[More students laugh.]* You see? Now, with a bodice—just stand up, please—it starts to be some kind of a shape. You see what I mean? Let's walk around so she can look in the mirror. Do you see?

Yes. Quite a difference. Wow.

You see the difference? Now you'll start to get a waistline, because you're very long waisted. So, you need something to push up the bust—

Right.

—and accentuate a hipline so you get an hourglass look. Now what that has immediately done: it has given you a little bit of height; it's certainly given you femininity; and it's definitely given you youth. Now you let it all drop and see how old you get. *[Many students laugh.]* Do you see the difference?

Yeah.

Besides your measurement is off. I can tell right now. The measurement of your hip bone to the one third measurement that you should be—

Uh-huh.

—you're short. Most all women are short. They're measured short. They do it to themselves. There's no support. There is no support. That's the problem. Any question?

Ah . . .

Your hair is a nice style, for someone else.

OK. What would you recommend, then, for a hairstyle?

Well, first of all, look at your face. Turn around and look at your face.

Uh-huh.

Do you feel that you have a full face here? Or do you feel that you have a very narrow face from the cheekbone to the chin? Is it quite pointed?

Yeah. Narrow.

Do you think your nose looks big?

No.

Look at it sideways.

Yeah.

Look at your nose sideways, as you go from the point of your chin up. Tell me if you think your nose looks big.

Very.

It looks very big.

Yeah.

Your nose is not very big. Your nose happens to be in proportion. The style of your hair brings everything to a point at your chin. Now when someone goes to look at your eyes, because you've made this pointedness with your hairstyle, all they can see is your nose and your chin. Then they see your eyes. Now to correct that, you've got to get away from this look.

Uh-huh. So, should I have more fullness here or what?

You [have] got to get rid of the hair on your forehead. Look at the hair—now, first of all, you see almost no forehead. Because you see almost no forehead, you see plenty of pointed chin. You see an accentuated nose and you see no fullness here. Hmm? All right. Now [the] first thing you do is take away the hair from the forehead. She has a short forehead. You need to have more face showing on her in order to get more fullness. The hair is, number one, too short. So, she would have to bring her hair more full. You see which—now everyone has two sides. No two sides of your body are equal. Your two hands are different. The two peaks on your hairline are different. Your legs are different.

Each part of your body, [its] measurement is a little different and looks different.

All right. Now, so what you have to do is look to see which is the prettiest side of the hairline. This is what you first have to find. All right. No, this is not the prettiest side. This is the prettiest side of her hairline. There's a little difference in the curve of where the hairline is. Therefore, she would want to accentuate this, bring this down and around, and fullness here, so she doesn't have the narrow head. See, the head, with the way the hair is, the head is very narrow. Because the head, in its illusion, looks narrow from the hair styling, her chin is much more pointed; her nose is more accentuated. Yes.

More fullness in the hair around here, then would, would—
This is where she needs fullness.

—tend to round it. [A non-volunteer student observes.]

That's correct. She needs—all of this needs to be pushed out and filled. This needs to be flattened. This needs to be filled and this here needs to be pulled. Can you see that? Are there any questions in reference to changing the look of the face on this person? Any questions?

Thank you.

All right. Because—does everybody see that this is very narrow looking, for the hairstyle? And with a very pointed chin, you only accentuate that situation. And the only way to correct it is through the hair. Any other question?

What colors would you recommend that I wear in my best interest?

In your best interest?

Yeah.

If you want to look the best—

Uh-huh.

—then stop the dark, drab colors. Now if you must—the skirt is beautiful, if it had a bright blouse. You see? Because the coloring just fades right out and she fades along with it. That is, there's no shape to see. Do you understand that? Now you can correct that with a different blouse. Definitely a bodice—

Uh-huh.

—because you need that to have—you see, as you turn around, just turn around this way. Can anyone see a waist? Can anyone see a hipline?

No. [A few students respond.]

Does anyone really see a hip?

No. [More students respond.]

Because, you see, it's nonexistent. The color is wrong. It doesn't mean that she cannot use the blouse. It does not mean that she cannot use the skirt. But it means that combination is disaster on her. Yes.

Yeah, that sleeve length, too, is not correct either, is it? [A non-volunteer student asks.]

Well, you've got to understand she has small shoulders. All right? Now if we want to narrow the shoulder, we lengthen the sleeve. Remember?

Right.

Now if—she's fortunate in the sense she has [a] very narrow shoulder-look. The shoulder-look is very, very narrow. Not a bit wrong. Therefore, she is good to wear and it will give her some width, balance here, that sleeve length, shorter. If she goes into full sleeve, then she immediately starts slimming this. And if she slims this, she must take corrective measures, then, to slim the hipline; otherwise, you go out of proportion. OK. You got all that down? *[Many students laugh.]* Any other questions? Yes.

What about her skirt length, because—

Way too long.

OK. What if she had—

Way too long! Stand in front of the mirror. Does everyone see it's way too long? Pull it up four inches, at least.

Yeah, but that's going—

Not above the knee. Stop—oh. There! It should not be longer than that. Because otherwise you have no shape. For her, she has no shape. You see? Now you [have] got to remember this: your legs are not your number one beauty asset.

No.

They look worse when you try to cover them with a skirt. Then they draw attention. What does show is a couple of stubs. *[Several students laugh.]* For her, a couple of stubs are showing. Which makes the existing legs, which are legs, but it's not her number one beauty asset. It draws the attention to the stubs that are there. So, you must wear the [skirt] there. You see? Then the legs will not be as noticeable because it is noticeable that she's trying to cover up the legs. And that draws attention to the legs.

Now if you accentuate your waistline, then they won't notice that your legs are not your number one asset.

Uh-huh. [The volunteer responds.]

What do you think your number one asset is?

My eyes.

All right. Let's go beyond the eyes. Your eyes are a great asset. That is true. What part of your anatomy do you think is, for you—each one has a different part that is their number one asset. Which one do you think is your number one asset?

I guess my face overall. I'm not really sure.

Oh, I don't think so.

No?

Turn around in the mirror and take another look. *[After a short pause, the teacher continues.]* We know it's not your legs.

No.

We know it's not your face. We know it's not your hair. Your shoulders are an asset, but that's not your number one asset.

My waistline?

When you show a waistline, yes, it's your hips. Pull all that blouse in and you'll see. Tighten up the skirt. Now! Now you'll see her asset. Turn around so the ladies can see you. See, once she has a bodice and this is pulled in, then you see a pretty hipline. So, the very thing that is her number one asset nobody ever sees because it's just totally draped and nonexistent, as if she had no hips at all. Do you see what I mean? Now if you tie or pull that in where it should be and put a wide belt or a bodice in here, then you will see what pretty hips you really have. They never showed before.

Hmm.

Do you understand?

Uh-huh.

Fine. Any other questions?

What color skin tone do I have?

Almost white. [A] very, very light skin tone. Therefore, you should consider—and because of the coloring of your hair—see, if you had that white skin tone with black hair, then you [have] got a whole different picture. But you happen to have it with very light hair. And because you have it with light hair, then you've got to wear colors that'll lift you up and brighten you up. You see, you need to wear colors that make you look fatter up here.

Hmm.

Heavier.

Uh-huh.

Then, you see, you'll accentuate your hipline, your waistline. And then you will see how pretty you really are. Yes.

If she wore a wide belt, the color of her collar, wouldn't that accentuate her waist and cut—

It would some, but, you see, this combination is too dark for her. She needs something light. Now, you see this color here. It's kind of a rust, wouldn't you say?

Uh-huh.

Now if she would wear a steel-gray blouse, steel-gray, with this skirt, and then on top of that wear a white bodice or belt, she'd look absolutely fantastic. Absolutely fantastic. If it was a steel-gray blouse.

Uh-huh.

See? And not a V-neck. Do you see this neck? See that neck? Now that's not your beauty asset. It's not a kangaroo neck, but it's not your beauty asset. Look, you want a bust. You have no bust. You want a bust, then pull this around and get yourself a bust. Even by closing this, it gives her a little upliftment. But you need support; you need a bust; you need to pull in your waistline. Do you see? Because when you're flat-chested, you've got to do something to give a different illusion. Yes.

Would a color like this help? [A different, non-volunteer student asks.]

Yes. A color like that would definitely help her. Absolutely help. Because, you see, this here is an absolute no-no, unless you got a nice sized bustline. This is a no-no, because this is how you look. And here's your bust. Way down here. That's how you look, see? Doesn't matter how you feel, but that's how you look. And besides her measurement, she's out of—off-center, see? Way off-center.

Could I wear padded bras? [The volunteer asks.]

Well, I think most women that I've known do. There are a few who don't. But, why, of course—look, no one is perfect. That's a very practical, sensible thing to do, as long as they don't look that way. And then you have to know what you're doing. But I think there are plenty of women in the church here that know what they're doing about that. I don't see you're having any problem. Do you?

Oh, no.

Well, there you are. But accentuate your waistline. You have a very pretty waistline. Nobody ever sees it.

OK. So, I can wear wide belts very well.

Now I'm glad you mentioned belts because it's a very important thing and most women don't realize it. Women must be extremely careful about buckles. That's an absolute no-no, unless you are very careful. The square buckle is very masculine and very manly. And you've got to be very careful about belts with buckles. Now they have some buckles that are feminine. You must be extremely careful. The best type of a look for a woman is—you notice that most women's belts, if they are made of suede, then the buckle is suede. You don't want to accentuate the buckle of the belt. Now there are some that are oval shape. There are some that are perfectly round. You [have] got to be very, very careful about a belt buckle because a belt buckle is masculine. It looks masculine. And it does something to your waist that you won't appreciate, if you really look at it. You must be extremely careful about buckles.

Thank you.

Uh-huh. Any other questions? Yes.

I'd like to know about the pleat of that skirt. The way it's fitted and then the pleat comes out lower on the hips. Is that a good style if you're broadening the hips in general? [A nonvolunteer student asks.]

Well, the thing is, this broadens the lower part of the hip. This style gives you a longer waist. Now if you want—for the women who are short-waisted, if you want a longer waist, there are several ways to get it. This is one of the ways to get a longer waist. Unfortunately, she already has a long waist and she lengthened it; her waistline, she lengthened even longer. Now if she had had a pleated skirt like that navy blue one, then she would have brought her waist up here. As it is, she lowered her waist down here and even made her waist longer than her waist really is.

Thank you.

It can be worn with a bodice, you see. Because the bodice will give that look. You can have macramé or whatever—any of those things. But you [have] got to remember that white goes with everything. White goes with—there is no color that white doesn't go with because white is the combination of all color. Be careful of black in a belt because black is the absence of all color. *[After a short pause, the teacher continues.]*

Do you see now why your hips look like they're here?

Uh-huh.

Instead of up here?

Uh-huh.

Because that skirt did it.

Yeah, because of all the struts down here instead of further up. Right?

Uh-huh. And because [if] you want to accentuate the hip, you can't drape it down there and accentuate it up here at a waistline. OK?

OK. Thank you.

Any other questions? Yes.

So much emphasis has been placed on blouses and skirts and dresses. What about the image you want to present of a working woman, an executive, where you [may] not be wearing a blouse and a skirt or a dress— [A non-volunteer student asks.]

But you might be wearing a suit?

A business image.

If you want to present a business image, then you need a jacket, a more tailored look.

Uh-huh.

A jacket and a matching skirt. And get the feminine part of the business look in some type, not too much, of some little frill in the blouse. Now because, you see, a woman looks very executive and looks very good in an office with her jacket and her skirt, ofttimes matching color. That's almost like a suit. What happens, she gains masculinity because she eliminates the little frill—not a lot, but some frill somewhere to maintain the femininity of the look. So many of them will wear an absolute tailored shirt with a necktie and it eliminates their own feminine identity. So, a woman can look very nice in a suit, executive work, very nice with a jacket, but should have some type of a ruffle somewhere. It doesn't have to be all over the blouse. But even, even a very small ruffle. Doesn't need to be a big ruffle, but some type of a ruffle somewhere on the blouse. Even if it's only a couple of inches put somewhere. That's necessary. Yes. Does that help with your question?

Yes. Thank you.

Yes. Yes.

Yes. Would—if she was wearing, in the same executive outfit, a plain blouse, would the introduction of a cameo or a necklace do the same thing?

A necklace won't; a cameo will. Now if she wants to wear a plain blouse, you see, the necklace will not give sufficient femininity to break the masculine vibration. A cameo will definitely do that. Did you ever see a man wear a cameo?

No.

It's absolutely restricted to the femininity of the women. Absolutely. . . Any other questions before break time? My goodness. Yes.

I'd like to ask about nylons versus pantyhose as far as a health consideration goes.

Well, years ago Dr. Waltham said very clearly that if the women ever became aware of what they are doing to their skin with pantyhose, they would never again buy another pair. Your skin does not breathe in pantyhose. There's no way that it can. Now you wear nylons; and so that much of your legs are covered. But your other part of your anatomy—is always breath[ing]. You know, you can have clothes on and the air, oxygen still gets to your skin. But when you wear things like pantyhose, there's no oxygen getting to very critical areas of your anatomy. And it's an absolute no-no as far as the doctor is concerned, [from] when they first came out. But that's up to each individual. Yes.

And can anything be done about preventing vein breakage in the legs and varicose veins?

Yes. Because, you see, one of the major problems with, especially women on that, some men, but especially women, is because the blood is not consistently flowing harmoniously through that part of the anatomy. And so, one of the major things that a woman must do—now why isn't it? Because the women have restricted the free flow of blood through their legs. They've done several things to restrict that flow. Number one of which is so-called pantyhose. And that only helps to add to the problem. Therefore, a person, especially women, should have their legs up more often. And they should see that their legs get some type of a massage, daily, *[The teacher can be heard patting what may be his legs with his hands.]* to help stimulate the blood flow because that's where that's caused from. That's the true cause of that problem.

OK. Thank you.

And how about in men? [A different student asks.]

In men? Men's problems—because, you see, what it is with men, some of them have that problem with their legs. They are not getting proper blood circulation. That's the major problem. With women, it's restricted by their pantyhose and things of that nature. Their shoes help to defeat the proper flow of the blood. And with men, they have that problem of circulation. *Some* men do. Most men don't. But some men have a circulation problem, and they should take corrective measures.

Now if you want to bring blood flowing through the system and get it flowing through to the surface so you don't have these problems, then you must pet [pat] your skin.[4] By so doing, you bring the blood to the surface.

Now remember, if you want clear and beautiful skin, you must nourish the skin. The skin has to eat, just like you have to eat. What does the skin eat to stay beautiful? It is nourished by the blood. If the blood doesn't flow harmoniously, consistently to the skin to nourish it, then your skin starts to, what you call, age. And we've already given, I think, class on how to properly care for the skin.

Now remember, when you put creams on the skin, you close the pores. I don't care whether they call them cleansing creams. I don't care what they call them. You literally plug the pores. Your skin has a multitude of pores. That's how your skin breathes. If you close the pores of the skin with all these various creams, then your skin starts to suffer from oxygen starvation. And as the years pass by, you start to see that your skin is not as smooth, as clear, and as bright looking as it used to be. It is dying. Your skin is literally dying from oxygen starvation and lack of nourishment. You correct that by bringing the blood, which is the nourishment, back to the skin and totally eliminating all the stuff you've been putting on that closes the pores of the skin. Any other questions on the skin? Yes.

Does that include makeup also?

It most certainly does. Because you've got to understand—not that you can't use makeup—but what you must understand wherever you put any cream, powder, paste, or whatever, in that area those pores are closed and that area of your skin cannot breathe during that time. Now unfortunately, they have cleansing creams and they have these creams and those creams. So, you put on paste or powder to look just so; then you use a cleansing cream to clean it off, but the only thing you clean off is the surface. You don't get down into the pores of the skin. That can only be scrubbed off with soap and water. And Ivory soap's the best cosmetic you can use. Yes.

It seems, at times, we have to use oil to remove mascara. And in so doing, are we clogging the pores around the eye and how should that be avoided?

The only way to avoid that is to wash the skin with pure Ivory soap. Of all the soaps available on the market, there is no better soap for the human skin, yet developed, than Ivory soap. A plain bar of Ivory soap.

And will that cut through it after you've used the oil or . . .

It will cut through it. It definitely will cut through it. The face or the skin should always, *always* be left with [a] cold-water rinse. Always left with a cold-water rinse. Then just take the wash cloth and—better—don't wipe—do not wipe the skin dry. Rinse the skin with water, not ice water, the coldest tap water, then just pat it; sponge it dry. See? With your wash cloth. Just sponge it dry. Don't wipe it dry. Then pet [pat] your skin and bring all the blood to the surface.[5] And you won't have to worry about your skin. But it will take time to correct all the stuff that's caked on it. Yes.

Well, what if you have an acne problem?

If you have an acne problem, it will totally eliminate that acne problem. If you don't believe me, here's the mother of a child whose skin today looks like a child's. Doesn't it?

Yes, indeed. Uh-huh. [The mother responds.]

And what does she do? Pet [Pat] the face with cold water every day?

Exactly what you described.

Every day! She's been doing it for how long now?

Hmm, I'd say about six years.

Approximately six years. You ought to see her daughter's skin. She had a problem, didn't she?

Yes, she did.

Acne—you want to remove it? That's all you [have] got to do: wash your face with soap and water; rinse it always daily with cold water; and pet [pat] the skin and you'll nourish the skin.[6] The acne will disappear. Any other questions? *[After a short pause, the teacher continues.]*

Time to close class. We'll see you at the next one. Thank you very much. And, my goodness, what time is it? *[After a short pause, he continues.]* One whole hour. An hour and a half?!

OCTOBER 10, 1981

Design Class 2

Now this class here, that we're having this evening, can be easily called, I guess you would say, an understanding of the temple of God, a restoration of your house of clay.

Is that working? *[The teacher asks the technician if the tape recorder is recording.]*

Uh-huh.

Fine. Now you've had, some of you, a little bit of understanding about what various parts of your anatomy mean. You've been given these various faculties. Little, if anything, has been said on the functions.

Now a person—first visualize your body as a house, for it is a house that you, in your evolution, have built. You alone, in your expression through eternity, have made the feet you have, the ears you have, the eyes you have, the nose, and each and every part of your body. Now the human body on this planet is the most perfected of all forms. It is the most evolved. It is the most, design-wise, harmonious form on the Earth planet through untold ages of evolution.

Now your house, the human body, is designed for perfect balance. That means, in design, your eyes, your hair, your nose, your teeth, your mouth, your feet, your arms, everything [is] designed as a perfect balance, perfect form. And now the question must arise: If it is designed in its perfection, then why is it out of balance? Why do some of us have small noses, large noses, small ears, big ears, small chins, large chins, and they are not in proportion with the rest of the house.

Now speaking very firmly and outspoken at this class, as usually is my policy, we have to start somewhere; so, we'll start with the efforts of getting the ladies to see where they're out of proportion, if they're out of proportion with the rest of their whole body.

Now as you would not take, in building a house, you would not put on a doorknob on a door that was not in balance with the basic design of the door. You wouldn't put on too small a doorknob. You wouldn't put on too large a doorknob. You wouldn't put the doorknob on partially and let it just hang. You would put it on securely so that the beauty of the door could be accentuated. And so it is with a lady's chest. Now it has to do with the Law of Harmony.

Without harmony, there is no beauty. Harmony is a perfect balance of design.

Now remember, the effect of the perfect balance of design is the goodness of life called health. Now if you don't bring about, through your efforts, an assistance to nature, to the house that you have created—you see, in building your house—and you have built it from the failure of learning the lessons of the past, in other lives. And you have learned [built] it through the many lessons that you have passed beautifully.

So, as you study your house of clay, place your attention upon the parts of the house that are beautiful. As you accent that and you place your attention upon that, you slowly but surely establish in your evolution the laws of harmony. You view the beauty, which is harmony, which is balance. And, of course, that that you place your attention upon you have a tendency to become, for it is the law. So, as you place your energy, the divine energy flowing through you, upon the parts of your anatomy that are in this perfect balance or harmony and not upon the parts of the anatomy that are discordant and out of balance, from lessons that have been flunked in evolution, then you will find, as you go on in this great eternity, you will once again enter the house that is the perfect beauty called heaven.

Now we are here in this moment, we are forming and we are deforming the house in which we live. As we do it today, our tomorrows reveal this. We say that our face is aging. We say that we're looking old and go on down the list.

Take, for example, a person that has an out-of-proportion-to-their-body nose. We'll start with the nose, for example. What is it revealing and reminding us of? We know that the nose represents reason and consideration. Does the size of the nose, being out of proportion with the rest of the house, does it tell us that we've had too much reason and consideration? God forbid, no. It simply reveals to us that the opposite functions to those faculties have been overaccentuated. And our little house is telling us that we need to bring that into balance.

I can give to you the function. But you can grow more beautifully by your effort to perceive what is opposite and contrary to consideration, what is opposite and contrary to reason. I'm first going to let you have the time necessary, hopefully, that you will value this little class enough to make the effort. Because in so doing, if you will do that, you will open the door of honesty. And you will look deep inside at what you fear is Pandora's box, and in so doing, you will face the lesson that you know you must learn.

So, you cannot, because of evolution, change, now, the size of your nose, because we have not yet freed our self from over-identification with the function that it represents. That's the only reason.

Now, then we can take the eyes, representative of awareness, and we can ask ourselves, "Now, my eyes are small. My eyes are large. My eyes are black. My eyes are brown. My eyes are blue. My eyes are gray. My eyes are green." And we can say, we can use one of the divine truths which say God's manifestation is variety, but we must ask our self the question: the eyes that we have, are we feeling good about them? If we do not feel good about the eyes, the awareness, the windows in our little house, then we must ask our self why. "What have I done with my awareness in evolution?" And when we ask our self honestly, we'll find out what we've done with our awareness. Are the eyes real small, that when you look [through] the window, you have to really strain to see? Or are they in proportion to the rest of the house? Are they beautiful or are they dull? How are the eyes? For they tell us what we've done.

Now we can look and we can see, "Well, these are the eyes that I came to Earth with. This is what I built over these years of evolution. I am not happy with these eyes. I am not happy; it is not my eyes. It's what I've done. I can change from this moment on what I'm doing. I cannot change what I have already done, but I can take a look and be honest with myself and, in that honesty, establish the laws necessary to have the eyes that I desire."

For when you look around the world, you will see the eyes, [and] say, "Oh, God, I wish I had those!" What it is telling you [is] that's what you used to have. And so, when you look at another and you see that which inside of you, deep inside of you, you wish so deeply, even in a split moment, if only you had those, that's telling you, your soul, that's what you used to have, until you flunked. And that's the truth.

Unfortunately, the mind takes that, when it looks out at the world and it sees other forms, and it says, "Oh, God, I wish I had that hair. How beautiful that is!" The mind gets it and then you have the function of fear and you have what is known as jealousy, envy, and all the list of discordant vibration.

Now in this day and age, you have an unrealistic phenomenon taking place with women. Unrealistic. The increase of breast cancer has reached staggering proportions, staggering proportions. Now you must ask yourself the question: Why has it reached staggering proportions? At the sacrifice—for example, say—you have built your house. Now say, for example, the only thing in your whole house that interests you—and stop and think. You have a roof, a foundation. You have doors. You have windows. Hopefully you have something there to keep you warm. You have a kitchen in which you cook your food. What type of sanity, God forbid, so far from reason, would anyone, having built an entire house, limit their self to the doorknobs of the house? Tell me what type of sanity are we talking about?

If you only want to live in a house that's made of doorknobs, has no doors, has no windows, has no roof, has no foundation, has no walls, no closets, no kitchen—it only has doorknobs. Because of our minds' overidentification with the chest of, in this case we're speaking [of] women, they have directed so much discordant energy to that area of the house, the disease, known as cancer, is revealing itself only, you understand, basically in that area.

Now we can go through every single part of the anatomy. There is nothing wrong with being attracted to a particular part of a house in its design. There is everything wrong, for it is discordant—it's contrary to the laws of balance and nature—to be so overidentified with a particular part of the house at the total sacrifice of the harmony, the health, and the balance of the rest of the house, you see.

Now, this overidentification, of course, reveals to adult people—it's an adult class—that a basic desire in the male species to revert to the womb of the mother for security is a predominant factor in the human mind. This is the true cause of the overidentification with that part of the house. It reveals to us a great need for something greater than our thoughts. When the desire, which is the divine expression, becomes limited by the minds of men and its need for fulfillment is greater than the need for God, you begin the path of imbalance of discord and disease. That's when your greatest wealth begins to disappear, for you have transgressed, in your error of ignorance, you have transgressed the natural laws of life itself that govern the balance of all nature.

You are a part of nature. Should the tree overidentify with the root at the sacrifice of its foliage, the tree would die. And so man, humanity, is dying daily.

Age, as you know age, is contrary to the perfected form in evolution of the human being. It is brought about from transgressions of natural law, not of harmony with natural law.

As man overidentifies with any function and creates an imbalance in the house of clay, he guarantees the Law of Discord and Disease. It is inevitable. It is inevitable. Now what happens as he overidentifies with a certain portion of the house, he has to consider, which he does not consider, the water center of the form in which the seat of emotions live. And in that center, which contains and controls all fluids of the form of the house of clay, he interferes and build[s] dams to the natural, fluidic flow.

I have revealed to you before the cause of cancer. Now you are getting an expanded understanding of how it takes place. If you want to know what's going on with your mind and the rest of the world, then study the location in the house that the discord is revealing itself. You have let the termites in. You know where they are. You know how to get rid of them. They eat away your house of clay.

As I said a moment earlier, when your desire for a particular portion of the house of clay is greater than [your desire for] the Power that sustains the house, then you suffer and will ever suffer.

Now, we start with the crown of the house of clay: the roof. We call it the hair. Well, the hair is the shingles. That's the covering. But without the shingles, of course the rain comes in and it's not a real roof. As you would not build a house from the roof down, only a fool will try to build a house, their house of clay, from the head down.

A wise man begins with the feet. And we all know what the feet represent. Surely, we know by now: understanding.

So, what do we begin with? We begin with understanding. Before a house gets a foundation, there must be understanding of its basic design. So, before we can get to the buttocks, which is representative of the foundation, we must begin with the feet; so that we can take care of the necessary building before the foundation ever gets poured. Because once the foundation is poured, and if there isn't understanding before it is poured, then the whole house shall never be beautiful no matter the covering. Because it's all in the understanding before you get to the foundation.

Untold centuries ago, this teaching was on this planet. Down through the ages there have been fragments still living today on your planet. And if you will look through ancient times, you will see there was a time when the feet were so very important: they had the very finest care. The feet became a beauty point to the house of clay. Unfortunately, the minds of men decided what beauty was and started to distort the feet and started to distort the true meaning, which is understanding, for the feet. But it is one of the many fragments that are still on Earth today, revealing the truth of the house of clay.

I know you're anxiously awaiting what is the function for this and the function for that. And I'm going to give you the opportunity to ask these questions. And then I'm going to show you the way to find the lesson that you've flunked. And I will start with you. You may have your question.

Since we're starting with the feet, may I ask about the function of understanding?

How do you feel about your feet? How have you always felt about your feet? Has it ever been an interest to you? Or are you, perhaps in honesty, more interested in another part of the anatomy? You should ask that which is of your inner emotional interest, not that which is appropriate for the class for someone else may ask that question.

Oh, OK. Thank you. Well, I'd like to ask about the nose.

That is a fine question. You know what it represents.

Right.

What does the nose represent? And what do the nostrils represent?

I believe the nose is reason and the nostrils are consideration.

Is there anyone to disagree with that? *[After a short pause, the teacher continues.]* There shouldn't be. You are interested in that part of your house because, you see, if you will search deep inside of you, you will find the function of concern and, in finding that function, will understand nature is designed to be assisted and never controlled by a mental world that does not in truth sustain it.

Thank you.

Next person, please.

I'd like to ask about the ears.

When in evolution we decide that what someone else may know we have always known, then our ears begin to reveal what we must, once again, learn to do.

Next one, please.

I'd like to ask about the hair.

When through the lack of the soul faculty of patience, where only wisdom can live, there is great effort for all good. Without patient, without patience one never experiences the harvest that is their just due. It is possible, through an acceptance of divine law, to bring about restoration, but that takes the total bowing of all judgment. And that takes great effort, great patience, and total image change.

Next person.

I would like to ask about the feet.

The feet. Hmm. *[The teacher pauses for a moment.]* Will you sense, hear, see, accept what, from fear, you insist upon refusing? When you reach that point in eternity when you know and accept, no matter what happens, there is something, there *is* an eternity, when the soul is permitted to rise and impinge that great truth upon the consciousness, all fear will disappear. Understanding will free us.

Next person, please.
How about the shoulders?
When we truly accept the beautiful faculty of possibility and in that acceptance of the faculty of possibility we graciously accept payment without judgment, we'll no longer be concerned, nor interfere, with the great strength of the faculty of courage.

Next person, please.
The legs.
The legs. There is a vast difference between patience and waiting. Waiting is a function of the mind, lacking the faculty of reason. It has no wisdom. Patience, where wisdom lives, is the total absence of the mental-emotional world. When we separate and bring about a harmony between the function and the faculty, when we know in truth the difference between waiting, a mental function, and patience, a soul faculty, the legs will respond in perfect balance.

Next person, please.
I'd like to ask about the hands.
The hands. It is difficult for the mind to accept, let alone to believe, for it takes a step into unknown dimensions, for they are unknown to the mind and shall never be known to the mind. The mind conceives; the soul perceives. And when perception is distinctly expressed and conception has the reins of reason upon it, then action will become perfectly, harmoniously balanced with reaction, and we will be freed from the function of concern. To do that which we know we must do and to do it without the mental gymnastics of contemplating our responsibilities in life—for to contemplate one's responsibilities is to fascinate with the weight of responsibility. And the weight of responsibility is the delusion that we are the doer. The only weight of responsibility we will ever know is the weight of self-glory, the delusion that we are the doer.

Next person, please.

I'd like to ask about the hips.

The hips. When the mental world enters the realm and the false belief that it can control all that it receives and denies that its receiving is dependent upon its sending, then discord, imbalance reveals itself.

Next person, please.

I'd like to ask about the ankles.

The ankles. When we try, from fear, which is mental control, to run away from that which we understand, because in the understanding we know the faculty of courage, the faculty of strength, the faculty of patience, the faculty of loyalty, the faculty of continuity—and all faculties are dependent upon our understanding; all balance is dependent upon our understanding—when we try to run from truth, we are weakened until we can no longer run. And then when we accept the truth that we know, then the faculty of strength will flow once again: we will no longer run. We will be still and we will be free.

Good night.

OCTOBER 25, 1981

Design Class 3

Well, good evening, ladies and gentlemen.

This will be Design Class Number Two, for the ladies and the gentlemen.

[The published titles of each class in this series are taken from the labels of the recordings. One possible explanation for the teacher identifying this class as class two is that the previous class, currently identified as Design Class 2, was included in this series only after this class was recorded.]

And we will start with the men this evening with the proper necktie. Now the reason, in choosing neckties, when you go to the store, you should never purchase a necktie that's on the rack, because you're guaranteed it's not pure silk. Now the cost of a pure silk necktie today is approximately $25. A necktie is an investment. Your suit, your dress is as good as your necktie. And it shows. It's the only part of your apparel, basically, in good dress, in which you can have color, in which you can give life to your suit, your shoes, your whole attire. So, your necktie is a very important investment. Your suit will look as cheap or as expensive, basically, as your necktie. You buy a few good neckties and it'll do your whole wardrobe. You buy cheap ties and they'll always look that way.

So, when you go to the store, what you do is look for the ties that are behind the showcase, under the glass, that have the lights on them. Those, most all of them, unfortunately nowadays not all of them, will be pure silk. If they're pure silk, then you will see a little tag somewhere on it that will say pure silk. This one I may have ripped the tag off. I don't like those advertisements. But anyway, it happens to be pure silk. If anyone wants to look at—this one happens to be a YSL.

You can get ties that are 80 percent silk and so much plastic, etc., but they will not tie and they will not shine. They will not look as nice.

So, we'll start with putting the tie on. First thing you do, when you dress, you [have] got your shirt on, you lift your collar. Now after you've lifted your collar, you put the tie up here. Do not button the shirt yet, because if you do, you start to break the collar down. You take your thumbs, you push it up and you can feel where the collar is to crease. Because if you don't do that, nothing looks more tacky than a necktie that shows below the collar in the back. So that's one thing you want to avoid.

Now after you've done that—do not button your shirt yet. You want the open movement for the tie. You take the tie and you get a basic balance, if it's a proper tie, approximately to the point of your belt, approximately. Depends on how long you are from the armpit to the hip. You turn the tie once. This is a double Windsor knot. A double Windsor knot is the best knot that there is because a double Windsor knot can be locked. By that I mean your tie will always look nice without pins and all those other things. You go around once; you go around twice. You come up under with your thumb. I hope you can see me there. Pull it through; open with your finger the knot, the open part, and push down in. OK?

Now, when you do this, remember, you want to fold it in here. Don't worry; it's pure silk and it's not going to make a permanent crease. You pull this down. I happen to like a little dent on the side. I always have. Tighten this up here. Now is the time to button your shirt. Now you button your shirt. Take your forefinger and your thumb—take your fourth finger and thumb, and push it up to the collar.

Now this is the most important part. You notice that the tie is not hanging even. It has exactly the right amount to straighten out the knot. So now you take your thumb on this, push it up under here. And you push. And you adjust your tie.

Now in that adjusting here, I like that over to the side a little bit. [It] depends; you can have a dead center one, like President Reagan, if you wish, but you're going to have to take a lot of practice. But a dead center indentation gives a chiseled look to the nose and the chin. You want to lengthen the nose and the chin, then all you've got to do is get a dead center indentation. I don't want to do that; so, I make mine to the side. And you just push that up there like that, and you take your thumb and you pull that down, with your thumb. Very easy to do. [For this demonstration,] it's taken me longer than I've ever taken.

Now you notice on my first tie here this evening, it's a little bit short, you see? Just a little bit on this, which means I just take this, I take this and I go like that. And we start again. So, with these particular pants, which are not my suit pants, and the rise is a little bit higher, I pull it out right there. And we go over again. *[The teacher reties his necktie.]*

You should have a perfect point. Both ends of the tie should be absolutely perfect. Absolutely perfect.

Now with this type of a tie and this type of a knot, you see, you must not show the shirt in this area where the tie's supposed to be. That's very tacky. It certainly is not dress. Now you take your thumb under here and you shape and you form the tie. Now if you want that here—if you want the center one, that's no problem: you just make an indent right there. You can easily do that, once you get used to the pull. I still want a side one. I've always had a side one. I consider I look better with a side one. That depends on how *you* want to look.

Now once this tie is put behind your vest, you will see that it will stay like this whether it's six hours, you're wearing it, or it's sixteen. Now [Student S], would you like to get me just a blue vest from my closet upstairs.[7] Just a plain vest. See, I got last minute notice, like you did.[8]

Now, if the tie is a little bit, when it hangs like this, a little bit long—it's not long because you're going to have to have this portion, you're going to have to have it—this is what your vest is going to do. Now, you see, you'll find a perfect point because your vest is going to take care of this. Your tie will always stay like that. You don't need stick pins. You don't need clips. Besides, it's not the best dress. If you want to wear a two-piece suit—I'm talking about a three-piece suit. If you want a two-piece suit, that, then, is the idea for a tie clasp that goes here so that the tie isn't flopping all around. That's when you wear a tie clasp. Now if you want to wear a tiepin, that is designed for a three-piece suit only; and it is designed to go above the vest opening, where the pin may show. Otherwise, it should never be worn. That's where it belongs.

OK. She'll be down in a minute with a vest.

Now the only material, in a necktie, that will lock in is pure silk. If it's a blend, it will not hold. It will slip. Thank you. *[The teacher receives a vest from Student S.]*

[The tape recorder may have been paused for a moment.]

—hold all day long, unless you're bending over a lot and making a phenomenal amount of movement. Then it will slip. But it will never lay perfectly flat again and you don't need any pins. All right?

That's the necktie. Now let's move on to purchasing the trousers or suits. We've already gone through the neckties. Oh, excuse me. I haven't completed. I've got to take the tie off. This is all you have to do to take the tie off. Within less than an hour there'll be no wrinkles. In fact, the wrinkles will be gone before you know it. Just hang it over the chair. Because that's [what] silk does.

Trousers. You will notice that your trousers, time and time again—there's one of two things that happens to trousers, to men's trousers. One of the big problems is that just below the belt line, across here, there's a batch of wrinkles or a wrinkle. And you wonder why that is. Now if that is not the problem, the other problem, on the other hand, is that the trouser in this area is so tight that it doesn't look proper. Certainly, [it] doesn't look classy. Now that's caused by not knowing whether you are a medium rise, a short rise, or a long rise. Now what do I mean by that? I mean very simply from the waist to the crotch, you're either short, medium, or long.

Now if you buy a pair of trousers that are medium or long rise and you are a short rise, if it is a long rise, what happens [is] you have these wrinkles underneath your belt here. That means there's too much material between the crotch and the waistband top. Now if you are a medium or long rise and you buy a pair of trousers that are a short rise, then you get these cheeks showing back here that looks gross, to say the least. So once you learn whether you're short, medium, or long rise in that area, then when you go to buy a suit—you don't want a salesman who's just trying to make money and make a sale—[don't let him] sell you, for example, a 38 regular when you know you should be a 38 short. Because if you do, the trouser in that area is not going to fit you properly. And it's going to mean a whole recut job—very expensive for a tailor. The best thing to do is to forget the suit.

Now in the suit, if the shoulders don't fit, don't get the suit. If it is a short, it says on the sides, like 40 short, and you are a 40 long, don't buy the suit, because no matter what they do to the trousers, they will never hang properly. It's just that simple.

Now on the cutting of the trouser, as you can obviously see these are cut for boots. When it gives me the heel, the break will just barely break, because I always wear boots, except in the house, I can't.[9] The trouser will just barely break. Now when they make this cut here, you don't want to over accentuate. You see, this is cut at an angle. It should be cut at a very slight angle from this point to this point. Not at a drastic angle. And you can tell that when you fold them in hal—hold them up, you can see whether the line goes pssht! or the line just medium goes across. That's very important in buying a suit.

Now buying a suit is a terrific expense. Therefore, you want to know something about the suit. Is it 100 percent wool? Well, what quality 100 percent wool is it? Can you take the material, squeeze it up in your hands (without the salesman seeing you) to see if the wrinkle comes out immediately or whether it's going to hold? Well, it's very simple. When you grab the suit and *[The teacher makes a sound that is difficult to transcribe]*, usually you do it on the sleeve of the suit and you twist that, you see, in your hands. And then you see. Does the wrinkle fall out immediately or have you left a wrinkle? If you have left a wrinkle in doing that, you know very well what you're going to look like after an hour's wear.

Now when you buy a suit, you see, the proper thing to do is you must remember the stores do not have the proper type of presses to press a suit. So what happens? Oh, they press the trouser and they give it a press here and there. But they don't have these things that fit up into the shoulder so that gets properly pressed out. So that means when you purchase a suit, unless it's from a very exclusive haberdashery, it's got to go in for a pressing. Because if it doesn't, it's not going to look right. And after you first wear the suit, the suit takes your shape. It begins to shape itself.

So, if you buy the suit—and what you will see—and there's another thing. Sometimes, usually it's pressing, but not always; sometimes it's the wrong suit; it's the wrong size. It's perhaps a long, when you should have a regular. It's perhaps a short, when you should have a long. And it's going to show in several places. It will definitely show in the trouser in the back. There's no question about that; it will show immediately. It will also show on the shoulder whether there is a natural drape here or it comes from the seam and it makes a nice indentation. Now one of two things are at stake: usually it's the wrong size suit. Whether you believe—you see, you say you look for a 40. Well, you look for a 40. But all 40s are not the same because some are short, some are mediums, and some are regulars. And the salesmen, either they don't know or they don't tell you. Usually, they don't want to tell you. So, you can take a look and you can take and put your fist inside of the shoulder and just hold it gently and you can see if that is in need of pressing or it's the wrong size suit. Because it is not class to have a suit and to have this nice big indentation here because you got the wrong size.

So, you have to learn patience. If you're going to invest hundreds of dollars in a suit, you might as well get the one that's going to look good on you. And it's not going to look good on you if it hasn't been properly cut.

Now there are several types of suits on the market. The YSLs are very popular. And they're a good suit. But you have to remember, they are basically a short-rise suit. So, being a short-rise suit, basically—they have different sizes. You must be very careful to see how the trouser fits on you. If you're a long rise and that's a short rise, now—however, you see, when you look at the suit and it says 40 or 42, whatever your size is, short. And you know that your measurement from under the arm pit to your hip on a man is long, then you certainly don't want to buy one that says it's a 42 short. You see? Now you'll probably look and see how a 42 regular fits. If you take it because that's the only one the store can get [and] you don't have the wisdom of patience, then you've just thrown your money away. That's entirely up to the person. I can tell you very definitely from experience that Pierre Cardin, which is fine material, it's a fine suit; it definitely is not for a short rise. They're all made for medium to long rise in that area.

Now are there any questions on this for the men? *[After a short pause, the teacher continues.]* The men don't have any question; we'll just move immediately on to the ladies.

How about— [A male student begins to speak.]

Haven't even got to shirts.

How about shirts?

Well now, there's the question on shirts. Nothing looks good if it's nothing but bags around your belt. Just absolutely a box bag. There's nothing attractive about it, whether you look in a mirror or somebody else is looking at you. Therefore, the tapered shirt is the best-looking shirt for a man, if the man has taken control over his fat. If he hasn't, then he must wear a box shirt. There are several companies that make tailored shirts.

Personally, myself, I'm happy to see it started last winter, gradually; it really took over this year, that the so-called pearl-buttoned shirts are really in. They are everywhere! Now it's a style of the '40s and '50s that has returned. And, you know, for men's clothes, when they get a return of style, I mean, they just go hog wild, the designers, and everybody and his brother starts producing them because the men don't take that many changes. The pearl-buttoned shirt, tapered shirt, [is] commonly referred to as the Western shirt, although it is not limited to a Western shirt. This happens to be a pearl-buttoned shirt and it happens to be a Mark Daniels, which is a good make. And they make dress shirts. They make sport dress shirts. So, when a Mark Daniels company designer starts making them, they're really catching on. The girl said to me "Well, old John Travolta really got that style started." I said, "Well, I don't know about John Travolta," I said, "but I've waited years for them to come back."

All right, now. Dress shirts, you [have] got to remember that the seam must come here, never down here. Never up here. And when you buy a shirt, say that you're a 14, 14 and a half, you [have] got to remember that you're accepting a 31 to a 32 sleeve, you see. You must have something here in order to stretch your arm and to move it.

Now when you're wearing a shirt and a coat, if it's a suit, you want the shirt to come just below the sleeve of the suit coat. So therefore, if you're a 31 arm, usually you'll have to—that's the only one you can get is a 32, unless they cut it. Be grateful for the 32 because it will come down just the proper distance under the suit coat. Now if you're getting a sport shirt and you find, well, that's a little bit on the long side. Well, it's very simple: if you pull it, it will hold, it'll tuck here, unless you start doing a lot of exercises, and then it will slip down.

All right. Now [a] tapered shirt is the best-looking shirt. Nothing looks worse, especially if you're wearing a vest, than to have all this material sticking out underneath the vest. It certainly is not dress. So, in wearing a suit with a vest, a tapered shirt is an absolute must. Absolute must. You asked about shirts.

Now, in wearing a suit, stay away from wide pinstripes. They don't make you look good. So, if you see—what happens when a person goes to a store, they like a certain color. But in liking the color so much, desire is totally blinding. So instead of looking at the cut and looking how it feels and fits on them and looking at the material and seeing if the material is going to wrinkle right away and they're going to look after an hour as though they've been in their suit for six months sleeping in it, they're blinded by the color. When you look, you have in mind, you have, number one: design. Number one: design. I beg your pardon, number one: material. What material is it? Because it's going to hold or won't hold. Number one: material; number two: design; and number three; color. But number one is material. And you [have] got to learn something about material because you're the one that's investing all of the money in the suit, whether it's going to hold or it's not going to hold. It's very simple. So, you check for the material. Does it wrinkle easily? Will it wear? Will it hold up? Is it a 100 percent wool? Is it a blend? How does the crease look? Will the crease hold up? You'll tell right away when you run those simple tests.

Then, after you're satisfied with the type of material, then you take a look at the cut, the design. How does it drape on the shoulder? How does it fit? If it has to have major alteration and you don't know or have an expert tailor for what is known as a total recut—now a total recut is when every seam, every pocket, everything is ripped out and the suit is recut to your size. That's called a total recut. Now if it is an expert tailor, he can do an expert total recut and you would never know—as if it came from the factory. In fact, it'll even be better.

Because what happens in the factories, especially on shirts, suits, men's trousers—[for] women they do the same thing. [They] do in all factories. You have a stack of material. Why, there might be one thousand layers of the same material. A gigantic, big cutting machine comes down and cuts it. Now it's very simple: the cheaper the shirt, the cheaper the trouser, the cheaper the suit, the more material is stuck under the cutter. So, the top layers, they get the size 38 short. And by the time the cutter gets all the way down to the bottom ones, hundreds of layers of material later, that one, well, you'd think that suit's a 40. Do you understand? Now this is—you see, you've got to understand how they manufacture the shirts, the trousers, or the suits. This is how they manufacture them. Now the more material they can cut at one time, the more money they save.

And consequently, it is better to spend a little money on fewer clothes [and] have something that looks good, feels good, will last for you than to get something cheaper. To save a buck, you're losing hundreds because you're getting cuts—you wonder why—you say you take a 28 or 30 waist, whatever. So, you try on one pair of pants and it's marked a 30. They fit great. You try on another pair of pants that's marked a 30 and you think they're 34s because it's the cut. That's where they save. That's part of the process of factories saving money—you understand?—and to beat the competition and keep the price a few bucks, $5 [or] $10 under their competitors. But you're paying the price in the material. You're paying the price especially in the way it's been cut. The more expensive the suit, the less material gets stuck under the cutters for cutting. And that's just the way that it is. Yes.

How about shirt cuffs? Button versus French cuffs.

The style today is the button cuff. Now, what you have to take a look at is how many suits' sleeves can you wear a French cuff in? There are few, if any. You have to get a very expensive suit, basically. You either [have] got to get a very expensive suit or a very cheap suit. The style of the suits today [is] not the wide sleeve to accommodate the French cuff. So, what happens? It's quite simple with the French cuff: you [have] got a suit not designed to accommodate [French cuffs], though French cuffs are still sold. You [have] got a suit designed to accommodate a button cuff—you understand?—in the sleeve, the entire sleeve. It is not wide enough to accommodate the French cuffs. So, what happens when you wear it? Instead of the French cuff and the cuff link falling graciously inside the sleeve, it's pushed and wrinkled. The suit was not designed for a French cuff. Now that's the situation with French cuffs. Personally, I like French cuffs. I got the cuff links for them, but none of my suits, the style today, will accommodate the French cuff. And therefore, I don't get French cuffs. That's the reason.

Because, you see, if you have a suit that has the width to the sleeve, you understand, then it's got the width all the way up to the shoulder. And it is definitely not—Excuse me—it is definitely not a continental suit. Because the continental suit, the sleeve is made narrower, as the leg is made narrower. And wearing a French cuff, the cuff itself is going to be wrinkled in here, do you understand? And anyone that knows dress will know immediately that that's not class.

Oh, now color. As far as stripes and stripes, there's a lot to be considered. There are many shirts that have all kinds of stripes. All right? You must remember it is difficult, to say the least, to wear a suit that has a pinstripe and on top of the pinstripe to wear a striped shirt, and on top of the striped shirt, God forbid, to wear a striped tie. I mean you're just striped out. *[Several students laugh.]* You look totally plastered.

Now if you have a distinct striped suit, your best dress is a plain shirt. Now there's many kinds of plain, tapered shirts or tailored shirts, they're also called. They have [some] where the material itself has a design of some kind of stripe or something. Fine. Then, you see, you can wear a tie, God forbid, not a solid and not a stripe. You can get away with a very subtle pinstriped suit and a striped shirt, as long as you don't have a striped tie. You cannot do all three. And you must be very careful to do the striped suit and the striped shirt. OK? Now is there any other question?

How about footwear?

Footwear? Well, no man in his right mind would wear a pair of shoes with a suit that wasn't highly polished because the shoe is next in importance to the necktie. Now with a shoe you cannot—with a suit, you cannot wear a loafer. So just forget it. If you're going to wear a suit, forget loafers. The two, they don't go hand in hand. There's no way possible that you can wear a loafer and wear a suit and be dressed.

Now if you want decoration, then spend $25 or more for a pure silk tie. Get the color there. Because the shoe, in order to show class, must be absolutely plain. That means freed from all [these] fancy designs and things. The freer from design the shoe is, the better the suit looks. Because then the eye is drawn to the suit, the necktie. And, you see, it, [the shoe, doesn't] hold the attention [or] make an obstruction.

How about handkerchiefs in the pocket?

Absolutely no. That is not dress unless you're super, super, super dressed. And that's only dress when you're going to some ball somewhere where everyone has that kind of dress and there's some delicate little handkerchief here. Otherwise, just on the street, working on a regular job—now if you were working on a job where you wear a suit, it's totally, totally out. The style is in and out. And nowadays it's definitely out, unless you're with a group of people where that is that dress. Because it is not class. Yes.

Do they foresee a return to hats?

Yes, but not for a long, long time. You see, trench coats are gradually making an indentation. Now the hat will follow the trench coat where climate permits for real dress. But the trench coat is just barely getting a headway again, as the commonly referred [to as a] Western shirt or pearl-buttoned, tapered shirts are really taking over this year. They started last year for the winter shirt. You've got to give Pendleton credit for making a dent again. Of course, they're limited to wool, you understand. But it's really in this year and it will hold. The trench coat is barely, just barely trying to get a foothold again. And they must take a real hold before hats come back. And only where weather permits. Yes.

Can you wear a pinstriped suit with a striped tie?

No.

If the shirt is plain?

No. Absolutely not. The way you can tell is to have someone besides yourself—because when we're in desire, it always looks good to us. I mean, I never met a person with a desire that their desire didn't look great. Now that's the way our minds work. But it is certainly not class. Because if you have someone, your wife, perhaps, look in the mirror—you got stripes going this way. Now I don't know of any suits with the stripes going this way. I know of no suits with the stripes go this way. Now, what happens is—so you got a suit, maybe it's just a subtle stripe, but it's a stripe. Then you got a necktie at a 45-degree angle stripe, correct? I never saw any neckties with perfect horizontal stripes. I've never seen any neckties with straight vertical stripes. Is that not correct? Why do you think the designers and the factories have always made them with a 45-degree angle stripe? Does anybody know why? Any of you men or women know why? Yes.

They have to cut it on the bias.

They have to cut it on the bias. That's right. Otherwise, it's not a necktie. Fine. So, all neckties have 45-degree angle stripes.

Now you take these stripes, they're all going *that* way, right? And then you come around and you got stripes coming down *this* way. Well, it just cuts you right off. It just—*[The teacher makes a sound that is difficult to transcribe.]* Now if you like to be [hung] by the neck, wear that type [of tie], because that's what it does.

Now you'll never see a shirt where the stripes go at 45-degree angles. No. And you'll never see a shirt, a dress shirt, where the stripes go horizontal. You will see a shirt where the stripes go vertical, as the suit stripes go. This is why, under the right, delicate stripes, you can wear a striped shirt and a pinstriped suit, as long as the pinstripe is not a solid, accented pinstripe. But you cannot wear a striped tie. That's why I explained that before. That's why I said that before. That help with your question? Yes.

How about a striped tie and a glen plaid?

No! Absolutely not! *[Many students laugh.]*

Now if you want to know what it looks like, don't put it on. Lay it down on a table or your bed. Lay it down. Lay the suit coat down, a glen plaid, and then take a nice stripe, that you think [the] color combination looks great, and lay it underneath. And you'll see right away. Just look at it. Take at least ninety seconds. You can't make it that long before you start getting dizzy. I guarantee you, if you want to know what your clothes look like, before you put your clothes on, you men, then just take your shirt, take your necktie, take your suit coat or your vest, preferably your suit coat because there's more material to look at, and lay them down and look at them for at least, try to look at them for at least ninety seconds. I guarantee you it'll be a miracle if you get past nine seconds before you go dizzy.

Now that's how people look at you. That's what's happening to them. They don't know what's happening to them. *[Again, many students laugh.]* They just know there's something they don't like and they will look the other way. So, if you want to know how people feel looking at you, do that before you ever put your clothes on. Yes. Any other questions? Yes.

Yes. Could you please discuss the colors of boots in relation to the colors of suits?

Well, I'm sure we all agree and know, you cannot wear a tan shoe with a dark suit. There's no way you can. You can get away with a cordovan, a dark cordovan, you can get away with a dark suit. Black for black. Black for gray. Brown for brown or cordovan for brown, depending on the shade of brown. And tan for beige and etc. So that's where you can use a cordovan with some grays, but not all grays.

Thank you.

OK? Anyone else have questions? Yes, the lady.

Must men always wear belts?

Do men always wear belts?

Must they always wear belts or do they—

If there are belt loops, a man must wear a belt to be dressed. If there are no belt loops, he does not have to wear a belt. But he certainly is not dressed with belt loops and no belt. Now if he has belt loops and suspenders and the loops show, then he's still not dressed. He can get away with no belt as long as the vest totally covers the belt loops, if there are belt loops present, because it won't show. Otherwise, he must wear a belt, yes. Absolutely. And it's a rare pair of trousers you'll find without belt loops. So, he'd have to have them tailored that way. And, believe me, they're not that classy because that's part of a gentleman's adornment, is the belt. So, don't be cheap on the belt. Yes, the lady.

Could you please discuss the width of the belt with store clothes?

The width of the belt is dependent on whether the man has no waist, practically, and he wants some kind of a waistline or whether or not he wants to shorten his waistline. And it depends whether or not it's a sporty look, whether he wants to look tall or he wants to look short. And so, there's a lot of factors. But basically, with a suit a man wears a narrow belt. Now you will notice that the loops in suits, in good suits, they're narrow loops to accommodate a narrow belt. If he's wearing a pair of slacks, then he has a little bit of a wider loop and, therefore, can accommodate a wider belt. The belt basically, what you have to do in the judgment—or consideration, rather, of the belt is that you don't want to wear a belt where three quarters of an inch of bare loop [show]. Because, what happens—it's very tacky looking. Say that I put a real skinny—you want to run up and get me a skinny black belt? The narrowest one. It's a YSL in my closet.

Should I stop the recorder?

Yeah. Stop the recorder. We can take a break. *[The recorder was stopped. The class reconvenes after a short break.]*

Part 2. OK. You'll have to learn that when you buy slacks, now when you just buy slacks, there are certain companies that make their slacks, basically, with a short rise. YSL makes a short rise. But not all of their sport or dress trousers [are] a short rise. So that you immediately tell when you put them on. And when you put them on, if there's all this wrinkle back here, you know very well that particular style is not a short rise. Basically, they make a short rise. You understand? Basically, but not always.

That's why if you buy a trouser, like a shirt, you try on each and every one. You never go to a store, as you know, you've been with me, and you'd never buy a shirt, even one that's in a package that you're going to wear under your suit, you never buy it and walk out the store. I buy it. I take all the pins out of it, take all the wrapping off of it. I go into the fitting room and I try it on. After all, I'm investing $23. So, you try it on. Now if you're going to be, at that time—say, you're going to buy two or three shirts: you try on each one because if you don't try it on, you may get stuck with one that was at the bottom of the cutter. Do you understand? And so, then you wonder, "What's the matter? I don't like this shirt." You don't know why you don't like it and you might come up with all kinds of justifications. What you don't like [is] it doesn't fit like the one you tried on. So, you try on your shirts. You see what I mean? You [try] them on, like you try on each trouser.

Now we're getting to the belts and this is the reason—I hope all you gentlemen can see—why you don't buy a reversible belt. I'll show it to the ladies and see how it breaks down. See the breakdown?

Why would it break down?

Well, it breaks down because this has been basically worn on the brown side—

Richard, you're not getting on the tape.[10]

Sorry. This has been—the reason that the belt breaks down is because the belt was basically worn [with] the brown side showing. All right. Now I'll put it on and I'll show you. Brown side showing. So, what happens [is] you pull the buckle and you put it in and you break all of this down, the coloring on the leather [on the opposite side of the belt].

Ahh.

So, you're not saving money by buying a reversible, though they got thousands in the stores and they're very popular. You're losing money. So, what you do with the belt: you buy the belt. You need a black one? You buy a black one. You need a brown one? You buy a brown one. You need a tan one? You buy a tan one. And that is it. Otherwise, this belt is not even a year old—you can pass it to show them how the inside breaks down. So, when you want to go wear it for a black belt, forget it. It looks like you had it fifty years. Oh, I'm sorry about that.[11] That's the reason you don't buy a reversible belt. Because you get one belt of each color and you save money. And you don't have to keep re-buying those things. That belt proves, from its breakdown, that I basically used it for brown. And it cannot be used as a black belt because it's so tacky.

I will try it on here to show you about loops, trouser loops. Notice that the black side, only, is broken down, because that's the inside. And that's caused from when you pull your belt to put it through the buckle, it's breaking down the inside. So, if you need brown and black, you buy two separate belts.

Shall I stop the recorder until it comes around?

Yes, if you want. They're just showing how the breakdown is.

Just—

All right. Put it in pause. *[The tape recorder was stopped for a time.]*

Ready? Now we're going to show about width. This is my other belt. Now I would not wear this buckle unless it was a sport outfit. God forbid, I could not wear it for dress, because it's sport. I happen to like it; so, I wear it.

Now we'll put on a belt that is not the proper belt for these trousers. Now, not only does it look tacky but more important than just looking tacky—and you see it's improper, you see? The width is improper. What happens is—

Can you back up a little bit, please?[12]

Oh, what happens is that in sitting, standing, moving you start breaking down the structure of the waistband. That's what's important. And it's worth having a proper-width belt, if you have decent trousers, decent pants, so you don't break down the waistband structure.

Now these trousers here do not have in them that buckram stuff, but you will find that many trousers at the waistband have that stiffness inside to hold them up. All right. Especially those type of trousers will break down right away. But even this material, see, it's doubled here, it'll start breaking down, and you've ruined a good pair of trousers before you ever get started.

Anyway, you don't buy reversible, time-saver belts. They're not worth it. They're just not worth it. All right.

Now are there any other questions? We're on belts, shoes—yes. The lady there.

Yes. I remember in years past they had a sleeve on a man's suit that had a slit in it, but it was an overlay. Was that for French cuffs?

Those were basically designed for French cuffs.

I see. Thank you.

Yes. Basically. But remember, French cuffs, you know, they have never been able to hold their style. They come and they go. You see? It's just like green for men. It can't seem to hold on. They try and try. It can't seem to hold on. Yes.

Could you please say something about tie clips?

Tie clips? Well, the only time, the only time that you wear a tie clip is when you're in a two-piece suit, you understand, or [when] you're in a sport coat and dress slack. And you don't want the tie—and the tie shouldn't be—flopping all over. That's when you wear a tie clip. Now, you never ever wear a tie clip up here, you see. Up here, you wear a tie pin with a three-piece suit above the vest. And the tie should never ever be flat. The shirt should never show up here where the knot is, ever. All right?

Uh-huh.

That's the only time you wear a tie clip. You wear the tie clip one button above the lowest button on the shirt. Now it goes between these two buttons on everyone. That's where a tie clip is properly worn. It never goes below it and it, God forbid, it never gets above it.

OK.

It goes from the lowest button that shows above the belt to the next button. Any space in between there is where the tie clasp goes, but no other place. And another thing with a tie clasp, you see, when you put on a tie clasp, remember, the tie is hanging straight. So, you [have] got a tie clasp here and the material of the tie is over here. You cannot put the clasp so it wrinkles the tie in this area. So therefore, a tie clasp is just barely pinching the edge of the shirt.

Uh-huh.

If it's doing anything else, it is not only tacky looking but it is improper. It just barely pinches the edge of this, because, you see, they're usually, they're not that long. They may be that long.

Uh-huh.

Maximum, a good tie clip. If it's one of those giant, long ones, well, those were made for ties about this wide, [and] they are not in style. And they didn't last at all in style. Yes.

[Thank you.]

You're welcome. Yes.

Who should wear a narrower tie and who should wear a little bit wider tie?

Well, now that depends, it depends on the gentleman's neck; it depends on whether or not he wants to try to add some height. You shouldn't have a necktie where the tie itself, the knot, is so wide that you see nothing but the knot. Because if you do that, you see, you don't see any of the suit and shirt or anything else. So, the width of a tie should not be so wide that it looks like the man is all neck. You see? There's more to a person than just the neck. I realize it's the symbol of self-will, but there is more to a person besides the neck.

And I want to speak and be right with you about plaids. Plaids are very nice. I have some myself. But remember, no matter what, they're sport. They're not dress. There's no way that a plaid shirt can be dress. All right? Yes.

How about under clothing?

Well, thing is—yes, that is a very important question. There is nothing attractive to any eye with a man's T-shirt. So, a man that wears a T-shirt, he has an open collar and the white T-shirt, the underwear shows, remember, it's not class and it's certainly is not dress. Now, when you—to not have that problem with your undershirt, because remember, it's underwear. You wouldn't think a lady was attractive if her slip was showing if she had an open blouse. In fact, it's most unattractive. It's certainly not dress. So, the same thing is with a man. You don't have a white T-shirt showing at your neck with an open shirt.

Now if it's the only T-shirt you have, then you've got to pay the price and button up the collar. If you're smart, you will go and at least get one V-neck T-shirt, because then the V-neck is not going to show any underwear here. Yes.

Ah—

And I'm glad you asked about underwear because nothing is more gross, and you see it repeatedly, than to have a nice pair of trousers—I try to watch it—and have the wrinkles of your shirttail showing. Now I am aware and [have been] for many years that a lot of men that have money, they don't have any tails to their shirts because they have their tailor cut them all off, and it's only down to here. So even though it's a dress shirt, [it] immediately goes to the tailor and it gets cut off; so, they don't have any problem with a wrinkle here of their tail of their shirt. They just get cut off.

Now some designers have come out with shirts that are cut across short so the men won't have that look with their trousers. Now the problem is that unless they get a proper fitting undershirt and it's pulled down, you understand, then—that deals with how you dress—then the shirt is put on and the undershirt is pulled way down and it's tucked in properly and smooth, then you don't have that problem which looks terrible. Any other question?

With sport wear, what kind of neck wear would be appropriate for sport other than a tie?

Other than a tie?

Yes.

Oh. Now that depends on the man. You can have—turtlenecks you [have] got to be very careful with. Men have to be very careful with turtlenecks because many men do not have the neck of a turtle and, therefore, should never wear a turtleneck. Because you [have] got to understand you [have] got to have a neck, depending on how wide the roll is. Now, a tall man with a long neck, he can—and doesn't have a gigantic Adam's apple here, sticking out—he can wear a fairly wide, perhaps a two-inch turtleneck. Because you've got to understand what it does to the neck. It immediately shortens it. So that you see this little face peaking up, just like a turtle. That's where it got its name: turtle neck. Because when you wear those kind of sweaters, when you wear those type of things, that is what it does to you: it gives you the look of a turtle. So, if you want to look real stubby and you don't have this nice long neck to deal with, then just wear a turtleneck, and you will look just like what it's named after: you'll look like the turtle, the neck of the turtle.

Is there any other question? Now you've seen the turtle when he just sticks out his little face, just barely, and you see this roll? Well, that's what they copied. They copied the turtle. And they made the turtleneck. Any other questions? Yes.

Well, along those lines, what do they feel about ascots?

Well, first—they're fine, depending on the man and how he wears it. But you've got to understand whether or not they are in style. Now I think we'll all agree, at this time, they are not in style. They're not. Now if you want something [to] accentuate, there [are] fine combinations of cream, off-white, not snow white, and black is excellent combination for practically all men. Or a dark navy blue with a slight cream color in a sweater or something is very sharp looking and very attractive. And especially if you have difficulty trying to wear different colors, you see. Maroon is also a very good color. That's very individual.

And you [have] got to go with each individual, what color that is, like I have with the ladies.

What sort of a neck on those sweaters?

Well now, remember, if you're wearing a V-neck sweater, if you're wearing a V-neck sweater, there's absolutely nothing you can wear, *nothing* you can wear underneath except a dress shirt and tie. So, if you [have] got a V-neck sweater for a man, that's the only thing you can wear. Don't try wearing anything else. Now you might think it's sporty looking to wear a V-neck sweater and an open shirt collar, but it is not good dress. It is not good dress.

Now if you want to wear a vest sweater—now there's a vast difference between a full-sleeve sweater and a vest sweater. You can get by wearing an open collar, if it is a dress open collar with a vest sweater. You cannot, it is not real class—remember that—you cannot get away, dress-wise, wearing a full-length sweater with a V and an open shirt. It just is not dress.

And you've got to be very careful, like, if you're—it is not street dress at all to wear a vest sweater or any other sweater and have an open collar. It's not dress, even though they show, in some of the stores, a pair of slacks, a sweater, and a matching, color-coordinate[d] sport shirt. Well, one thing about that, if you want to be known as a person without any initiative thinking, go buy the whole assemble, the whole thing. It's all been color coordinated by the designers for you and it looks blah! If you like something that's plumb color or lilac or some of these other oddball colors, they have those available. OK? Any other questions on the men's department? *[After a short pause, the teacher continues.]* I guess all the women are waiting for facials. Yes.

In reference to the Mark Daniels brand on the tailored shirts—

They are one of the companies that have tailored shirts.

Are there any others that are recommended?

Well, Mark Daniels is a good brand. When YSL comes out with the pearl-buttoned shirt—don't worry, they will, because all the companies are getting on the bandwagon while they're moving. After all, they're in business to make money. So, the designers *this year*, this year the designers are all coming out with the pearl-buttoned, what they call the pearl-button shirts. The reason they call them that, they used to look like pearl. Now, of course, they're plain glass, but they are—some of them—are colored and some aren't. But they don't have the pearl look like they used to; otherwise, they'd cost a mint.

And also—

Daniel Hester is coming out with them. That's another good make. The Daniel Hester, however, remember, the Daniel Hester, like the Pierre Cardin, is basically designed for taller men. I mean, not [a] 6-foot [man] necessarily, but certainly not 5-6 and a quarter. I can tell you that. *[Mr. Goodwin was just over 5 feet and 6 inches tall.]* Because the shirt's cut differently. It has a long rise in the shirt.

Shirts, you know, the rise, you see, you're talking about the rise here and how to buy your trouser—now you [have] got to consider—you haven't even considered the rise from this point to this point. Because when you put on a shirt, even if it's tapered, if it's the wrong rise here, it just, it just doesn't fall right. It looks terrible. Because that's also—because this depends on where this cut is in the material. You see, you can tell when you put the shirt on, you understand, and you just let it fall down here; you can see. Does that carve in here or is it carving in down here and then it's swooping out down there? Well, you know very well that that was made for a tall man, you see? And you don't want to buy that shirt. But that's why you try the shirt on before you ever leave the store. Because those are the things you see in the dressing room and you see right away. You see, if it's a tailored shirt, then it's got this cut, you understand? It's tailored, tapered, to fit your particular body, you see? You're either short, medium, or long, not just here, but here to here. So, you can see right away how it fits.

Thank you.

Otherwise, you don't make the investment. Yes.

Now if a man has narrow shoulders—

Yes?

—and his hips are, he's not in proportion. Is there something, like, that, to accentuate—

Why, of course. The good tailor pads the shoulders. That used to be very common practice. Now it's more difficult. Some of them don't even know how to pad the shoulders. It was very common practice for many, many, many, many years. If the man does not have the shoulder, you know, that he should have to fit the hip, then they pad the shoulder. The good tailor takes the lining out, and they put the padding in properly. Then he looks like he's got shoulders. Yes.

How about on shirts?

On shirts? Then he's got to work with design. You want to know what gives you shoulders? I don't know if you can see from there. See this mark here? The material?

Yes. [Several students respond.]

See the material?

Uh-huh.

That gave me shoulders. I happen to like these. I like these shirts not just because they give me shoulders because I like the way they fit and they're not all baggy, hanging down over my belt, see? Things like that give you shoulders. That's what gives you shoulders.

Epaulets will give you shoulders, you see. Anything that draws the eye to thickness in this area, you understand, or strength in this area, heaviness in this area, gives the illusion of shoulders. OK? Now if you have—if you don't have something here in design or otherwise, then you don't have the shoulders.

You see? That's how you correct having [narrow] shoulders. And if your shoulders are too wide, then you go the other way, see? You get the plainness to eliminate them.

You just answered my question.

Yes, you just got to go the reverse way.

Uh-huh.

You want everything that just falls and drapes here; so, there's no [attention drawn to] the shoulders. So, it will balance this out down here, you see. See?

But you'd be amazed at what the proper width belt will do to a pair of trousers. Makes all the difference in the world. And you know, there is nothing good looking about baggy trousers, you see. Sagging busts on a woman are equal to baggy trousers on a man. And that's the comparison. They're the same. And they look just as great. All right now, ladies, do you understand?

Uh-huh.

Yes.

Can loafers be worn with sport jacket, slacks, and a shirt and tie?

Absolutely not. The moment the tie went on, the dress shoe has to go on. The moment you put the tie on, you must have the dress shoe. Not a loafer. You cannot properly dress with a necktie and not have the dress shoe. The necktie guarantees the dress of the shoe. Loafers will not make it with a tie. There's no way they can. Open shirt? Yes, they'll make it. A loafer goes with an open shirt. Sport shirt or open shirt, then you wear your loafer. Yes, someone else had a question? Yes.

A lot of the sport coats, they're, like, it's not like a suit, it's looser, I mean, as, that's more casual, right?

It's a sport coat? Yes.

It's a sport coat, but most suits have the real tight cloth. The sport coats are kind of open. They have, like, a rough finish.

A looser. Yes. That is—that's sport.

A lot of them have small designs, a herringbone or check.
Yes.
Can you wear stripes with that?
Depending. Now there's a lot of factors there you [have] got to consider. That depends on what kind of tie that you're wearing with it. Is it a very delicate stripe? Is it a very bold stripe? Is there something in the stripe of the tie that will pick up the color of the material? Because if it doesn't, then you can't. It depends on the weave. Is it a real open, course weave or is it a medium course weave? So, there [are] several factors on whether or not it can go with a tie that has a stripe in it.
Also, on that course weave, is a wool tie OK?
Well, you see, I'll tell you one thing: a wool tie, you just have to understand, is not a dress tie. Never was a dress tie. Never will be a dress tie. There is no way to make a wool tie a dress tie. There is no way. A wool tie is a sport tie. It's limited to sport wear. It can only be used with sport.
By sport—Excuse me.
Sport means not a suit and a sporty look. A wool tie is strictly a sporty look and should never be worn for dress. It is a sport tie. Definitely a sport tie.
But—
Now if you wear a wool tie and then on top of that you wear a woolen sport coat, you [have] got to be really, really careful because all of a sudden you look like you weigh 200 pounds. You're adding phenomenal weight. Now if you can carry that much weight and the color is coordinated properly, then you can get away with it. Wool ties are very difficult for men to wear. And I guess if you go to the stores, you'll notice they're not overly popular. I've yet to find a wool necktie in a showcase. Has anybody here found a woolen necktie in a showcase? You won't find a wool necktie in a showcase. You'll only find pure silk. Unfortunately, they're trying to mix some of the combinations, silk and something else, into them. But you will not find a

woolen necktie under a showcase. There's a reason for that. Yes. Does that help with your question?

Yes.

OK. Everybody had enough with the men's design? *[After a short pause, the teacher continues.]* They have?

I'm sure we're gone way over the tape.

Then shut off your tape. We'll go out to the kitchen. We're going to have a coffee break and do a facial.

OCTOBER 27, 1981

Design Class 4

This class [is] entitled "Spiritual Centers of Communication," the sound system of the human anatomy. *[Again, the published title of this class is derived from the label on the audiotape.]*

Now there are eight sound speakers in the human body, the house of clay. There is one central power center for that sound system. The speakers are located—and are of equilateral triangular shape. One is located with the apex downward over the left chest. One is located with the apex upward over the right chest. One is located—if you will draw a line between the top of your cheekbone straight across, equilateral triangle, to the center area of your mouth, is another speaker. The other speaker, the other—they come in, as you understand, in pairs—the other speaker is from that point equilaterally, to this point of your forehead. That's four speakers.

The next set of speakers are located at this point here at the front of the head equilaterally to the back, top part of the head. And the other pair—the other speaker to that pair is located from this point to the back of the head.

Now there are two other speakers. One is located with the apex pointing toward the toes on the bottom of the left foot. One is located with the apex pointed to the heel on the right foot.

The size of the spiritual communication centers or speakers of the human anatomy may be determined—for they are all identically the same size—may be determined by measuring the line from the top of the cheekbone, and all speakers in the anatomy are exactly of that size. They are all triangular, equilateral triangles.

The spiritual power center to the speaker system is located in the area of the sexual organs.

I note some of you are taking notes, but it's also being recorded. If you wish to know whether or not you are utilizing the speakers, all the speakers of your body or you are utilizing them to their fullest or only part of the speakers of your body, you may determine this when you speak by very lightly touching the area of the rib cage. If you feel a vibration or movement when you speak, then you are using those speakers. The same applies to the location of all the speakers of the human body.

Now, what we must understand is quite simple: energy flows from the vital body. In order to entertain or have a thought in a mental world in our mind, energy is used to form the thought. That energy, also, is used and utilized to maintain and to sustain that form. Now in the sound system, which is color—and, as we have said before, color is sound.

Many people can speak for many, many hours. They have no hoarseness; they have no problem with their throat. The reason for this is they are using the speakers of their anatomy whether they know it or not. Unfortunately, these speakers have been suffocated through errors of ignorance, especially the speakers of the chest. Covered with flesh, like a blanket over a regular fidelity system, you're suffocating by not keeping the flesh supported properly so that the sound vibrating from the area of the chest, from those particular speakers, can come out clearly and distinctly.

Now in the testing of whether or not you are using these speakers, simply touch these areas of their location.

Now I'm going to give you a few moments to absorb that, and I'm going to let you have your questions before we go on. Are there any questions? Yes.

I would like to know how we can retrain ourselves so that we can properly place our voice to vibrate.

Well, visualization, you must understand that visualization is an instrument through which energy may flow. Now you already know that energy follows attention. How do we get attention? What is the process that takes place? If you think of something that is of interest to you, energy, attention goes to it.

Therefore, if a person wishes to utilize certain speakers—now, for example, when a person is speaking, they will have—or singing—they will have experiences, sometimes, in certain parts of their anatomy. Sometimes they think their toes tingle at a certain note or a certain pitch. Or there is a certain kind of a freezing or sensation at the top of their head or even the back of their head. Or they feel something in their chest. Or there is a sensation in the area of the nostrils. These are the speakers that they are not used to the sensation of them being activated or utilized.

Most people use only the midrange. For example, there is the base, the midrange, and the treble. Just like the speakers. A good speaker—a speaker was originally copied from nature. Man is the world['s], the universe's greatest copier. He copies the things he sees. He copies the things he senses. He copies the things he feels. It is long ago—the word that they call the lost word isn't just a matter of understanding; it is a matter of application, and we do not have the result of the word we speak. It's not the word we've lost; it's the art of the word that we have lost.

Because we do not—we are under the delusion that we speak from the throat. That is not where we speak from. That is where we think we speak from, but [it] is not where we speak from.

Now if you wish to take a few moments, we can shut off the recorder and I will show you myself whether, whether or not you can feel—

[At this point, the recording is interrupted. The recording begins again as a student is speaking.]

—*only be able to hear that if you really used your vocal cords. Not if* . . . [Background noises make it difficult to accurately transcribe the rest of the student's words.]

That is correct. The vocal cords must be used. But, you see, most people are simply using [a] very little bit of their speakers. The sound does not emanate from the feet. The sound does not emanate from the speakers of this area here. The sound is not fully emanating from the area of the chest. The sound is not emanating from the head. And they do not have the sensation because the sound emanates from the whole being.

Now, in the spiritual realms, that sound, which is color, is known as color and *is* color and it does not—you cannot lie in spiritual realms of consciousness for the colors are universal colors. And therefore, everyone knows the color. The language is the language; there is no way—there is no covering. So, whatever is spoken is viewed as color. It comes out of the body as color. It's coming out as color now. We do not see the color. We *think* we hear the sound.

You see, my friends, the sound is taking place in the ear, in the *ear* of the listener. That's where the sound is. We think that the sound—without the ear, there is no sound. The sound takes place in the ear. The vibration from the speaker is an emanation of color. It is transmitted to what we think is sound. If there is no ear, there is no sound, but there is color, for color *is* sound. The sound takes place here. It does not take place anyplace else. The speaker is an emanation of color, of vibration. Only here does it get transmitted [into] what we understand to be sound.

Now, it's question time.

Do each one of the speakers have to do with a level of consciousness or do they have any specific significance?

Oh, all speakers are affected by levels of consciousness because energy, you see, is—a person can speak; a person can sing. And at the time they're speaking or singing forms are being created because concentration is not there, you see. There may be a partial concentration.

Now, the power for all of these speakers, you understand, and its location and what it represents, it is the power center for the speakers. Energy, as I said earlier, is dissipated from the vital body, from the power center by thought. So, if a person is speaking and their thought is not the word they are speaking, then it does not have the power of the word, for the energy from the vital body needed to power the eight speakers is being dissipated to go into the thought forms that are being created and shaped, maintained, sustained, and [for their] movement. That comes from your vital body. Therefore, concentration is the key to all power, for when you have the full utilization of the energy of the vital body, when it is directed to one thing and one thing only until only the essence remains, then the lost word is no longer lost, for the art is there. Do you understand that? *[After a short pause, the teacher continues.]*

I think singers, especially, should be aware of a certain stage of growth of people in reference to singing. They call it puberty. You call it an age when the voice changes. But what you don't understand, the power center at that time is in the process of dissipation into other areas of consciousness. And so, what you understand to be sound starts to change. The reason it starts to change is very, very simple. The energy is not the same degree or amount of energy that it was before. In other words, you might say a person, a young boy is going from a soprano to a baritone. What is happening is the energy—more energy is required for the higher vibrations, the soprano, the treble, than is required for the baritone or the bass. More energy is actually utilized out of the power center.

Now when that energy is dissipated at thought forms being created by a mental world at the time a person is speaking and singing, you understand, or even when they are not, that is being drained, that energy, and therefore, from the high pitch, from what you would call a treble, you move down into the other pitches. It takes more energy for soprano than it does for baritone. Whether you understand that or not, I know someday you will. Yes. Go ahead with your question.

My question was answered. [After a short pause, the student asks a related question.] *How about listening?*

Listening? That deals with another whole class. Now you're talking about the ear, where the sound is actually taking place. The color leaves your body. Here in this physical world this transforms it into what you call sound. Now whether or not you are the one speaking and you think you hear that, which without the ear you cannot, but with the ear you do. The ear is required in this world. Otherwise, it is only color and you view it; you cannot and do not hear it.

Yes, I want to get to [Student Q]. Yes.

Why is it, then, that some people, they can speak very nicely, but when they sing, they can't hear the note on the piano? They—it's—

They cannot hear. They can speak—

Uh-huh.

—but they cannot hear. Because the lines of communication of the centers [are] not clear. You see, for example, if you do not have a harmonious flow of energy throughout the sound system, if a portion—or in varying degrees—is dissipated into other areas of consciousness into other forms—you follow me so far?—

Uh-huh.

—then the listening ear, the listening ear, where the sound is really transmitted in the ear, is distorted. It is distorted in their ear. Therefore, they are, you might say, tone-deaf. They can't tell one tone from another. Because, you see, if a person, if they wish not to be what you call tone-deaf, then the person must learn more of the art of concentration, for a portion of them is not there. Now they may consciously try for years, but that never, you understand, do they overcome—not that they can't, if there is true concentration.

Concentration is not just a matter of a mental gymnastic; it is a matter of total self-control. You see, one must be able to control not only the conscious mind [and] the subconscious mind but any and all dissipation of energy from the vital body to the creating forms.

One must become that which they concentrate upon. In other words, a person may say they are lost in what they're singing. They are no longer there. Now when a person is no longer there, that simply means that their energy is not dissipated to an awareness of their surroundings because they now are that which they have concentrated upon. And being that which they [have] concentrated upon, there is no awareness of anything else for they have become the thing itself.

If a person truly, in the art of concentration, for example, a singer, if they become the song, they are no longer anything else. And when they become the song, that is, the essence of the song, then everything within is united to that one purpose. For that moment, they become the very thing that they have concentrated upon. Now a song is not aware of a room. A song is not aware of a body. A song is not aware of a sky or a bird or a tree. A song is aware it is a song.

A word is aware that it is a word. And because its full awareness is of what it is, it is not anything else. In order to be aware of anything, we must direct energy to it. And it is in the directing of the energy to it that we are a house divided, and the word returns unto us void. We are a house divided. Stop and think of how many divisions [there are] in the house when one desires to accomplish anything.

Say, one wants to, to learn a note. We all understand that middle C—middle C is where one should begin. That's where one should begin. Because that is the range—from that balance point, they may move up and down. But a person should never move higher than they move lower. A person thinks when they speak they may only move that way. No, they're speaking and moving this way as they're moving *this* way. They're moving in both directions. However, more energy may be poured into the right side of this sound than is [poured] into the left. And consequently, we perceive that a person is soprano or a person is baritone or whatever name we have given them. The truth of the matter is that more energy is being poured in that direction although the other is still vibrating equally. Except it does not receive as much energy and, therefore, is not perceived. This is why it is possible for a soprano to reach a very high note, but it is also possible to reach a lower note. It depends on where the power, through concentration, is going. Does that help with your question?

Yes. Thank you.

Yes.

No, no. [A student may be indicating that he no longer has a question.]

You had a question earlier.

It's answered, again.

It's answered. Yes.

OK. Well, we've had at least one notable singer who was deaf.

Yes?

Who never heard, technically never heard himself.

Technically.

Yeah. But yet, his notes were correct. He could deliver a good song and not hear himself. Was he—

Were you mentioning Johnnie Ray?

Yeah.

Yes. I happen to have known him. Yes, he was absolutely deaf.

OK. Well, then how did he work that out with himself?

Well, it's quite simple: you see, he himself spoke and he sang. And the listening ear could not understand because he was physically deaf, surely, he should have been tone-deaf. Would everyone not agree? *[After a short pause, the teacher continues.]* Does it not show us that tone, so-called, deafness is something we have been educated to? We have been educated to it. He didn't have the problem of being educated to it. Now you might say, "Well now, this person here, they're born tone-deaf." Now we may have merited a body in which we seem to be tone-deaf; then we educate our self, from acceptance, that that's the way we are as this energy is dissipated into these various forms in the sound system. Yes, he was quite an education for the music world. Although he was, he was a good singer, I don't—he was a popular singer. I think in the '50s. I guess it was the '50s. Yes.

Is there an exercise for developing the potential of the speakers?

Absolutely and positively. That's been given to you some time ago. It was highly recommended, years ago, that middle C, that you practice an "Ah-uhm" on middle C until such time as you could gain full concentration, for that is the very important key to movement throughout the sound system. The simple "Ah-uhm." Now when that is properly done, you will feel it, you think, in your entire anatomy. You're actually feeling it in eight speakers. That's where you're really feeling it.

Thank you.

Uh-huh. This is why when a person, sometimes they reach a certain note and they think they feel it in their toes; it's actually the speaker at the bottom of their feet. That's where it really is, but the sensation may be in the toes. The sensation may be in part of the nose or the back of the head, those are where the speakers are located.

"Speakers" is the best word that we can bring to you to understand for something to relate to. Yes.

The easiest thing that I have found to really get in touch with all those so-called speakers is the humming.

Oh, yes.

Because the humming vibrates everything, if it's done correctly. If it's—

That was given some time ago. There's a certain hum—were you given a hum?

No.

That you were never—oh, then it wasn't given. Fine. Because that, yes, because one is more receptive to a hum than they are to anything else. But why is one more receptive to a hum? Is one's ear more receptive to a hum over a physical speaker or to music? What will cause the ear to instantaneously be attracted to sound? A musical note or a hum? And if so, why? *[After a short pause, the teacher repeats himself.]* If so, why?

Well, I think it would be responding more to the hum. [Student R responds.]

Why?

Curiosity is one thing. For a clear note, it is immediately identified. But for a hum, it's not as easily identified. And therefore, you have to—it's lower; it's softer. You have to pay more attention. You have to direct more attention to it to hear or to, to get it. [Student R continues.]

Thank you. [Student Q].

With a hum, though, it has to do, really, has to be situated up in here to be able to vibrate, because if it comes from the throat, it's not really a true hum. It has to be situated up in the front of the face.

Yeah. [Student R agrees.]

And it's a clean, it's a very clean, true sound. [Student Q continues.]

Well, I was talking about the listener, not the hummer. [Student R clarifies.]

But it is the ear of the hummer that is hearing the hum.

Oh, I thought the question was, If somebody heard a hum or a spoken sound—

Yes.

—which would they be more attracted to? [Student R responds.]

I see. Whether or not it's their own hum.

I presumed it would be somebody else's hum.

There is a vibration in that particular speaker that is more noticeable than the vibration of the other speakers. That is very true. Surely, you've heard people speak that these speakers are the predominate speakers, and it sounds like they're speaking through their nose, I mean, if it is overly emphasized. Yet all the speakers are being used. But if it is overly emphasized in that particular speaker, then, you see, we think this person is talking through their nose.

But when you hum, you feel a sensation in that particular—in those speakers, those two speakers, is what is happening. Why is the hum, the awareness of it, emphasized in those particular speakers? Why aren't we aware of the sound that's also emanating from the ones in the feet? *[After a short pause, the teacher continues.]*

I guarantee you if you will stand and be still and hum, you will be aware of the hum in other speakers in the anatomy. The only reason that it has been a rare occasion for most people, most all people, any awareness of the other speakers, is because they've really never paid attention to them. When it has happened and they've had a sensation, they credit it to something else. That's why we have—you see, the mind has nothing to relate to, to these speakers. But the mind does have experiences when it had a sensation here, when it was singing or speaking, when it had a sensation in the bottom of its feet or foot, when it had a sensation here in the forehead or when it had a sensation over here in the area of the cheekbone. The mind can relate to times when it had these sensations. But not having, yet, the information or understanding of what's taking place, it has always credited it with something else.

Yes, you wanted to finish with—

Well, the question, I think, was why are they more aware of the nasal sound of a hum. [Student R continues.]

That, that particular speaker? That's the question. Why do you think they are?

Well, the mouth is closed and the sound is directed more up.

Well, let us say, perhaps, we might understand that the sound is emanating more clearly from the speaker. Perhaps if we would consider that possibility, we would gain more understanding. Yes, because [Student Q] had something to say.

No, no, no. I agree. No, you know . . .

Oh.

Well, I was going to raise my hand to mention about vibration. And well, we have this exercise that we've been given about standing and . . . well, anyway, there's a certain vibration that seems to emanate as we stretch that affects certain parts of our body. [It is difficult to transcribe one word.]

Uh-huh. Uh-huh. You have been given varying exercises to help you be prepared for the classes that are here and the ones yet to come. But if they have not been done, then they have not been done. But it is not because you haven't already been given them long ago. So that you could have that awakening; so that it wouldn't come as such a shock when it came.

Now if a person will stand up—for example, let [Student Q] stand up. Let, let [Student Q] hum. And close her eyes and hum, to see if she can be aware, which I'm sure she can, of varying speakers within the body or sensations. Now if you will, I think you would feel even more comfortable if you stepped out in the kitchen in order to have more awareness of just you. Any place where they don't look at you.[13]

OK.

Not that there's anything wrong. But you just hum and when you do, close your eyes and in the process let everything else disappear. That's when one becomes aware of these other things. Go ahead.

One solid note or . . .

Solid note because awareness comes quicker from one than many.

OK.

[After a short pause during which the recorder may have been paused, the teacher continues.]

Did anyone agree that sounded like a speaker?

[A student responds, but it is difficult to transcribe her comment.]

Or didn't it sound like a speaker to you? Well, it did to me. But anyway, that's your ear not mine. Now did you, because you only had a few moments there, did you have any sensation in any part of your anatomy outside of the one that's the strongest?

Well, I always, I've always felt I sing with my whole body. I've always felt that. I never paid attention to my feet. Would you say—

Start paying attention, because you'll feel the sensation. It comes out of all—those eight parts.

That was interesting because I have never felt, but I've always said that you sing with your whole body. But I've never paid attention. That was, it was interesting about the feet.

You will find—the best way of awareness is to stand on a hard floor.

Uh-huh.

A hard floor in bare feet or thin stocking feet. Because the sensation—you will be able to detect the sensation quicker than if the foot has a slipper or anything on it.

Uh-huh. Thank you.

Now you can shut that off. And if there's questions, you are free to ask them.

[The recorder is paused.]

One must become aware when they speak or when they sing. What is the difference between speaking and singing? A person speaks and then a person sings. But there's a difference. One says, "That's singing," and one says, "That is speaking." But what is the difference?

The range of vibration. [Student R responds.]

The harmony of flow is the difference between speaking and singing. The harmony of flow. Now there are many techniques one adds to get the harmony of flow, but the—a person speaks, a person speaks at a high pitch, low pitch, midrange pitch. But a person in what you call singing has the harmony of flow. They don't move from a low pitch to a high pitch, from a high pitch to a higher pitch. There's a harmony of flow. That's the true difference between speaking and singing is the harmony of flow. To attain the harmony of flow one goes through varying techniques to accomplish that.

Now what does one mean by the harmony of flow? Yes.

Why is it, then, that some people speak with a very high pitch when they in truth don't really sing that high pitch? They sing lower.

Because when they sing, there's some harmony of flow. When they speak, the harmony of flow is not there. Now think what happens when a person speaks. When a person speaks, there are many forms being created. There is much energy being dissipated. When a person sings, the chances of less forms being created is very great because the very process of singing requires more attention. And because it requires more attention, there is some degree of the flow of harmony. Perhaps not a lot, but some, because it requires some degree of concentration. And it varies with each person, how much concentration is there.

But speaking, how many people concentrate when they speak? It's a rare person that concentrates when they speak. They say many things and two seconds later cannot remember what they have said, let alone what did they mean by the words that they used when they spoke. They don't even remember what they meant. And ofttimes we speak one thing and we manifest another, for the forms created in the words we speak are discordant and contrary to the very words we are using. They are totally contrary.

Therefore, as I said, in singing, in the harmony of flow, there is some degree of concentration. That does not mean that all singers understand the word and, in singing the word, form the harmonious shape in a mental world of what the word means. What one might call a good singer, not only do they form the word but they harmoniously form the shape, for it is vibration. And it is not only in a physical world but it is in a mental world. Yes.

A lot of people, when they normally speak, their voice may be on an average of a lower pitch. Yet, when they get excited or angry or upset, the pitch of the voice rises.

Always.

What is that due to?

It never lowers. Because the excitement creates forms. The excitement—let me clarify something—is the effect of forms. The excitement doesn't create forms. The forms create the excitement. Perhaps that will help you. Yes.

When some people, then, when they speak, they stutter or they [are] looking for the words or they just pause and all of that.

It's the battle of the forms being created and drained from the energy of the vital body through the power center.

Is that the same with stuttering?

It is indeed. To such an extent, to such a battle of discordant forms—you see, you can take a person who stutters and if you are an instrument through which, though momentarily, you have helped them to enter a realm of harmonious forms, the stuttering disappears. It just disappears. The moment they become consciously aware that the stuttering has disappeared, it returns immediately, for being mental forms they are subject to a mental world and a mental king. Yes.

But if they really work on it, those people that stutter—

They can overcome it.

—can overcome it.

Definitely. Absolutely and positively. If they gain in understanding of the true cause, which, from lack of concentration, is created forms that are discordant with each other, and they are battling for energy as the voice, the mouth is trying to speak and the sounds are trying to emanate and the war goes on.

Take, for example, a person singing. They can be singing quite beautifully, quite beautifully. All of a sudden something happens. They don't know what's happened. Something's just happened. They almost lost the words that they're supposed to sing. They might say, "Oh, they forgot." No, it is recorded in the memory par excellence. We did not forget. Other forms are demanding energy and draining it so that the energy required for the continuity or the flow of the memory pattern in its expression is being disrupted and interfered with. Because there is not sufficient energy for that, and there're several other things that are going on. That's how we seem to forget.

Returning to the high-pitched voice of the excited person, why is the pitch always high and never low?

The forms of which excitement is an effect are created from a very high pitch originally. Now, you take, for example, sensation is never a low pitch. Sensation is always a high pitch. For example, if you were listening to something, to a sound, the lower frequencies will not, seemingly, excite you. It requires high frequencies of sound to tempt and affect the senses. It requires high frequencies. Never low frequencies. Low frequencies calm the senses and will even cause so-called sleep. High frequencies are the instruments through which the senses are excited, alerted, and activated. Yes.

Ofttimes listening to music or something, a person may get a sensation, generally up and down the spine, from listening. And what is that the result of?

The feeling or the sensation that comes up and down the spine? You're talking about the listening ear?

Well, I'll give a personal example: listening to a beautiful piece of music or something, and then all of a sudden, [you] just get a tingling sensation up and down the spine.

Because you've permitted yourself, without conscious thought, to become receptive [to] or to become that which you listen to. As the singer becomes the song, the listener becomes that which he listens to. That's when you become it; that's when you go beyond the limit and limitations of the mental forms in a mental world, then you become it. See, concentration is not only something you project; it is something you receive, and it is something that you become when it *is* concentration. [Student Q] had a question.

We were talking about the high and low pitches. Is that why when people hypnotize somebody, it's a very monotonous kind of a low voice?

Always. It is because low frequencies, low frequencies dull the senses. High frequencies activate the senses. Midrange frequencies, they do a little of both and all you [have] got to do is to listen to any song that's a midrange frequency and it's neither exciting or . . . *[The teacher makes a sound that is difficult to transcribe but suggests a dullness.]* It just doesn't seem to have it. There has to be the movement from low frequency to high frequency; otherwise, the ear will close it out the best it can. It is the fluctuations that truly excite the senses—if you wanted to call it excitement—[that] create the forms. It is the fluctuation of frequencies, from high to low. Yes.

It's interesting when you go to a place where [there's] a lot of singing going on, say, like the opera or whatever or wherever you want to go, and when there is sort of a talking kind of a singing, you hear people coughing and they're shuffling their feet and they're moving around. But the minute they start going up the scale and they become very, very, very high, you can hear a pin drop.

Because all the senses are activated.

And, and—

Of the listening ear.

—it's dead silence. Of course, it's like very, very high pitch.

It's the frequency. It is the high frequencies. Remember this—and it's important as far as senses are concerned—see, we teach, and have taught, that concentration is the key to all power. Place your attention upon that you wish to become, not on that which you wish to overcome. Concentration is going beyond the form to the essence.

Now, when the ear is listening to sound or vibration, it is creating, constantly, shapes and forms in a mental world, the listening ear. Now we're moving to the listening ear. The listening ear is doing that all the time. As the frequency, the pitch or the frequency, increases into higher frequencies, as that happens, the forms created are not only less forms but they are stronger forms. They are fewer forms, but they are very strong. And we experience what we call an excitement. That is our awareness, that excitement, of this process that's taking place within us.

Now if the pitch reaches what we may consider super-high frequencies, then our concentration, our forms become from a 100, to 50, to 30, to 20, to 10, to 9, to 8, to 7, to 6, to 5, [to] 4, to 3, and if we ever get to 1, we become the note itself, the frequency. For that frequency is within us. Even the listening ear becomes that frequency. That's when a person says, "This singer was *unbelievable*! Just unbelievable." What was unbelievable was the listening ear and its ability to become that which the singer was singing, for that's where it took place. That is concentration. That is becoming the singer. That's what really happens. They become. They adore the singer because the mind, which can only relate to its limits of possession and can only relate to division and separation, cannot mentally relate to being the person because it has its own identity and knows that it is not. So, it does not understand that it has become *in its consciousness* the very note that it admires. That's when we move to the essence of anything. Yes.

Is the human ear different from, like, a dog ear? Like, I mean, you can sing a high note and crack crystals.

Absolutely.

But a dog, you have those dog whistles that have such a high frequency the human mind cannot hear it, but the dog hears it.

The human ear hears it, but the mind does not record it.

Ahh.

The human ear does hear it; the mind does not record it in the sense of conscious awareness, in the sense of conscious awareness. The ear of the dog, highly sensitive, is no more sensitive than the ear of the human. The ear of the human is more evolved. It *is* more evolved. But you must understand that the deafness to those high vibrations has been created by a mental world. You see, for example, in these high frequencies of which all people respond by what they call excitement. Now some people, when they hear a high soprano, it just— *[The teacher makes a sound that is difficult to transcribe but is suggestive of irritation.]* What is grating at them inside is an excitement that is not in keeping of what their mind has judged is pleasant excitement. It is the mind that judges, "This is a pleasing excitement. This is a terrible, irritating excitement." The mind is what does that. The human ear does hear the high pitch that the dog hears, but it does no longer have the conscious awareness of it.

You know that some people can hear a very delicate sound, and many other people do not hear. They all hear. But one has trained, let us say, reeducated their ear; their mind is what they've reeducated. And therefore, their energy, their attention, their concentration is going more into those areas of consciousness and not being so dissipated by other varying forms at that moment. And therefore, they are aware of that very delicate, high-pitched sound. They are aware. Yes. Any other questions? Yes.

I was going to mention about vibration. And we hear something like an operatic aria by a soprano or baritone or tenor and if it's harmonious, [we enjoy it]. And yet, on the other hand, we listen to some other music which carries different harmonies, very inharmonious to each other. Therefore, we dislike some music. And therefore, also, reveals the levels of consciousness that we also are expressing on.

Because some music is discordant to certain levels of consciousness because the forms of that level of consciousness are not harmonious with the forms that are created by the listening ear. So, some people like country western. Some like classic. Sometimes we like classic and sometimes we don't like classic. That reveals to us—you see, sometimes we think, well, we always like classic. That is not true. Sometimes certain levels we are in don't like classic. And all we say is, "I don't want to hear any music at this time. I don't want to hear any music." Because the level we are on—say that the selection we have or that we're used to is classical—it doesn't want to hear anything at all because it doesn't even want you to know that this particular level doesn't even like the music that you like so much. That's the truth of the matter. Yes.

I've lost the question now.

Well, that that is lost shall be found, just like your glasses. Yes.

Now we all have soul talents. Some in instruments, others in voice, others in many different things. And yet the very thing that we desire seems to always be ever far away from us. And we can't—only because, I guess, we have judged, then, the lack or the impossibility of it, or say the defender of the minds to be able to get through that particular area to go into, say, other levels of consciousness, of our soul's expression—

Because it's because we don't want it that much. That's the reason we don't have it. Now stop and pause and think. We always get what we really want. But because we are not making the effort, perhaps, greater effort to be aware in our self—the law demonstrates to us clearly: we always get what we really want. So, say that we want this here, and we will not admit to our self that we want this, but there's something over here we want even more. So, when it comes to the desire for this fulfillment, it's totally continuously drained to sustain this over here.

As the law clearly demonstrates in all of nature, as the leaf falls from the tree to once again nourish the tree, [that], once again, new leaves may come; everything in its season. So, we must learn that whenever we desire, we must always prepare to let go. For it is the things that we hold that stand in the way of the things that we desire. Now, you should take note of that. It is the things that we hold that stand in the way of the things that we desire. Now remember, we're talking about holding things in a mental world. It is the things that we hold that stand in the way of the things that we desire. And that, of course, reveals a house divided, which cannot stand.

And I think if we will all pause in consciousness and whenever we have a desire for something and it just seems beyond our grasp, we will see clearly the things that we hold that are standing in the way of the things we desire. And we always know inside of our self what it is we hold so tenaciously to that are in the way of what we want.

Because, you must understand, of course, that we say that we hold a certain way of thinking. Well, what is it that we hold? Do we think it's just a thought passing through the mind? It is forms that have been created, and it takes energy to sustain them, for them to live in that mental world. And so it is those armies and those forms that we hold to that are standing in the way; in other words, [they are] draining the energy necessary for the new forms to have birth and life and movement. This is why we teach, and all ages have taught, in simple words of the day, that we cannot have our cake and eat it, too. We cannot hold to that which we used to desire that has served its purpose in our life and is now standing in the way of something else that we desire. There's no way that we can have both. There is no way. For, as the teaching goes, the cup overfloweth.

Try to understand that it takes energy from your vital body to create forms. It takes energy from your vital body for the forms you have created yesterday to continue to live. It takes energy for new forms to be created to fulfill that which you desire. And it is only a lack—those little new forms, you understand, they can hardly crawl, let alone run and serve and fulfill your impatience because there isn't enough energy. The forms of yesterday are still living in their feast.

You know, when we speak of the law, remember, when you speak of the law of nature, you see, of which we are an effect of that law, all of us, what do you think you're speaking of? Some subtle nothingness that you cannot relate to? They are forms. The servants of the law are the forms of the law. The law is not some straight line that goes out and comes back to you. You send out from your vital body pure energy. That energy takes the shape and the form that you have created through your thoughts and your desires and everything else. Now they become a living, moving entity. They are the servants. They are the ones that fulfill the law. It's not some straight line. They go out into the universe and return with their kind. And their kind always comes back to us, after racing all [around] out there, cold and hungry and they have to sit down and have a feast. And that takes energy.

It is only the past that is the shadow of our future. It is only the past. And it's only a shadow because we continue to feed, which is perpetuating the law of yesterday. We perpetuate a law by feeding and sustaining the forms, the servants, of the law of yesterday.

Time to shut it off.

Now we can have a few minutes discussion—*[The recording ends.]*

NOVEMBER 5, 1981

The Art of Evolution

Tonight's class [is] entitled "The Art of Evolution."

As beauty is in the eye of the beholder, so art is in the soul of God. Now art is not limited to painting, to singing, to carpentry, or to plumbing or to any particular field of endeavor. Art is the expression of the soul faculty of harmony, rhythm, and quality. Art is an instrument through which the seeing eye or the listening ear is enabled to open the door of imagination and enter the spheres of perfect harmony, where peace reigns supreme.

Whenever the artist is concerned with the effect of their effort, they steal from the viewer the indispensable ingredient for opening the door of imaging or imagination. It is commonly referred to as an artist who has overdone their writing, their painting, or their particular form of soul expression. Concern over the effect of any endeavor places the endeavor into the mental world of consciousness, guaranteeing the duality of expression and the bondage of form.

For art to be art, the instrument through which it is being expressed must be free from the bondage of a mental world. And in order to accomplish this freedom, the instrument of the Divine Expression must move quickly, for the spirit of freedom is a spirit of spontaneity. It is in spontaneity, in those moments that we experience inspiration, for in spontaneity is the ability to be free from the shadows of the past, from the bondage of yesterday, commonly known as judgment.

Without quality, there is no good; without good, there is no God; without God, there is no inspiration; without inspiration, there is no true art.

Now to continue on with our class and speaking on the art of evolution, we will take a few moments to discuss the art, the evolution of life on the planet Earth. Some time ago we stated that you will never find the missing link in [the] evolution of man on the planet Earth. The reason that we made that statement is quite simple: the link does not exist on the planet Earth because it never was on the planet Earth.

Eons ago highly advanced civilizations, from other universes and other solar systems, seeking to strengthen, physically, the forms that they inhabited—for they were highly advanced mentally. Their mental bodies being greatly refined at the expense and sacrifice of their physical forms. And realizing that their civilization, without change, would come, in time in form, to an end, and being a highly advanced technological civilization, they sent out their great crafts into the universe with one purpose in mind: to find forms with which they could crossbreed and, in so doing, guarantee their survival and the continuity of their race. In that great endeavor, they traveled faster than what you call light to many solar systems and many different planets. They found, eons ago, conditions suitable on the planet Earth for the possibility of a crossbreeding to strengthen the physical forms of future generations. They accomplished this in various parts of the planet Earth: eleven specific locations.

The crossbreeding with the highest evolved of the animal form with the extremely refined mental forms of this particular civilization brought about a form known to you today as humans. The crossbreeding, giving the necessary strength for survival on the planet, also brought to the form what we know today as the animal instinct. However, it has served its purpose.

Historic records record, even to your present day, civilizations that disappeared without trace in the blinking of an eye. They disappeared not over a period of years, months, weeks, or days. They disappeared in a matter of hours. For in the master plan of this highly-evolved race of people from other solar systems, they came to bring the crossbreeds out into the universe to inhabit other planets, other places, and other times. And so, your historical records and the findings of your archeologists are baffled with the strange but absolute disappearance of one civilization in ancient times after another. One of the many examples is the Mayan civilization. No trace, nothing. They simply, seemingly, disappeared.

And as you study the forms, the so-called forms of the human on your planet today, you will see that some are more evolved, more refined than others, for this crossbreeding went over the land and covered many areas of the planet Earth.

And so it is, the art of evolution, the art of anything, man can only be a part of; he shall never be the whole. And in the art we have earned in our evolution, let us not forget the responsibility not only to our self to be a clear channel for pure, unadulterated art but to remember the responsibility that we have to the listening ear, to the viewing eye.

Let us remember that whatever we serve is forever serving us. So let us awaken, for the time has come. The days of sleep are over, for sleep is a service to a realm of darkness that you cannot see, that you cannot hear. It is a part of the animal instinct within you. It shall come to an ending someday. Seek not for sleep to rejuvenate. Learn to rest that you may forever have conscious awareness, for only in conscious awareness do you have the ability to express the soul faculty of reason. The light only shines in conscious awareness. It does not and cannot shine in the sleep of satisfaction. As satisfaction is a function expressing the animal instinct within the human form, remember, it guarantees regret, for the animal is not satisfied for long. And when it is not satisfied, it is flooded with regret.

Laziness, like sleep, is a function of the animal within you. You are only part animal. That is what your soul has earned. And to spend most of your divine energy directing it to the service of the animal instinct within you is contrary to the refining process of evolutionary incarnation.

The planet in which you reside, being the planet of faith, you all have an abundance of. But through laziness, you do not consciously, moment-by-moment choose wisely where you will direct that great power. It is from laziness [that that power is] being directed to the animal instinct within you, and it is your only suffering. It is your only struggle. It is your only despair. It is your only hopelessness. It is your only lack and limit.

Let the fires of purification, not the fires of lust, light your way to freedom. For the fires of lust are the fires of the animal within you, and the fires of reason, that transfigure and transform your life, are the fires of conscious awareness.

Learn to rest for you have forgotten the way. But remember, that that is hidden shall be revealed, and that that is forgotten shall be remembered, as that that is lost shall be found. You have lost the light and, therefore, often mistake the light of lust for the light of love. They are as different as bondage and freedom, for that in truth is what they represent.

There is no tomorrow for those who do not accept today. As you continue to live in that which has gone, you cannot accept that which is; and not accepting that which is, you cannot experience that which is to be. Therefore, you experience what has been. But in that consciousness of laziness, there is a divine principle that does not fail. For repetition, the repeating of your errors of yesterday, guarantees an evolution and a freedom from them.

There is a better way. It is not necessary to continue to repeat what has been. It only takes a little effort in placing your consciousness in what is, for there, in that moment, in *that* moment is the power of God, constantly available to those who are willing to live in the eternity that they are. To move in consciousness away from what is, is to lose the power available to you.

I see that you are interested in the various locations of where the ancient civilizations from outer, outer space brought their colonies to crossbreed with the higher animal forms of the planet Earth. And so, it is South America, China, Tibet, India, Egypt, Greece, and North America.

Good night.

[After a pause, the class continues.]

Now ask your question.

The question was that the—

Yes?

—the beings that were mentioned, their physical and mental abilities were mentioned, but what about their spiritual evolution?

They're highly refined. Through the vehicle [of] attention you direct energy. As you direct more energy to any particular form, the form is refined through the fires of purification. It's called hybriding. And when, through direction of your energy, through attention, that is imbalanced with your grosser form, the gross form begins the process of deterioration. Now we have directed, and direct, most of the energy to our gross form, which is at the sacrifice of our more refined or higher, more delicate forms. So, we don't have to worry about directing more energy to the dense form. We do need to be interested in directing some energy to the more delicate, refining forms and vibrations because we're out of balance in that respect.

Any other question? Yes, [Student B] has a question.

You mentioned civilizations that just disappeared, and I think the Mayan civilization was being used as an example.

Uh-huh.

Was that because their dense forms deteriorated or was it because they were taken back to the original planet?

Not to the original planet. They were brought here to colonize and to crossbreed. When that purpose had been fulfilled, the ships came to pick them up. Then they were taken to other planets on which they could colonize more. You see, their forms had to be brought into a more dense state in order for their race to survive. And we're on the verge of repeating that same process. We're quite a ways from what they actually did, but we are headed in that direction in keeping with the law. Yes, [Student R].

It's been mentioned in archeology—
Uh-huh.
—that they believed that the Mayan civilization practiced human sacrifice. And I'd like to ask what the Friends' definition of it or what their explanation of it is.

Well, in reference to the practice of the Mayans, known to man as human sacrifice, [it] was nothing more nor less than the survival of their crossbreeding process. Now in order that they may have as healthy a form as possible for the survival of their race, those forms which had what we would consider defects or not healthy or in the best interests of the survival of the civilization were, what we would understand, sacrificed. They were not sacrificed in the sense that the race was highly evolved and changed its suit of clothes, its body, like we change our coats today. So, if you look at the civilization in its high state of evolution and considering that the physical, dense form is just a suit of clothes that they were consciously aware that they were wearing for a time, it was not what you would consider a horrible thing. It was a release from the gross form, and the people voluntary chose and sought that release. Yes. Knowing that the civilization as a whole [would benefit and] was in the best interest, they had no problem whatsoever in being candidates for that particular, what we call, sacrifice. It was not a sacrifice. It became, through a loss of its true purpose, a religious ritual. That was never its birth nor its intent. It became that. Yes.

Approximately how long a time did that civilization remain here, after the crossbreeding, before it was removed?

The average was three to five centuries.

Thank you.

Three to five centuries. Yes.

You said that these beings started crossbreeding in Egypt and Tibet and South America. How long ago is that then, because Lemuria blew up 12,000 years ago.

Uh-huh.
Right?
Uh-huh.
And Atlantis blew up 12,000 years ago.
Uh-huh.
And those people from Lemuria supposedly came over to South and North America.
Uh-huh.
And the Atlantean [people] came over to Egypt.
Uh-huh.
Did, then, these beings come at that period?
Before. Before.
Before Atlantis and Lemuria.
Before Atlantis. Before Lemuria.
Which is way past 12,000 years ago.
Absolutely. Like all of evolution, it rises and falls. We are, as a civilization, we are, in spite of what appears, we're on the rising cycle. Yes.
Von Däniken's, some of his theories, he had some writings—I believe from South America to substantiate it—that there was a scheduled return of those beings—
Uh-huh.
—to this planet in the year 1999, I think. Was he correct?
He's too early. Too early.
All right.
Yes.
It seems that we are, like, the ancestors of some of the people left behind that didn't go to another planet. Is that correct?
That is correct. For the purpose was: for the survival of their particular species, crossbreeding was necessary and colonization of this planet was the effect. And many other planets and many other solar systems.
Are we—
We're in the process of doing the same thing.

Are we, like, descendants of the weaker ones since they left some behind?

I wouldn't consider that we are descendants of the weaker ones. I would consider that we are descendants of the ones more capable of surviving in gross vibrations. Yes. *[Many students laugh.]*

Thank you.

Thank you, Henry Kissinger. [A different student remarks, which results in more laughter from the students.]

Yes.

Well, you hear so much about, like, the Devil's Triangle.

Uh-huh.

Or over in Japan—

Uh-huh.

—they have the same space, where they have actually seen, outer space vehicles go into the water.

Uh-huh.

And disappearing and whatever happens there. Is there really, like, a hole in the Earth that they go into or . . .

I'm sure you are all familiar with or have heard of what is called in the universe as a black hole. What you are not familiar with, nor understand, is what is called, in a planet, as a magnetic hole. We mentioned some time ago it is a magnetic pull and that's exactly what it is. What goes in does not come out in a recognizable form. Yes.

But when the ships and planes that actually disappeared and there's absolutely no trace of it, have they been picked up and moved to another planet?

No. No. They have been transformed by a magnetic field into forms unrecognizable by the inhabitants of the planet, of this planet.

So those unrecognizable beings—

Or forms.

—forms, have then moved on to . . .

That is correct. That is a method of transportation. There are no cities in those places in the bottom of the ocean.

No, but I just thought maybe—

There are no beings living down there in recognizable form.

To our eyes.

That is correct. Those are called magnetic holes. Black holes or magnetic holes are nothing more than *[The teacher pauses for a long moment before he continues.]* —we'll discuss it at another class. Go ahead with any other questions you have. You remind me. *[The teacher may be addressing Student R.]*

Yes. [Student R responds.]

Yes.

I'm wondering if—what transpires when these people become, so that we don't recognize them as forms, is that a form of apport? Is that what . . .

Well, yes . . .

. . . molecular structure? [The student paused in her question and, as the teacher began his answer, the student continued speaking, which makes a complete transcription difficult.]

. . . but that word is reserved to other experiences. It is a change in molecular structure. It is an acceleration of the vibration of the form, and that acceleration process is indispensable to an artist in order to be receptive to inspiration.

Turn off the recorder and I'll be right back. *[The recording pauses.]*

Whereas inspiration is the smile of God traveling faster than the speed of light, one must, in order to recognize it in consciousness, raise the rate of speed of their consciousness to be harmonious with inspiration, which travels faster than the speed of light. Therefore, to receive that which is, the Light, one must become the Light. Are there any other questions? Yes.

Is there any relationship between these beings who originally came to the planet and the great spiritual leaders in our history, such as the Buddhas and the Jesus and the Mohammeds?

Yes, there definitely is. And in reference to the—we prefer to call them intelligences. So many people look at the word *being* in not the most positive manner. In reference to the intelligences which left their homeland, you understand, though they traveled faster than the speed of light, it still was a great, vast distance, uncomprehendable to the present human mind. And therefore, the intelligences that left the homeland, the ones who finally landed upon this planet were the copies or clones of the originals. That process took place on their ships through space and time.

You see, without identification, there is no time and there is no space. But without identification, there is no individuality; however, without individuality, there is formless, free Spirit. Therefore, whenever you rely, (the word meaning "depend"), whenever you depend upon your mind for anything, you are depending not only upon that which is limited but you are depending upon that which is bound. And when you depend on that which is bound, you can only have bound or payment experiences.

To experience freedom, you must become the freedom that you are. To become the freedom that you are, you cannot depend on that which is bound, for a house divided cannot stand. To depend on what you know is to bind yourself to the chains of creation that demand, in keeping with their dual law, payment and attainment.

Overidentification with individualization is the guaranteed bondage of life. *[After a short pause, the teacher continues.]* What did I say?

Overidentification with individualization is the bondage of life. [Student R replies.]

The guaranteed bondage. [A different student corrects Student R.]

It's the guaranteed bondage of life. [Student R corrects his error.]

Say that again that you may be free in understanding.

Overidentification with individualization is the guaranteed bondage of life. [Student R responds.]

Overidentification with individualization is the guaranteed bondage of life. Now, perhaps, you understand why self-thought is your most destructive thought. For self represents the epitome of individualization; it also represents the epitome of separation. That that is separated is never whole and shall ever be in need. That that is separated is never whole and shall forever be in need, want, and desire. *[After a short pause, the teacher repeats the sentence. Some students may have been taking notes.]* That that is separated is never whole and shall ever be in want, need, and desire.

Any other questions before we conclude? Yes, [Student B].

I've heard it said that an artist frequently doesn't know where he's going when he started painting. He doesn't know how it's going to turn out or he's started writing and he doesn't know where he's going.

Uh-huh.

How does that spirit of spontaneity . . .

Spirit of spontaneity, we are receptive to the spirit of spontaneity at an accelerated rate in consciousness exceeding the travel of the speed of light. Therefore, the mind cannot know when it is receptive to and recognizing what we call the spirit of inspiration. They may see it or know it after, never during. This is why it is critical for an artist, in the art of any profession, to have no mental activity, for mental activity is the obstruction to inspiration. The guaranteed obstruction.

What so few of us realize, let alone recognize, let alone accept, is that in what we call inspiration, the smile of God, those forms, those intelligences who, in their evolution, have perfected that particular form of art expression in the spirit of spontaneity are able to express. And that's the only time they are able to express. At no other time. All other times the artist is controlled by the shadows of the past and what it has already offered to them. Nothing greater, ofttimes lesser from the experiences of their early days of unfolding their particular art form. Never greater. Only greater when they are receptive to what is called the spirit of spontaneity. Then God smiles through his angels' efforts. That's how God smiles. Yes?

In this planet, there have been cycles when art has risen in full bloom—

Uh-huh.

—across the world—

Uh-huh.

—and was profuse.

That is correct.

And then it withered and has gone.

Uh-huh.

And it seems to be a cyclic thing. And what is it that controls or governs that cycle? And are we near another such a cycle?

What governs it is man's need of knowledge. What governs man's need is his overidentification, of course, and separation from the whole. Therefore, when man, as a civilization does, it begins to identify, it begins to recognize what it calls individualization, it begins to become self-important, art suffers. All art. Because the opportunity, the door of opportunity to inspiration, to the acceleration of the consciousness, has been clouded, never completely put out, but definitely clouded. All art, music, all art form reveals that to us as we study history.

Now many people, as the ancient Greeks have done and civilizations before them, outlawed certain art that they knew beyond a shadow of any doubt was contaminating the populace of their particular countries. And they did that for the survival of their civilization. It isn't that they liked or disliked the music. It's they knew where it was coming from.

But when we came to this planet, we got a brain, and as we go to school, we try to learn all kinds of things and—

The brain came from the animal in the crossbreeding.

But the brain never stops. I mean, it's constantly working.

The animal is ever alert. It's called survival. It is the animal within us that is constantly in need. It is the animal within us that is separate and individual. That's the animal within us. Yes.

Could we ever stop the brain activity? I mean, when we try to sit and meditate, I mean, it's just moments that it can be very still and then just stop . . . [It is difficult to transcribe the last few words.]

That is from a lack of effort in demonstrating the great power of concentration. It reveals a definite need of daily, moment-by-moment effort to become aware of the thought process, which is in control. That takes flooding the consciousness. One chooses what they desire to flood their consciousness with and because they are attempting to control the animal within, repetition is the law through which the change can be made possible.

And that may take years.

It could. It could, but it has to be done someday for that's the Law of Evolution. Better here while you still have the strength of the animal to use and not have it use you. Presently, the animal within us uses us. And through effort, daily effort, in flooding the consciousness with the thought of your choice, you'll gain control over the animal by using the strength of the animal.

One looks at a so-called enemy and does not, if they are wise, battle with the enemy on the enemy's terms. One studies the enemy and uses the force of the enemy to defeat the enemy. It's an ancient art; China and Japan teach it very clearly in some of their different techniques. You must learn to use the force of the animal that has you in control to control the animal that is controlling you, for the so-called higher self or higher vibrations of consciousness within you do not have the brute strength to battle the animal on the animal's terms. So, you must understand the animal that the animal's force may be used against it.

As I have said on many occasions, learn to use the function of anger to serve the greater good within you, but when you *become* the anger, then you *are* the animal and cannot defeat the animal within and, therefore, cannot be effective in defeating the animal without.

He or she who backs off to what is called forces, which is the full expression of the animal within any form, is doing that not to another but to themselves. The defeat is within and is experienced without.

The animal, designed to serve a purpose of survival of the form, must be used for the purpose for which it has been designed and for no other purpose.

The animal is not a reasoning, thinking, calculating, planning intelligence. The animal is an emotional, reacting, thinking being. It does not plan. It does not organize. It does not calculate. It does not reason. It reacts to its emotions. Any person reacting to their emotions is expressing the animal within them and is the victim of the animal expression. Yes.

You are saying that the animal has the emotion; but what is it, then, in us that can organize and plan? What is that? That's not an animal. What is that then?

That is not the animal. Planning, organizing is the faculties. They are the expression of the faculties, using the animal force to fulfill them. The animal within us does not plan, organize, think, consider, etc., etc. We—it uses, the animal within us, to have the experience in a physical, gross form.

In and of itself emotion has no light, has no reason, has no consideration, has only need. The animal instinct has want, need, and desire. The reason that the animal instinct has those functions is because it is designed to survive and serve a world composed of functions. It is not a bad thing, nor a good thing;

it just is. Emotion, which is the animal expression, expresses only in keeping with what already has been. It cannot foresee. It cannot plan. It cannot use a faculty of reason for it is beyond its realm of consciousness.

The animal instinct, designed to serve our soul and its survival of expression on this planet, is not being used wisely. We become the emotion; we do not use the emotion. We become the animal; we do not use the animal. That help with your question?

Yes. Thanks very much.

When you can use the function of the animal, the anger and all that it has to offer, and then, as you turn off the water facet, turn off the function and in that instant once again experience the peace that passeth all understanding, then you are using the form for the purpose for which the form has been designed. That takes what is known as self-control, which is given birth through the power of concentration. Be the observer, never the observed. The awakened intelligences constantly observe the animal forms for they are responsible for them.

An animal expresses what man calls love in keeping with the law of the animal's survival. And an animal is very loyal to the hand that feeds them and very patient when the hand is empty, for an animal never fails in its loyalty once the loyalty is established, for it represents their survival. An animal does not think, the animal within us and the animal without, the animal does not think, "I like this person because they're very intelligent. I like this person because they don't get angry. I like this person for this or that." The animal likes you in keeping with the law of the animal's survival.

And in the process and the design of the Infinite Intelligence, as the animal instinct is being refined, think of what's happening with an animal who likes you, becomes attached to you, you're the hand that cares for its survival, the hand that feeds it: the animal begins, through the process, to express the soul faculty of loyalty. As we all know, functions are only undeveloped faculties. Yes.

Which [is] the closest animal on the Earth? Not, not in the water, like I said the dolphin's very close to the human intelligence, but on the surface, what is the animal?

The elephant.

The elephant.

The elephant is a highly evolved species on the planet. Highly evolved. The highest of all animals on the planet, including the water [animals]. The elephant is the highest evolved and, unfortunately, becoming extinct. Yes.

Is it spiritually evolved?

Yes. Does anyone know how long it takes for a little baby elephant, how long is the mother elephant pregnant? Does anyone know?

Seven years.

Two years.

Two years.

Two years?

Twenty-four months. [Many students respond.]

Anyone else know? *[After a short pause, the teacher continues.]* Two full years. And in that time, there's a great deal of evolution taking place. Two years, the mother is pregnant. Does anyone know what all elephants, no matter who they are, if an elephant is shot and dies, what they do with the elephant? Does anyone know? Yes.

I think I know. I think they go to a burial ground.

All elephants are carried by any elephant passing to a hidden burial ground. No elephant is ever left in the jungle or anywhere. Any elephant passing will take whatever is necessary to drag the corpse to the burial ground, which is ofttimes hundreds of miles away in the jungle. And to this day they have not been able to find the elephant burial grounds, for they have sought for centuries for the tusks. They have not found them. The elephants are so intelligent and so clever they hide those giant corpses where no man, to this day, has been able to find. To this day. Now that takes a very highly evolved animal with thought, planning, organization, and the thing that we seemingly reserve to the human animal. No burial ground has ever been discovered by any human animal. In all their searching, they have yet to find the elephant burial grounds. And, of course, there are many. And when you think an animal as huge as an elephant, leaving such distinct tracts in a jungle, which, surely, they would be able to find, [a] corpse being carried, sometimes hundreds of miles— do you know why they can't find the tracks? Do you know what the animal does? Does anyone know? Yes.

It goes back and covers them up.

They have, as the animals are carrying the corpse away, the elephants, there are other elephants that put all the brush over every single track. They walk backwards, those elephants, as the other ones carry the corpse to the burial grounds. That's why man can't find any tracks.

Sounds like a bunch of Indians.

Pardon?

Sounds like Indians. That's . . .

Where do you think the Indians learned their tactics? Yes.

Were the elephants present when these other intelligences came?

Yes, they were present. The elephant is one of the oldest animals on the planet. One of the oldest.

Then, why did they crossbreed with, like, the apes rather than the elephants?

Because it was not suitable to the form. An upright form was indispensable for certain reasons governing energy and for the continuity of the species. We have more mobility than the elephant. We do not have more loyalty for our own species, unfortunately. We have less consideration, whether we like it or not. We have less care. We have less love. We have less faith. We have less interest in the survival of our own species.

Though the elephant is, unfortunately, becoming an extinct species, it will never be extinct. It will never be extinct. It knows how to survive. Before the dinosaurs, were the elephants. They survived the dinosaur age. They survived ages before that. They'll survive long after man has gone.

It is the only animal on the planet that the intelligences in spiritual form are able to work with. The only animal, including man, on the planet that the spiritual intelligences are able to communicate with freely and work with. That's because of the animal's evolution and refinement of having an awakening of what we understand to be soul faculties.

It is not as mobile, perhaps, as a human form, but whether we like it or not, it is superior. It does not kill animals, only in keeping with survival. It does not eat animals. But it certainly does keep the jungle alive. Without the elephants, the jungles would choke themselves to death. There would be no trees. There'd be no vines. There would be nothing, for the trees and the vines would choke themselves to death, would receive no light and would die in time. It is the elephants that keep the jungle alive, for that's their home.

Now surely, we'll all agree a form so huge must have great intelligence to move through dense jungles and be able to hide from the greed and insanity of the human species.

Any other questions before we conclude? No other—yes?

As far as raising our rate of vibration for inspiration faster than the speed of light . . .

Uh-huh.

. . . could you, maybe, help us understand how to do that as related to being at peace?

Well, I've already explained how to do that many times. Overidentification with self is the obstruction. Self-thought is the obstruction to inspiration. It is the obstruction to all good, for in self-thought, you are individualized; you are separate and cannot be whole. You cannot have both. If you wish wholeness in yourself in any situation, then you have to remove that which is keeping you from the wholeness. That which is keeping you from the wholeness and the healing is your own separation.

Thank you.

Now if you have a situation in your life that is falling apart, so to speak—and that's a good description because it's part, not whole—then it's a very simple process, a very simple process: eliminate the separation that's caused the problem in the first place: the overidentification, the individualization, the total reliance and dependence upon a part.

Whenever you see a part of anything, you cannot view the whole, and you cannot be what you do not see. And if you want to be what you do not see, then you must enter the realms of imagining, pass through the doors of imagination, and enter the wholeness that waits. Now that technique, if you wish to call it a technique or tactic, it's taught in much grosser form by what man calls positive thinking, believing is being, and all those different things. But the principle of the law is there and works for those who believe it. You cannot be what you do not believe. If you believe that things are bad, they will get worse. If you believe that things are good, then good they shall be, for you move yourself from separation to wholeness. You cannot experience wholeness and be separate. It's like trying to mix water and oil. It does not work and there's no way that it ever will.

Same simple truth: he who sees the obstruction never finds the way, for you're seeing the part of the thing: the part you choose to see; therefore, that's all that you can be. And being that's all that you can be, that's all you can experience.

Because I believe in good, I experience good. If I didn't believe in good, I could not experience good. That's why I have taught don't believe that something's going to work out. You throw it into an indefinite future. Believe that something *is* working out, then you bring it into the present consciousness of eternity where you have the power. You do not have the power in that which is going to be; you have the power in that which is. So, if you're going to change that which is, you must *be* that which is in wholeness, through your belief.

Your belief has made you separate. Only your belief will make you whole. You see the parts of things and, therefore, cannot experience the wholeness of them. But you only see the parts of things because of your dependence upon them.

As man depends upon his parts, parts is all he can experience. So, when we depend upon our mind, we are depending upon a part, a vehicle that the wholeness is using. And because we're depending on a part, we experience parts. That help with your question?

Thank you very much.

Any other question before we have refreshments and conclude? *[After a short pause, the teacher continues.]* All right. Class concluded. Shut off the recorder, please.

APRIL 14, 1982

Special Seminar 1A

[Once a year, usually at the beginning of June, the American Legion required the use of the log cabin on Sunday morning, when Serenity Spiritualist Church services were held. Special Seminar 1A was held at the Serenity temple at the time when services would have normally been conducted at the log cabin.]

Some of you are aware that the topic for discussion today [is] "Freedom from Fear Through the Law of Disassociation."

We understand that fear is faith in the human mind; that it is a reliance upon what our thoughts are able to accomplish. In that understanding, we find that we believe in many things; that our beliefs in these things are in a constant process of changing. Sooner or later in our life we see that we are not the thought that we believed in a year ago, a week ago, or even a moment ago, for our thoughts appear to be in a constant state of change.

We understand that there are 81 levels of consciousness, that there are 40 soul faculties and 40 sense functions. We also understand that a function is only an undeveloped faculty. Because of the very nature of the human mind, its nature to gather and to store information and experiences, whenever we permit ourselves to identify with the thought of I, instead of the true I which we are, when we permit ourselves to identify with the thought of I, we then believe in the thoughts that we have had in our life. And in that believing, we find our self a house divided because of the contrary thoughts and the contrary experiences that we have already had in life.

When we understand that we, our true being, we are not the thought, but we are the power that forms the thought—we are that which uses the thought—if we will remember that we are that which forms and moves the thought and we are never the thought itself, then we will have a more harmonious and abundant life to live.

It is through our overidentification with the thought of I that we become the victim of the thought that passes through our mind, for in so overidentifying with our thought, we lose the light of reason that knows that we are not the thought but we are that which uses the thought. In awakening to that demonstrable truth, we must not permit our minds to deny the demonstrable Law of Personal Responsibility.

So often in our lives we make an acquaintance and establish what we call a friendship. If we understand what friendship truly is (use and not abuse; respect the right of difference), then we have an enduring and lasting friendship. If we understand friendship to be abuse and not use, if we understand it to be not a respect for the rights of others, then it is not friendship, and it is destined to fall for it is built on the shifting sands of time and illusion.

We believe we are here. We believe we're on an earth plane. We believe all these things. And when we evolve and something happens, experiences in our life, and what we believe in no longer serves us well, then, being the victim of the belief, making the error of errors, becoming the illusion, we suffer the consequences and experience what we call a struggle. There is no struggle to what we are. There is only struggle to what we think we are. And so it is that sometimes we think we are this and we feel just wonderful; and then there are times we think we are that and we feel just terrible.

So, the first step in awakening, of course, is the daily effort to gain control over the human mind, the vehicle that we are using. So the vehicle that we are using, that was designed by the Infinite Intelligence to serve a good, just, and useful purpose, we must stop believing that we are it and, once again, become aware that we are that which is using it. Then we will not have to suffer these ups and downs and these various seeming struggles of life.

It is the very nature of the human mind to believe. Therefore, when we permit our self to overidentify with our mind, we must pay the consequences of what our mind has to offer. If we use our mind wisely and if we consciously choose the thoughts, which are the vibrations that we wish to experience, if we make that effort to gain control, once again, of the vehicle that we are driving in this world, the human mind, then we shall indeed be free, for that is the Law of Disassociation: to awaken that you are not the thing, that you are the user of it and not to be blinded by belief that you are the thought that is in your mind. For if you were the thought that is in your mind, then you would be many things, for many thoughts do we entertain in the course of one day.

As we awaken to that truth, that we are the user of the thought, we are the former of the thought, but we are not the thought itself, as we awaken to that in the light of reason, then we pause in our daily thoughts and activities and we choose which thought we will use. And we do not permit again the thought in our mind to use us. That is disassociation through an awakening of the soul faculty of reason.

We have come to Earth to serve a purpose. The purpose that we have to serve is not within the realm of the mental world to inform us. We all know, when we are still and when we free our self from the belief of the thought of I; for when we free our self from the belief of the thought of I, then we awaken to what we are and not what we think we are. For in so doing shall we then serve the purpose for which we have entered this earth realm. We cannot fully serve the purpose of our soul until we still our mind and awaken to the soul that we are.

We are not the mind, nor are we the body, for if we are, then it is indeed a sad god that we attempt to believe in. For what God would put anyone through such trials and tribulations? It is our belief that we are the thought that is our trials and tribulations. We have been granted by our divine birthright to choose wisely which thought, at any time, we choose to entertain within our consciousness. We have, by our birthright, the freedom and the truth that we are. But we cannot find that 'til we give up what we *think* we are and then, by so giving, awaken to what we are.

Now I'm going to spend a few moments at this time to permit you to ask any questions in reference to freedom from fear through the Law of Disassociation or any questions that you have of a spiritual nature. If you would just be so kind as to raise your hand. Yes, the lady in the—

I wish that you would speak on loss of memory as applied to the elderly.

Thank you. In reference to what is termed loss of memory in reference to the elderly, it is the kindness of Nature herself, designed ever to preserve, to use and to preserve. It is that divine Nature that permits some people who, at a point in their life, are tempting an imbalance in their mental world and their physical world that they seem to express a certain type of loss of memory.

Now we all know that in the course of our life it is indeed difficult for us to forget, to forget something that disturbs us. The difficulty in forgetting that which disturbs us reveals to us that, through our belief, we are the victim of our thought. That is the great difficulty for us in forgetting. Now it is stated in this philosophy, and [in] other philosophies, to forgive is human; to forget is divine. And how truly spoken, for it takes the Divinity that we are to gain control over the mind that attaches to whatever it gathers; it takes the Divinity that we are to gain control over the mind to forget. So this process—of course, there are very many medical terms for what they call senility or forgetfulness. It is a way of their freedom when the experiences in their life have become so complicated, when the house has become so divided that they forget what has been and who is in their life. Does that help with your question?

Thank you so much.

You're welcome. *[After a short pause, the teacher continues.]* No other questions? Short seminar. Yes, please.

If you're constantly having thoughts of, fearful thoughts of bad things happening, how do you deal with that?

Yes. First, in reference to having thoughts, fearful thoughts of bad things happening, we must be honest with our self and we must find within us what it is that we are getting in the experiencing of fearful or bad thoughts. What is the need within our personality? Does it offer to us an excitement of our senses? Does it offer a challenge to our mind? We must remember, there has to be something that we, a part of us is gaining in order for us to experience those types of what are called fearful or bad or negative thoughts.

Now we understand that the sense functions, the so-called animal part of the human being, is ever fighting for its own survival. As we make the effort to free our self from the entrapment of a mental world, the mental world of which we have become a part [of], through our belief, that mental world begins the battle of battles. It introduces into our consciousness all types of doubts and fears and horrible, seemingly horrible things.

The only control that fear has over us is our fear of it. As Franklin Roosevelt so wisely put it, the only thing to fear is fear itself. It is a mental world battling and fighting for survival.

And so it is on the spiritual path or the path of freedom from creation, freedom from the animal part of our being, freedom from what some call the lower light or the greater light, the lesser light, the brighter light—it doesn't matter what they call it. Whenever we permit our self to believe and, by believing, overidentify with form, creation, the mental world, we must pay the price.

How do we deal with these thoughts? By recognizing first that we are not the thought. We are that which is experiencing the thought, but we are not the thought itself. If we will always remember, regardless of the experience or the thought, that we are not the thought, if we will remember when we are dealing with people, "That is not the person. That is the level of consciousness that they are in at this moment. But I have known them in other levels of consciousness at other moments. So therefore, I know that that is not the person. It is the level of consciousness they are at this moment in," [we move along the path of freedom]. That does not relieve us, or them, from the Law of Personal Responsibility.

Either through the error of ignorance—and usually it is through the error of ignorance, the person has chosen, not consciously, to enter those levels of consciousness that are not only detrimental to themselves but detrimental to all who are around or about them. But remember, they will not be there forever, for they are not the thought; they are not the level of consciousness.

Therefore, we look around at our friends and associates, we see that they have changed. What we do not see is we have changed. And because we have changed, we look at them and we see that they have changed, for they are different somehow. But we do not stop and pause and think; but we are different somehow. And so it is with any thought, with any fear.

We must remember that by the law of coming into our consciousness, it is destined by the very same law to go, for that that is given birth knows death, and that that knows death knows birth. And so, our thoughts are in a constant process of birth and death. My good friends, suffering is in birth and suffering is in death. As long as you believe the thought that enters your mind, as long as you insist on believing that, you shall suffer for you shall be born in your identification to a thought only destined to die to the same thought some moment and someday.

So why should we here, entering this earth realm with a purpose to serve, to fulfill our life, to awaken to the demonstrable truth, why should we continue to suffer, to continue to be born and to die?

You see, we concern ourselves, sometimes, about what happens when we leave the physical body. My friends, that's only a death in thought, and it's only another birth in thought. But we're dying and we're born moment by moment by moment. Sometimes we meet an old acquaintance and they're really dead. They're not the way they used to be. Yes, they have died to the way they used to be, and they're born to another way. And this process goes on moment by moment by moment.

But let us remember, the thoughts that we serve are the experiences that we have. And the greatest freedom and the only freedom that we will ever know is the freedom which is the effect of the Law of Personal Responsibility. When we say to our self, regardless of what experience we have, when we say to our self, "Something inside of me that I am not, perhaps, consciously aware of at this moment, by the very law has brought this experience into my life, for the law, demonstrable and clear, says that like attracts like and becomes the Law of Attachment."

And so it is with myself when I look about at my students, I say, "Well, I've got to work harder on myself because I don't like what I'm seeing." But I know I could not attract them if it wasn't something inside of me, for the law says and demonstrates in life no matter what we're in, we shall grow or we shall go. So we grow and go constantly within our self. Does that help with your question on fear?

Thank you.

Yes. The gentleman back there, please.

Yes. I'd like you to expound on the relevance of dreams.

Yes. Thank you. In reference to dreams, there are several causes of dreams. The most common being the effects and disturbance of the mind from the functions being activated during a so-called unconscious state. For example, a person eats and their digestion goes on and on and on for hours after, and not considering that process, they eat and then they go to sleep. And it takes several hours for all of that food to be digested. Now when that takes place after you're in a state of sleep, your mind starts to interpret that in many different ways. That's one type of dream that's quite common.

Another type of dream is the dream of suppression. Now, ofttimes in our jobs and our experiences we want to say something to a certain person and a thought rises in our mind and says, "Oops, I better not say that. I might offend them. I might even get fired." Now because what happens with us, we take that feeling and that thought and we suppress it. Now that's the worst thing that we can do with our feelings and our thoughts, is to suppress them. The human mind can take so much, and then a great deal of that energy pushed down into the so-called depths of the subconscious, that energy gets released and we have various types of dreams. That's another type of dreaming.

Then, of course, there is, which is on rare occasions, unfortunately, the dreams that are prophetic, as we enter into other realms of consciousness while we are asleep.

I personally am not a believer in the process of sleep. I am well aware and have been for many years, the more we awaken spiritually, the less we sleep mentally and physically. And I am a firm believer in that for forty-some years because I have experienced its benefits. But we must remember, my friends, because, you see, rest is what benefits us; sleep does not. You know, you wouldn't think of going out with a pickax and digging for eight hours; and yet, we seemingly go to sleep and utilize more energy than it would take to dig a ditch with a pickax. We use more energy. It is released from our unfulfilled desires, from our suppressed thoughts and judgments. And so, you see, there's little of that time that's spent in so-called sleep that is restoring the health and goodness of our mind and body.

Now we can, through a little effort, become more consciously aware as we're going off to sleep [and] take control of our mind, and in time, through effort, through the powers of concentration, we can enter the realms of consciousness consciously that we choose to rest in.

Unfortunately, for so many of us, we go to bed, we put our head on the pillow, [and] there's many different types of thoughts; many of them we're not even consciously aware of. We seemingly go to sleep, but what we really do [is] we enter the realms that have predominant control over us through our abuses of those realms; and we become the victims during what we call sleep. Consequently, we wake up, sometimes, in the morning and we think we didn't sleep at all. We're not a bit rested. We wake up grouchy. We have bulling spells in the morning and we have all kinds of emotional forces and things. And we wonder, "What's the matter?" And our mind immediately tells us that it's something outside, and we go down the whole list of something's wrong with someone else and that's why we feel terrible; even though we don't see them upon our awakening, our minds are very clever and they blame some experience we had with someone yesterday or what we have to face [that] day. So that is not beneficial to us. It is very common. It is extremely detrimental. And someday, of course, we will all awaken to what's really going on when we *think* we are asleep. Does that help with your question?

Yes. Thank you.

Yes. Now the lady on the aisle had a question, please.

Yes. I understand that hospitality is a soul faculty. What are the other two to make the triune faculty?

That has not yet been given. However, I would like to say one thing in reference to the soul faculty of hospitality. Hospitality is not possible without the faculty of generosity. And generosity and hospitality are not possible without the faculty of responsibility. Perhaps that's helped with your question.

Yes, the lady in the back, please.

Could you speak a moment on when we realize our thoughts that are not in our best interest and we say, "Well, I realize that I'm not this thought," and the benefits of choosing a new thought that is in our best interest?

Yes. And what was the question in reference to?

Would you speak on choosing wisely a new thought to replace . . .

Yes. Well, first of all, you need the incentive to move to another thought. And if a person finds themselves the victim of a thought, which they are consciously aware of, [that it] is not in their best interest and is certainly not going to reap a good harvest for them, however, they find themselves the victim of the thought, then, of course, they must have incentive: incentive to themselves personally to move to another thought. So, first of all, there has to be the incentive.

Now how does one get incentive? Well, one gets incentive through the divine expression called desire. Now I've seen—I know we'll all agree, if we have the right desire, we have all the incentive in the world to do what is necessary to fulfill another thought. Would you not agree?

You're right.

All right. So, in that moment, we choose wisely: we choose that, "Well now, let's see. I must have incentive. I must have the endurance. I must have the strength, and I must direct this divine energy into a thought, into a thought pattern that will prove itself to be constructive and beneficial for my good." You understand?

Yes, sir.

Therefore, you take a look around through your consciousness and you find a desire that has a very high priority. Now once you find that desire, you cast the light of reason upon it: it's called educating desire.

There's nothing wrong with desire when desire has the light of reason over it because when desire, the divine expression, has the light of reason over it, it has total consideration and all the soul faculties to support it, you see. After all, you must remember that desire is the expression of the Divinity. It is when man's mind registers desire that the light of reason goes out, and he believes he is the desire: that puts the light out. That's what puts out the light.

So, in choosing in your consciousness a thought that is beneficial, you've chosen a desire; and you cast the light of reason upon it so that you have at your disposal all of the soul faculties: consideration, tolerance, etc., responsibility, and down the list. Now if that desire that you have at that moment, under the light of reason, does not prove to you that it will be in your best interest, go through your list and choose another desire, for there are many there, of course, for all of us to choose from. Does that help with your question?

Thank you.

Yes. You're welcome. Yes, please.

Does there come a time, through this practice, that one can, that one reaches a point where you don't go on that avenue of the negative thought? I mean, do you actually get to a point where you don't go down those paths of the negative thought, where you can actually be free of it?

Thank you. Remember this, my friends, positive and negative are opposite ends of the same pole. It is only thought that makes them so. Therefore, through the Law of Disassociation, when we free our self from the negative, we free our self from the positive. And we become that which we always have been: we become aware of what we truly are. That is the Divine Neutrality.

We are not the thought; we are the user of the thought. We are not the judgment; we are the victim of the judgment. Nothing's either good or bad, but thinking makes it so. For, you see, the Living Light Philosophy teaches a God of divine neutrality, sustaining and supporting all of life. And who are we to judge what is good or bad when the Divinity itself is not a judge? For if it [were] a judge, there are many things it would not support, in our thinking. I'm sure we would agree. Does that help with your question?

Yes. Thank you.

So, if you want freedom from fear through the Law of Disassociation, then give the greatest gift you have to give and that, to God, is the gift of self. For the gift of self is the thought of I, and the thought of I, the self, is the crown of the house of judgments. That's all that it is.

So, as we, in our daily efforts, continue on with conscious awareness to remember that we are not the thought, that we are greater than the thought [and] we are not experience, which is the effect of the thought that we have entertained, [we begin to awaken that] we are greater than all of that. When we awaken to that simple truth and demonstrate it, this word called *need* will no longer exist. We can only experience need in the realm of delusion that we identify with. Because, you see, my friends, how can we experience what is known as need, the lack of that which we desire, if we are That-Which-Is? If we are That-Which-Is, the Divinity, there cannot be need. Need is an effect of our own delusion. It is an effect of our identification with the thought of I. You see, through the thought of I, the house becomes divided, our house, and we separate our self from the universal whole which we are. So, this is why we teach: you do not annihilate the I. That is not within your power to do. There is no annihilation to truth. You remove from your consciousness the thought of the I and then you will awaken to the I that you are. Does that help with your question?

Yes. Thank you.

[After a pause, the teacher continues.] No more questions? We will have brunch. *[After another short pause, the class concludes.]* Thank you very much.

JUNE 6, 1982

Class January 15, 1983

[The following teachings may have been given to a very small group of advanced students. In this volume, as in other volumes, a series of five asterisks indicates that the tape recorder was stopped and then restarted.]

Truth is not yours or mine. It is the Light. It is Divine. Therefore, all who turn to Light, though short the stay and dark the night, deserve the right to have the Light in their time in need of darkest night.

*****

That composed of mineral, that is the vibration and element thereof, is of the heavier and gross vibration and creates great static difficulty in the necessary frequencies of communion.

*****

Plants, living plants, flowers, especially flowers, have the highest frequencies and are so conducive to the best reception.

*****

If you must have minerals, have gold or copper.

*****

Divine intelligent energy, the life-giving fluid, blocked in all humans in the water center, becomes available to the feast of has-beens and to-bes, who are placed in their parameters by agreement with has-beens, may be released through a breaking of the dam by activation of the center of fire. The usual process is descent through and out of the earth center. But the spiritual path of illumination takes the fluids in the fire center and by the sheer power of the inner will—not the conscious will, the inner will—sends the great power, the *prana*, the life-giving energy back through the water center, the air center, the electric, the magnetic, the odic, the ethereal, and celestial realms of consciousness, and the peace, the joy, the love, the fullness thereof is guaranteed.

*****

The thoughts of men are just like beavers. For example, when man enters the veil of illusion, which takes place by the thought of I, he enters in consciousness from the air center to the water center. The thought of I is a self-multiplication process and, therefore, diligently working, like little beavers, builds a dam across the river in the water center; thereby being the source of supply (the river) for the multiplications of the thoughts of I, man experiences the e-motion or motion of the I in illusion.

*****

Thought, a chain reaction. It only takes one thought to awaken thousands of has-beens. It is a process that is instantaneous. Man thinks he has one thought. Does not realize that one thought is inseparable in the water center from all related forms that have been created. Now man, in his awakening and unfolding, as he broadens his horizons, his one thought, which is connected ofttimes to thousands of thoughts, is now related, through the bridge of broadening of one's horizons, to all thoughts within the horizons. Therefore, man must learn how to establish intelligently a protective force field. This discussion we shall carry on with you at another time. Good to see you.

Dr. Bronson.

[Like Isa Goodwin, who is Richard Goodwin's mother, Dr. Bronson is an angel who would occasionally express through the mediumship of Mr. Goodwin.]

*****

The egg, child, of which you speak is the egg of an eagle, not a chicken.

JANUARY 15, 1983

Class January 17, 1983

[The following teachings may have been given to a very small group of advanced students.]

In the year of the Light one-thousand-nine-hundred-eighty-three. From the Book of Life, Book One, Volume One, page one.

Long ago in a garden of glory, the elephant roamed in the abundance of life. The eagle soared in the freedom of space. And day passed and dusk grew nigh. The eagle, in its excellent sight, viewed this great and massive form. Its movement, its massiveness intrigued the sight of the eagle, and it descended from the great sky above to earth and landed upon the trunk of the elephant.

A communion, a friendship began to grow. And in the friendship and exchange of the thoughts of life, a bondage of the forms of thought began their birth, their strength, and their denial. And in that, [those] ever-increasing walls of ignorance, the elephant began to feel a restriction of his need to roam and to enjoy the glory of his jungle to which he had become accustomed.

The eagle, used to the freedom of its flight, to the thrill and to the sensing of its movement through air, began to look again to the sky, with which, by nature, it was familiar. And so, one day the eagle, viewing its homeland, took flight and did not return to the land of the elephant, to the glory of the garden, with which, by its own divine purpose, [it] could not be imprisoned. And the elephant, with his great strength, destroyed the wall that had surrounded him and kept him from the abundance of the great jungle that he so enjoyed. And the elephant began to roam. And once again, the eagle began to soar.

And so, once again, the elephant and the eagle awoke to their love of truth, to the wisdom of keeping it (truth) separate from creation. For in that great awakening, the elephant became aware that he is not only an elephant but he too is an eagle, and in that awareness, he too could fly; he too could experience the vastness of space. He too could view beyond the things of his nature and limit of form. And in that day, a new life within the elephant was born. And that life is the life of memory, of memory par excellence. The divine principle, the elephant became.

I am that which is. I have never been that which was. I shall never be that which is to be, for I am that which is. And my love of truth, my love of that which is, which I am, shall ever be, for while in flesh, I shall not forget. And when I am the eagle, I shall forget, for then I shall be formless and I shall be free. But while I am yet the elephant, I shall give forth, my friend, the eagle, and in so doing, in that giving am I freed from bondage. For keeping truth separate from creation, my love of truth shall be the fullness of my life. And in the fullness of my life, joy, the eagle, the elephant of which I am, shall be.

And so, my children, the love of truth is the domain of your spirit. And the love of your flesh is the domain of the land of flesh. Be not tempted to mix the unmixable. Be not deceived that truth shall not ever rise again. The joy of life is the separation of life, for that which is must return unto itself. That which becomes must change and return unto the source of its beginning. Let us, then, tempt not to mix oil with water. Let us respect and, in the respect, grant the right of return of our soul to the Light which it is.

Wanderer in the land of the flesh, soldier in the land of the spirit that you are, be ever watchful that you may always be what you are, that you may not love what you think you are for that is the great division; that is the great separation; that is the love of truth.

Over the vastness of space lies the curtain of illusion. But remember, my children, it is only a curtain and the Light, your light, shall ever pierce its obstruction to your view if you will ever remember the Light is first. The Light is the Divine Principle. Love is its expression. Life, its joy. Be not forced by the lack of the Light in the imbalance of its effects, for effects are cause and repetition of experience, for repetition is the continuity of the Law of Cause.

And so, when we experience what we know as irritation, remember, repetition wears the form and wears it well, wearing away the limit of our love. For he who loves his adversity equal in passion and desire as he loves the form of his bondage shall awaken within to the Light, to the love of truth, and shall be bound no more, for Love Divine is the province of the Light. It is and cannot be. It is and has not been. The form reveals the limit, and in the revelation of the limit do we lose the love of truth that we are.

From the river of life, we flow into the ocean of love and rise through the mist of creation to the rainbow of promise of the Light, the truth that we are. And while sailing along the river, may we never forget the many ports we visit serve only that which we have become familiar and secure with. Destined, O Light, you are, by the nature of your being, to return to the port from whence you have originally sailed.

So, winds of time and waters of life, your purpose is being fulfilled, for the captain of your ship on the boat of his soul has the Light and the power to reason. Chart well your course through life that you may know you are in truth the master of your ship, the captain of your destiny. For in so knowing are you lifted in consciousness to pass through the great mist that is upon you, to never lose sight of the gateway to heaven. Through the rainbow of promise you shall return, for promise, the open door of the Light of God, must ever be your true love. And then your journey through time and space shall be the Peace, the Power, the Light, the Love, and the Life. And you shall not fear, nor be disturbed with all the things along the shore that tempt, that weaken, that hold and bind, for that which tempts is that which weakens. And that which weakens is that which binds.

Let the sails of your ship, the reason of your soul, be the direction in which you, the captain, may sail. Serene upon the sea of time is he who learns and applies that which is his divine right to chart the course and, in so doing, fail not in the storms of life. Be not tattered in your sails. Be not torn in their purpose, for you are the captain. You must never forget, for in so doing are your sails lost; your ship, without anchor, moves aimlessly along the river of life; your efforts discourage for there are no longer sails to encourage; and you lie, a ship upon the sea, without direction within your power, without hope, without possibility, without encouragement to enter the port, your home, where you know is the fullness of your life.

Ofttimes, as captain of our ship, in our sailing on the river of life, hoping for land, we view a mirage. And as we sail closer, in sadness and shock do we find it to be a whirlpool in the waters of life, a whirlpool of mental substance. And disappointment overcomes us; unless in that experience of disappointment we awaken to who we are, we sink in the whirlpool of a troubled mind and are lost in the illusion of mind.

Awaken, O soul, in the illusion of time and be secure in your love of truth, for though new to your mental substance, it is destined to rise supreme. Concern not your mind with what has been. Concern not your mind with what shall be. Seek not what is not within your domain to seek. Satisfy, O mental substance, yourself with the flesh that you are. To rise and to fall is the nature of your being. Let the nature of the soul be not infringed upon in its divine right to the love of truth, which is its domain, its right, and its joy. Enter, O mental substance, to the limits of your creation. Do not tempt to cross your limits and be what you shall never be.

Light everywhere shall shine. Before it, all form shall bow or be consumed. For form, thought, must not be permitted to deny the limits of its pleasure. It cannot, it shall not become what it can never be. Separate yourself, O form, separate yourself and be in the land of your home. Tempt not to cross into the formless and the free.

Soul to soul I shall ever be part of one that's part of me and not the limit of that I use, but the fullness of the Light that serves and returns to its source to serve again.

Wherever I go, whatever I do, no land shall be the homeland I am, for home is not restricted. Home is not the bondage of time. Home is not the reference, nor security, of familiarity.

In losing the purpose that we are, we experience contempt for what we thought we were. And that contempt, that irritation, is only our efforts to, once again, be what we are, not what we think we are.

Across the great universes a speck of light moving in consciousness, serving its purpose, never to stray from the duty, from the purpose of its being. Alone is he who views creation. Alone is he in the viewing, for in so doing, identifies and is lost in creation by denial, in mental substance, of the consciousness he is.

We shall not find in our search without that which is forever and a day within. Truth we are. We cannot become. Love that which you are and, in so doing, view it everywhere you go. For what you seek reflects what you think you are. It cannot reflect what you do not think you are. Be the Light unto yourself and all shall come in keeping with the Law of Love, for love returns to the Light from whence it has wandered. And that which is born and grows in darkness becomes diseased from error and direction of its love to the mist of creation, its loveless direction, and did not see, for a time, the Light of its true love. *[When the teacher spoke the word "love-less," there was a significant pause between the syllables.]*

Ever through the mist, the promise of God whispers its gentle and sweet harmony. In that promise is the joy beyond words. In that promise, the joy becomes fulfillment. Becomes as we, in awakening, ah, the honesty that is the Light within.

Be of good cheer. Know beyond doubt what you are. Suffer not in the question of what will become. Wonder not that you may know. Design not that you be not bound. Plan not for there is, by far, a greater intelligence. And when you know not, when all plans and design of mental substance have brought unto your life the inevitable disasters and destruction, be of good cheer, for in their destruction there is less to tempt your Light; there is less to obstruct your view.

Blessed are those with no things in consciousness, for they see clearly who they are. They are filled with the joy, not limited by it. The love, the effect of the Light, is without limit for it has no design. And without design, there is no destruction; there is no disaster. There is upliftment. There is peace. There is happiness. There is the greatness beyond the mind: the bliss, the ecstasy that you are.

The land of the flesh is birth and death. Be it thought or physical substance, it is first thought. It is thought and form within your consciousness. It does not in truth exist. You make it so. You create it with your power in mental substance. Everything you think you seek, everything you alone in mental substance have created. Therefore, in your search for truth be not deceived by your search which creates in your consciousness forms, obstructions, to its realization. Accept your fullness. Permit not your mind to create its form, for then it is no longer fulfillment.

Stop the seeking. Stop the searching. Accept you are. Accept the joy. For in your search for it do you form and deform, by mental substance, by lack of control, obstructions without number. Pause and accept. And in the will of God, that which you are, the awakening, the ecstasy of life, the joy of your soul, the happiness of your heart, you shall know you are.

*****

[The rhythm or cadence of the teacher's speech during this class is somewhat different from the other classes. He has relatively long pauses after speaking a few words. With regard to the stanzas below, there is a slight change in his cadence that suggested that formatting. However, it may be helpful to read the stanzas as prose.]

> I wait in consciousness. I wait to be.
> And in my waiting and waiting, no thing do I see.
> And then I awaken in the wisdom of my patience
> I know that I no thing shall ever be.
> And in that awakening, I am not bound.
> In that awakening, truth, I am free.
> Only in my impatience, the possibility of change,
> Do I become and therefore be
> And in the being bound to thee
> The effect, the cause, the design I see.
>
> O love divine a servant be
> 'Til selfishness imprisons me
> And warps the reason of my mind
> Into the madness of blind.

Be. Do not become. Be. Do not begin. Be. And do not end. Be, that you may see. And in your being, all things shall serve, for you no longer become what you can never be.

Let the becoming, which is the love, serve what you are, the Light. Enter not delusion. And Light you are serve love. Love must ever serve Light. For when Light serves love, mist and darkness are the destiny.

When you return to what you are, you will free yourself from all things. And in so doing, all things shall serve you well. May your light so shine upon the shadows of time that your veil of delusion may disintegrate before your view, and all that you have sought, or thought you ever would, shall be your stream of consciousness ever moving, ever flowing through the great ocean into the mist passing through the rainbow, paradise, heaven, you are.

Good day.

JANUARY 17, 1983

Class January 19, 1983

January 19, 1983. This is Richard Goodwin speaking personal to all his students on Earth, in all worlds, in all times, in all places.

Several years ago, the seeds of deception entered into the garden and in the shadows of the temple of Light, Serenity. Over those years, through great effort and my love for God and all souls, I tried to be a good gardener in God's garden: to weed it well. And yet weeds have great tenacity. And finally, I had to prune them, to clip them that they may not grow so great as to consume the beauty and the joy of God's garden.

And time has passed, and I have pruned them to the very best of my ability. And approximately six months ago, two of the weeds came closer and closer to the Light and began to flourish in its warmth and compassion. They grew with the rapidity of a mushroom and began, in their ignorance, to cast a shadow upon the Light of the temple in the garden. And as they grew and the shadow descended upon me, I prayed and did all that I could without permitting my Light to descend into mental consciousness, the shadow of truth.

As the method is legal if the motive is pure and no shadow is cast upon the love of truth, my silence was not only required but demanded. And one day, as there is for all of us, the day when truth crushed to earth must rise again, I cast the Light upon the little souls, smothered by the form of the mushrooms of flesh. And with great effort to control of self, I continued on to serve the Light of God and took from the darkness the essence of the Light and gave unto all of you the benefits, the good that can be freed from the darkness of creation, of form, of mental substance.

I have been hopeful, in these latter days, to be encouraged that the darkness of deception, being lightened by the Light into shadows, may someday, once again, their soul shine through and the Light free their eternal being.

It is with sadness in my heart that I must, by order of the angels who guide your temple of truth, reveal to you the principle, but never ever the personality, for in your present state of growth and evolution you would be, controlled by mental substance, instruments to serve the darkness and drive from the Light of Truth their humble, eternal souls. That, I would never be, with God's divine help, an instrument of doing.

The true and only cause of my physical decline is what you may understand to be insufficient energy for the harmonious movement of my vital body to keep balance, harmony within the bodies of my soul on Earth. As my compassion continues to utilize vital energies from my being to continue to assist, to encourage, to help, and to inspire the entrapped souls, the depletion is my decline in the earthly bodies to remain with you in the physical world.

And so, in serving my God, as servants before me have demonstrated and proven, I am not without, nor have I ever been without, nor ever will I be without, in my service to the love of Truth, the Light of God, my Judas, my betrayer, my deceiver. I love Truth and am ever willing to pay the price of creation that those who come unto to me may be granted that and that only that shall free them.

The great, ever-increasing darkness of deception within the love, the light, and the beauty of the temple of God, the increasing darkness and deception, I have battled and continue to battle in realms of consciousness and have, unto this moment, been, in my love of God, victorious. But as the Law of Balance can never be transgressed without its penalty, I am reaching, with but four degrees left, the borderline in which the process of my decline and departure from your earthly realm is irreversible.

I am not saddened for my journey. My heart is heavy and saddened because my mind believes that I have failed in my efforts to teach and to demonstrate that the love of God is more worthy, more valuable, more lasting, and so much greater than the love of the flesh of earthly substance. However, there is yet available to me four degrees. My life, my soul, my spirit is not dependent upon the flesh of earth and, therefore, is not within the power, nor control, of the realms of mental and physical substance.

My mental body and my physical flesh is at the mercy of the laws and the kings, the rulers, within whose realm my soul is presently serving. I have, in these latter months, made great effort within myself to conserve energy, knowing the price that would be paid if I did not. I have, and I continue to do, to direct what energy [is] available to me to the teachings that I know in my heart will free you long after I have left your world.

As the deception, wearing many garments, continues to grow, to flourish, the energies available to me for the great battle for all your souls, those energies are little left unto me. And so, my children, though you cannot be instruments of the great God and King of Kings, you cannot be those instruments until you make your conscious choice: Who, in all your needs, will you serve? Who, in all your wants and desires, will be the master of your soul? Who, my children? Only you, moment by moment, can decide.

My life, eternal, unbroken stream of consciousness, shall continue. My flesh, my mental body is at the mercy of the realms I battle. If the deception, wearing many garments, continues to flourish—only four degrees are left unto me and then no law can change that which is irreversible.

I pray not to remain on Earth. I pray not to leave Earth. I only pray to serve my God and complete my job, be that in Divine order for me.

My fellow students, I do want you to know that I do understand, that I do forgive; forget is the right and the domain of Divinity. I would not presume unto myself I have ever arrived. I know in my heart, my soul, and, yea, even my mind, that it is the great sadness of life in form, the great insatiable need for God, which is goodness. And so, in those realms of darkness, that need turns to an unbearable need for power. And my heartache is that power, O God, which is yours, shall never be ever fulfilled in the form of mental substance called need.

And so, I leave my day in God's hands. Your days, hopefully, through your constant prayers, [are] in God's hands also.

It is my responsibility to now share with you the sincere wish, desire of the founders of your temple of Light, Serenity, that upon my demise from your physical world that it be disbanded, that all assets be converted to cash, that all teachings revealed unto you, including, after my departure, the higher teachings of the initiates, be printed and distributed throughout the land of flesh, throughout the Earth planet. For those who are awakened shall read, shall study and apply. For those who [are] yet controlled by the need of goodness, limited in mental substance in the twilight zones of life, the great Light revealed shall return unto itself. And any form in the way shall be purified with the glory and the fires of heaven.

And so it is, my friends, my last will and testament to be recorded on paper as soon as possible, for the days are few.

In reference to my personal belongings, there's little of earthly substance that one might consider mine. My clothes, God brought to me through the kindness of my students. They were purchased, it is my belief, in the hopes they may serve the purpose of their design. Therefore, my few earthly threads, I have cared for to the best of my ability that they may, in my care and consideration, represent my value for the kindness and consideration of those who were the instruments through which I had received them. I wish them to be given to the only student I have who is of similar size, [Student R]. May he so, in the use of the threads, awaken to the spiritual truth of the Law of Consideration, Kindness, and Care that they may represent the continuity of that beautiful spiritual law.

My ring, which also came to me from my students as a birthday present, represents, in its color and in its design, the understanding necessary for a soul to have, through their efforts of the control of self, through their love and dedication to God. [Student R] is second in command of the ship of destiny of the Living Light Academy. It is in keeping with the spiritual, demonstrable laws that he should receive the spiritual symbol of the authority, the dedication to the purpose for which the Light on Earth took the form in shape in earth of the Serenity Association.

There are a few other personal things. My elephants, I believe, may serve well my dear friend, [Student S]. And it is my wish that she receive them, to use them for the spiritual good for the freedom and the upliftment from the twilight zones of mental substance. Other personal items, though few in number, I wish them to go to [Student Q], to [Student H].

And above all is my wish that those who remain behind on Earth will unite in their love of truth, that peace and harmony may reign supreme, that God's love may be their love and they fulfill the will of God, demonstrate, from freedom of judgment, freedom of mental design, that God's love, our love of Truth, shall meet and joy, fulfillment be theirs.

JANUARY 19, 1983

[In the vast majority of the recordings of the classes of the Living Light Philosophy, the vitality of Mr. Goodwin is clear. In this class, however, what is clear is both his dedication to the Light and his utter exhaustion. Despite the seriousness of his health condition, he continued to serve God and the ministering angels without missing a single devotional service at the log cabin. This is one of two recordings of Mr. Goodwin's last wishes. The second recording of Mr. Goodwin's last wishes was made on September 21, 1988. Mr. Goodwin passed to the higher life on February 24, 1989.]

Class January 21, 1983

January 21, 1983.

Now, we're discussing deception: that it is not possible to deceive until we first deceive our self, in keeping with the demonstrable truth that we cannot grant to another what we have not first granted to our self.

Now I will make sure that this [recording] is available at private times for note taking. And you can, perhaps, take the essence of the things that have impact upon you.[14]

Ah, it was—what day? Wednesday? Today's Friday.

Yes.

Wednesday? Wednesday, at the request of the Council, I recorded, in keeping with my responsibility to this temple of Light, my last will and testament. I did that after several heart attacks. I did that because out of a hundred degrees, I was four degrees from death's door. Now I had no fear, because there is no death. I did feel a great responsibility that things had not been taken care of in reference to what few personal possessions that I have. And where I would like them to go: to people who I feel might benefit from them. And also, my wishes concerning the organization; of course, that's in the hands of divine and man-made law.

I also explained, at that time, that the great wave of deception that had entered the temple of Light was the true and only cause of my departure.

Now I realize that you, perhaps in ignorance, do not seem to understand what you are, first, doing to yourself, and, second, doing to those with whom you come in contact in the temple of the Light. I explained earlier that when we believe that we are fulfilling a spiritual commitment, when we believe we are doing a spiritual duty and, in that belief, perform duties, thoughts, acts, and deeds that are serving the opposite of spiritual duty and spiritual commitment, that we put a cloak of goodness, of

Light, of truth over the form of what we're really doing and establish the Law of Self-Deception.

Now I have taught for years that honesty will lead us through. And I have asked for years that creation, by demonstrable truth, be left out of the temple of truth. You cannot mix truth, formless and free, with creation and expect to have truth. What you do have is Light obstructed by the shadow of form, known as the lesser light, the deceiver of all deceiving: you establish the Law of Deception, a shadow cast upon the Light of Truth. You then become an instrument of discord and are destined, absolutely destined, to experience disaster.

No man can serve two masters. There is no possible way to serve truth and falsehood because to attempt such a service is to divide in consciousness oneself. There is weakness in division. There is strength in unity.

Now let us pause in this greatest of all self-deception. I have taught for years that truth needs no defense, for truth is. We justify, we excuse, and we defend deception with those instruments of justification.

Who, we must ask our self the question, are we deceiving? We believe we are deceiving the person or persons that we're talking to. But truth crushed to earth, in time, shall reveal we are only deceiving our self.

The formless, free Spirit, that which you are, the Consciousness which is God, enters an expression of itself. The expression of the great Consciousness is Love.

The motion of the Consciousness is will, divine will. And so, divine will, pure, formless, free, infinite, intelligent, moves an expression of itself known as divine love.

With the intercourse of divine will with the expression of itself, divine love, we know the birth of the intercourse to be—what, [Student R]? *[After a short pause, the teacher continues.]* Will, love manifests what?

Truth.

Life!
Life.

The will to love, the expression thereof, *is* divine, *is* desire, *is* design, *is* perception, *is* form, and forgets the source of its birth, knows itself and, in knowing, conceives, known as mental concepts. And so, we find spiritual essence expressing itself, forgetting its source, becoming mental substance.

Now mental substance conceives and deceives. Spiritual essence perceives and prepares, for full is the remembrance of form, but not the form, for it remembers it is a covering for its source to express. Being a covering with remembrance, it is free from need, for in its remembrance, divine will, total acceptance, keeps a conscious awareness ever present of the source from whence it came, the sustenance which it is. Contrary to mental form which has forgotten its source, knows its need for sustenance for survival and is ever filled with want, need, and desire.

We view in life many things, many forms, many people. Our view is ever dependent upon and relative to the shadows of what has been superimposed on what is, and the illusion becomes our reality. For example, a boy meets a girl and then departs. Views him not for ten years past. A meeting takes place once again. She views him through the shadows, the forms in her consciousness of how she conceived him ten years past. The boy doesn't fit the conception of her shadows in her consciousness, and she experiences he now has grown a bit taller, looks a bit older, perhaps, now has a mustache, and a process takes place within her consciousness. He does not fit exactly the shadows of the past views that still remain on her river of consciousness. Adjustments must be made within her consciousness in order for the present form to fit. So new shadows in consciousness are created. Old shadows are adjusted or crack and decay.

We go to the store. We view a chair. We desire the chair. We create the shadows, light, dim, or dark, ever dependent upon the degree of desire we permit to flow through our consciousness in the form, in our consciousness, of the chair. If the desire is great, the blindness is in keeping therewith. If the desire is not so great, the blindness is not so great.

We purchase the chair. The shadow in consciousness is now established; weak or strong, dependent upon the degree of the desire. The weeks, the months, they pass. Sometimes it is only days. We look at the chair. We see a defect. We are not happy. We did not see the defect at the time of purchase for our view was dim; our desire was great.

We now have, as we always have, the divine right of choice. Create a new shadow, including the defect that we have discovered, or return the chair for a replacement. Dependent upon other shadows in consciousness will we choose what to do, for it is the shadows in consciousness that will make the choice, not us, for we are blinded, in varying degrees, by desire and cannot see the shadows that dictate what we shall or shall not do.

Should we decide, victims of other shadows, other desires, other efforts, other justifications, which are defenses and protectors of self-deception, [should] we decide to keep the chair with the defect and create new shadow forms in consciousness, time passes and we view a terrible scratch on the chair. We know we haven't scratched it. No one else has scratched it. And we are very upset. We have adjusted, in our desire, from the shadow of the chair to the shadow of a chair with a defect. Now we have, again, choice: create another shadow including a scratch or return the chair. Usually, we are so controlled by shadows in consciousness, we once again create another shadow, superimposing it upon the chair of our reality. We now, slowly but surely, as the shadow solidifies in consciousness, we resign our self and keep the chair.

The months pass, and one day we realize that two of the springs in the chair have collapsed. The chair, the original shadow, still existing in consciousness, has already adjusted enough, and we experience what is known as frustration and emotional upheaval, for all shadows, all form, all identity is designed in the element air and descends into the living waters of the water center, where motion, to our personal experience e-motion, motion within—for emotion, its meaning, is motion within—we experience emotion. These are the shadows going to war for we have decided to now create another shadow including two defective springs.

Shadows formed by design in the air center, giving [given] birth in the water center, solidified in the earth center, activated in the fire center, rise up to battle; a new shadow is entering.

Remember, shadows have no sustenance without the energy flowing in your river of consciousness. Therefore, by their very nature of mental substance, they fight for their survival. Finally, the battle within is won. You are relieved, gradually, of emotional upheaval, and the chair remains. You have accepted, by the creative process of a new shadow superimposed with other shadows; the chair remains an illusion in your reality. For reality is a conscious realization of passing events, and passing events are the shadows moving on your river of consciousness.

And so, the months go by and one day you are shocked. One of the legs of your chair has collapsed. You experience, once again, at the view of the collapsed leg, an emotional upheaval.

For the shadows through which you view the chair, having the intelligence of your mind, for they were created by your mind, know what you think and [they] prepare for war, for the battle that is to come, for you are thinking of how to repair it and, in that thinking, are creating new shadows in consciousness.

And so, you attempt to repair the broken leg, having discovered that it was improperly made in the first place. Another shadow, the greatest of all shadows, denial of personal responsibility, you blame the store and not your lack of effort to thoroughly investigate. And so, in your efforts to repair the broken leg, you are as successful as your ability and willingness to control the self, for in the self are the created shadows of your consciousness. Without self-control, the shadows battle, and your work, your job lacks the goodness, the quality which is the expression of your soul.

Finally, with the collapse of the other leg of the chair, in disgust with the battles raging within your being, you get rid of the chair. When you get rid of the chair, you no longer view the chair. The shadows of your consciousness, imprinted upon its very aura and essence, go with the chair and you feel good. You're free from the trauma, the frustration of your own emotions. You feel a great relief. So relieved do you become, the banner of caution must rise. And it clearly says, in parentheses, my students, "Bladder beware" end of parentheses.

My friends, the chair and this example is a living demonstration of receiving, holding, and relieving. The temple of your soul reveals that part of your anatomy is known as the bladder. So, bladder beware. It represents within your consciousness self-control.

And now, as we understand the wisdom of bladder beware or caution, we can clearly see that the lack of effort to investigate thoroughly everything, presume nothing, is indispensable to personal responsibility and will free us from the destiny of disaster because it frees us from self-deception, from sellout to what is commonly referred to as time-pressure.

We often experience what we call time-pressure but do not understand what pressure we are experiencing. Because there is no time in space, because time, the conscious awareness of the illusion called time, is dependent upon reference, and because reference is ever dependent upon form and because we create many forms, many shadows in consciousness, when the forms rise up in consciousness for their sustenance, we begin to experience pressure. And because they are the instruments through which we experience the illusion of time, by reference, we call that time-pressure, when more justly it should be called lack of self-control: lacking in our effort to control self, which is the covering of the multitude of shadows we have created.

Through our efforts to control self, we become captain of the ship. And being captain, we wisely chart our course on the river of life. We see the many shadow forms in the various ports we pass as we sail along the river of life. We make intelligent decisions, for we are on the river, freed from the bays, freed from the ports. And being freed from the ports in the bays, where the shadows are created, we choose wisely which port to enter. We take with us personal responsibility, the light of honesty, the dawn of reason, the ability to transform what we alone have created. And in that ability, declare and demonstrate our divine right to take charge over all creation within the just and rightful domain of our consciousness.

Therefore, the shadows, our servants, do not become belligerent [or] demand and order us to do anything, but patiently wait for the orders of the captain of the ship of his soul that they may receive their sustenance in keeping with the light of reason that transfigures them from devils of greed and ignoramuses of need to little angels of care, kindness, and consideration, for the captain, the master, freed from bondage, they know would not attempt to bind them, to starve them. Therefore, there's peace in the ports of life. There's harmony and love divine for there is total consideration. There's wisdom in creation. There's joy of life, for the demonstration of personal responsibility of the master transforms the shadows, and from the lesser light of darkness grows the greater Light of Truth.

And so it is stated that truth crushed to earth shall rise again. Forms of darkness, by the light of reason are you transformed, by the love of God are you transfigured, by the divine will of total acceptance do you, in evolution, become the angels of Light.

JANUARY 21, 1983

Class January 23, 1983

[This class, as well as several classes given after this date, was recorded on a microcassette recorder. During many of the microcassette classes, the recorder was often paused. A few sentences might be recorded and then the recorder was stopped. The class may or may not continue while the recorder was paused. When the recorder was stopped, an audible sound was recorded on the tape. Typically, the teacher would silently signal the vice president to start and stop the recorder; so, usually there are no spoken words to indicate a break in recording. As a result, many of the microcassette classes do not read like the previously published classes. As an aid to understand the microcassette classes, the instances when the recorder is stopped are indicated by five asterisks. The pause between teachings could last a few moments or several hours. So, sometimes adjacent teachings are closely related, but often they are not.

In addition, some recordings, but not all, were edited to remove some of the more personal topics that were discussed. In a few classes, the transcribed teachings had to be reassembled from multiple tapes. While great effort was made to present the teachings in the order they were given, there is the possibility that some teachings are out of order because the proper order of the teachings could not be established from the surviving, edited tapes. The personal, hand-written notes taken by individual students during those classes were consulted to aid in establishing the order of the teachings.

Although some of the microcassette classes may seem incomplete, they are complete transcriptions of the surviving recordings. Also be aware that some of the teachings were given only to a very small group of advanced students, while others were given to a larger group of students.

This class records an exposure, which is the process through which the levels or forms controlling a student were exposed to the light of reason. Although exposures were very common and often occurred whenever students were at the temple, they were rarely recorded. Whenever the behavior of one or more students interfered with the rights of the Serenity Association, there was an exposure. That behavior could take the form of an inappropriate attitude, an emotional outburst, a disturbance of any kind, or a failure on the part of the student to fulfill their spiritual duties, such as bringing a pantry item or properly preparing a brunch item for the Sunday brunch. This process helped the students to face their personal responsibility, and the true cause of the disturbance was exposed. Whenever forms are exposed, the first expression is often a justification for or an excuse of the behavior that triggered the exposure. Although exposures were often difficult on the uneducated egos of the students, they were extremely beneficial: the process freed the students from their overidentification with those limited forms that caused the disturbance and they were able, for a time, to express more of their true being. One student described the process of exposure as rather like getting a shower on the inside.]

[The following teaching may have been given to a very small group of advanced students.]

Experiences in the mind are reflections or effects of movements in consciousness which are shadows of the past.

*****

[The following teachings were given to a larger group of students.]

What happens is really quite simple: you start to see the effects of lesser light, known as disaster. Now when man moves from abundant good to form and limit, he experiences what he calls lack. He experiences lack, need, because the great power that flows through the divine will of total acceptance is being denied, and obstructions, known as shadows, forms created, [are] called from the past. Therefore, the great power, limited in the vehicles through which it now has to flow through, does not and cannot flow as abundantly.

The church is the living demonstration, the academy, of this process daily. For example, today revealed many shadows in the way of the abundant good or flow of God. We had very low attendance at our brunch. Our bake sale revealed the living demonstration: one of the lowest in our history. And we go down the list and see that the shadows, the forms created, the forms called up from the past in the consciousness of the participants within the academy, who, by their presence, become the academy and [determine] what Light is able to flow.

Now if you understand that basic principle, then you will understand how much Light can shine because, in keeping with the brightness of the Light are the forms of justification, the defenders of self-deception, the false security called reliance upon mental substance or self-reliance, creating the obstructions we see.

Thank you.

*****

—not going to erase it. *[The teacher refers to the microcassette recorder.]* You don't have to worry. This isn't the higher teachings. You can leave them on. All right, now—

*****

We now see how a person, meriting an experience where they have to part with a dollar, a few dollars, a few hundred, or a few thousand, for it is the principle of money and never the amount, serves forms, shadows of past experiences and what they have offered to them in times past. They expose themselves to other people and whoever is not strong in the Light within their consciousness at the moment, through the law that like attracts like, becomes attached and a part thereof, the vibration. Now stop and think what we are doing to our self. And we're doing it, fortunately, in one respect, here in the Light where it can be revealed, for only in revelation is there truth, is there freedom, is there a way shown unto us.

Now. Now. [Student H]—

Uh-huh.

—the evidence reveals that, supposedly, you were not aware of [Student A's] condition at the time of her entering the kitchen. Is that correct?

When she first entered the kitchen—

*****

Are you getting the student's transcription—comments? *[The teacher addresses the recording technician.]*

OK.

And then I'll delete it.[15]

I really wasn't because I hadn't seen her before she came in. [Student H continues.]

All right. Now [Student A]—that's all right. Leave it on. *[Again, the teacher addresses the recording technician.]*—you were speaking—[Student H] spoke to you about three dollars for the photo—

Uh-huh.

—fund that you owed. You already were weakened by the shadows in control of your emotions, is that correct?

[There is no audible response from Student A.]

And did you agree to pay that three dollars?

That's right.

Yes. And you didn't feel badly about that?

No.

All right. Now [Student P] said what to you when you exploded? *[The teacher continues to question Student A.]*

I don't think I exploded. I just, I just didn't think . . . [Student A speaks very softly and several of her words are difficult to transcribe.]

Can't quite hear you.

I just felt that she was interrupting.

You felt that she was interfering or interrupting. *[Student A continues to speak as the teacher speaks, but it is difficult to transcribe her words.]* That's all right. Because, you see, you had that feeling.

Uh-huh.

Now let me explain something to you. If you, your life energy, your vitality, is in process of serving shadows that they may animate, they may move, within your realm of consciousness—and remember, the life—the river—the, the water center where the life is—for without water, there is not life on this planet. In your water center, you have all of these shadows from the past who are moving on the waters, disturbing the waters, and you experience what you call bad feelings and are very sensitive in your emotions.

Uh-huh. [Student A acknowledges.]

All right? This happens to all of us. And while they're all out there in your little bay of water in consciousness, jumping around, swimming around, eating and doing everything they want to do, another army jumps into the same bay of water. [Student P], in this case, interjected life force through the spoken word. You became irritated, would you say?

Yes. [Student A responds.]

Well, you were annoyed; you were upset. A little bit hurt. Did not your pride get slighted?

It's not the first time she's made—

I understand, [Student A]. We're going to get right to the point. It's not the first time she's did [done] it. And that's important because you already have shadows that immediately rose up, jumped into the pool of the water center, for they exist in consciousness, all asleep.

Uh-huh.

And they woke up when she did that to you, when you merited that. They woke up; they jumped into the pond or the pool, now, along with the money dudes who are jumping in there, eating. So, the money dudes get upset because another troop has jumped in. And your pride is slighted; you feel hurt and you're certainly emotional.

Yeah, right.

What you don't understand, and hopefully this evening will reveal, because you're getting a class of truth regardless, what you don't seem to understand is when she interjected that, she woke up your shadows that don't appreciate being imposed upon. And her army jumped into your pool of water or bay. It depends on how big it is, of course, how many jump in.

Well, that's not where it ended. You had a few other shadows swimming around down there with the money shadows of the past. And those few others, not as many as the money ones, the sex ones were doing their number eating at the same time. I've been in the business a long time; I do know how these things work. So, these little sex dudes, they were down there. Actually, there was about eighteen, twenty of them, compared to two, three hundred of the other, money ones. And they're jumping around swimming down there and here comes this regiment, this regiment of money entities jumping into your pool because they're hungry and they want to eat.

Right.

The bridge has been established. You have permitted the bridge to be established.

So [Student P's] regiment of money [forms], all those dudes, they rushed in where angels fear to tread. Right into your pool. Following them, dead on their heels, came all her sex ones, from just a suppression of a few weeks ago. And in that instant, [Student P] experienced a relief, a little feeling of good, and a zinger. And there's a lot more to a zinger than what people realize. She had her little pride, had a temporary, momentary charge of energy. Did you realize that?

Yeah. [Student P responds.]

You felt good in the instant. Did you not?

Uh-huh.

You felt real good in that instant because in that instant all those dudes, living down in there—you understand?—hungry, they went phew! *[The teacher makes a sound that is difficult to transcribe but suggests very quick movement.]* in a split second. Now, perhaps you can see why teasing, tempting, and all that stuff is . . . *[Again, the teacher makes a sound difficult that is difficult to transcribe, but suggests that that activity is forbidden.]* if you want and love the truth that frees you.

Now look what comes out of this process, happening to you trigger-happy people all the time. As recent as a Friday night, just a couple a nights ago, the armies called the zingers came from that chair and banged me with the whammy of whammies under the guise of a Mediterranean raccoon. Well, it was called something else. I finally evolved it, finally, with God's help, I evolved it from a Mediterranean *r-a-t*, to a Mediterranean raccoon, to a skunk! And when the skunk finally got created in consciousness, here—it was a huge skunk. I had him waltz right over and he did his number in keeping with the divine Law of Personal Responsibility.

I am responsible to all things created within my universe. That which is alien and foreign to it, that tries to shoot me down, gets sent on back. Sometimes it takes a little while to get it back. Fortunately—my own beloved sister—yes, put it down for posterity *[The teacher may be addressing the recording technician.]* —my own beloved sister shot her zinger, which was that army, because *she* was hurt, in her need, at that time, to ask the question, if you can call it a question, "Do we *have* to excuse our self from the dinner table?" I said simply the truth, "That's the way I was brought up. I don't know about you." We had the same mother.

Now, let's find a better way to charge our so-called pride, the crown of our ego. I've never taught to annihilate it, but let's find a better way to give it the charge that it needs so that we can feel God. There are better ways than the crown of the ego to feel God. There's a million different ways, and divine will will show them all to you. But [with] divine will, there are no obstructions, for divine will is total acceptance.

How are you doing with your tape there? *[The teacher again addresses the recording technician.]*

Just fine. Just fine.

Fine. Fine. Make sure we get—I get some of these written down for posterity; then you can erase it.

Now, [Student P], the revelation of this little, seeming innocent incident is most beneficial in helping all of us, of course, with the truth. Why do you think, instead of working with, a few weeks ago and to this day, working with your sex problems and working with your money problems, why do you think that effort was not successful for you? I believe you made some effort. I happen to know some of my Council's made some effort with you. I happen to know I made some effort myself. Why do you feel that your efforts went in vain, that you worked so hard for and received nothing? Or were those regiments three regiments instead of just one? *[After a short pause, the teacher continues.]* Come on, [Student P], you're using up my tape over here. Got to respond a little faster or go buy me some—

*****

She's now ready. Go ahead.

OK. The only thing I can think of is— [Student P begins.]

You're going to have to speak up. [The recording technician interrupts.]

Louder!

The only thing I can think of is that it wasn't totally cleaned up. I mean—

Didn't [Student S] work with you? Are you awake, [Student S], or are you sleeping over there?

I'm trying to be awake. [Student S replies.]

Trying to be awake? You want to stand up or something?

May I get some water?

Certainly.

Thank you.

Put it in a pause mode. [Student S] is going to get some water so she can stay a—

*****

Go ahead. Go ahead, [Student P], with your explanation. The recorder is on.

Ah . . .

Speak up. You're using up my tape.

Ah . . .

You said you felt you hadn't been cleaned up.

Well, I thought I had been and all this, you know, hasn't been.

What's the demonstration this evening, which is the revelation? Were they cleaned up and you went back and entertained them again and did nothing but feed them? What was the problem? Was there any honesty that would lead you through the darkness within, because that's where it exists in order to be without? Was there any little lamp of honesty that you carried down into those chambers?

Well, I think there's one more thing I should discuss with [Student H] privately.[16]

I see. And therefore, we're lacking, with the lamp of honesty—

Uh-huh.

—in reference to your sex problems and your money problems, is that correct? Or did the money ones get solved? No, they couldn't have. A whole army just, just went over the bridge.

Uh-huh.

[Student A] is responsible because she is the one that helped establish the bridge. When your armies saw there was a bridge to go eat, they didn't waste no time running across that bridge. Now this happens all the time, friends, everywhere. This is why it's so difficult for people, you know, I understand, married people, relationships, situations, involvements, go down the list, and I'll tell you it is difficult. It can be, and it can be beautiful: it depends on how awake you are of where these armies are moving, you see? But if you accept the wonderful truth that frees you, personal responsibility, then you can say, "Damn it! I built another bridge out there! And look at me now. I was feeling lousy and now I'm at the bottom of the barrel. How many bridges did I build? Could one person have so many armies to run across?"

Go ahead, [Student P].

Well—

And you're not even married to her! *[The teacher is addressing Student P and referring to Student A.]* She's a woman. God, stop and think of that! I can't imagine what kind of bridges are between you and [Student H]. Ha! Ha! Excuse me. Ha! *[The teacher uses "Ha," as an exclamation; there is no laughter.]*

Well, the other thing that, between [Student A] and myself was I was in the bathroom this morning with— [Student P speaks softly.]

Speak up so I can—

I was in the bathroom this morning combing my hair before church service.

Yes?

And I was having a conversation with [Student Z].

Yes.

And [Student A] very rudely interrupted and I was annoyed. Fit to be tied.

Did you—

And I think that's where the whole thing started.

All right. That's good. Now, you see, here's the law going on: tracing it right through the chain, the links that we establish through association, involvement, and go on down the list, and finally marriage. Now, you believe that this morning [Student A] interrupted you. Is that correct?

Uh-huh. [Student P speaks softly.]

Can't hear you.

Yes.

That's correct. Did you, in the light of honesty, which would lead you through your own darkness in consciousness, did you lift up the light of honesty and say, "[Student A], now I feel, here, that you have interrupted me and interfered with my right to express with another person at this moment." Did you lift up the lamp of honesty that truth would free you? Did you say that?

I never got an opportunity to.

Opportunity, like the hands of the clock, is ever dependent upon what we alone establish in the control of the shadows of darkness within us. When they're under control, opportunity presents itself. But because we only do that periodically, like the hands of the clock meet every so often, so it is we describe opportunity like the hands of the clock. Action moving in the realm of illusion. That's what the truth means, in perhaps clearer terms. Action in illusion.

When you take action in illusion, you stop, momentarily, the clock of time. When you stop the clock of time, through eternity you enter infinity where God, Light, Truth *is*. That is when you are what you are, not what you think you are, not what you think you've been, and not what you hope to be.

Opportunity is ever with us to a wise man. So, in the midst of disaster, we may capture the divinity: if we stop the clock, the illusion does not move, for *we* in that moment are in control. *We* move, not the illusion. *We* become the captain of the ship. It is no longer adrift. It moves to the port of our call or it drops its anchor in the security and . . . of responsibility. *[The teacher speaks a word, but it is difficult to transcribe.]*

Thank you. Close. Concluded.

*****

Turn it on. *[The recording technician had turned on the recorder just before he spoke.]*

Now you saw here, hopefully you have seen from the demonstration of two of the students what happens when a bridge of rapport is established. Now because these two students have known each other for some time in the academy and in the church, a bridge, known as rapport, is established.

Now perhaps you can understand that I have many bridges to spiritual realms of consciousness established for a long, long time. I have, also, through exposure, through my work on Earth, established very strong bridges with you students; the strongest bridges [are] with those who are closest to me. When you [are] serving various shadows of your past experiences, in any way, your armies, hungry and upsetting you—and so many there are, at times, fighting within your consciousness, causing great storms on your ocean of the water center, for that's what it really is, a great ocean—they run across the bridge. And that's commonly known as being the target. They run across the bridge to get as much from my ocean as they can get.

That doesn't matter whether or not you're a thousand miles away or ten. Of course, it is a greater impact with the life-giving force of the spoken word. Therefore, within the temple of Light, a prophet must be open to all his bridges of communication to the lands ethereal of the spirit world. The guardians at the portal, now serving, the majority of them, the bridges to the higher realms of consciousness, they must stand guard that the deceiving earth-bound entities in the astral world do not come across the bridge which has been established in rapport to the realms ethereal, leaving few, very few guardians at the portal at the bridge on the earthly realms and mental substance realms of consciousness.

There is a Law of Self-Preservation. There is a Law of Survival. There is a Law of Personal Responsibility. Therefore, the prophet is responsible to the duty and to the work that, in his evolution, he has come to Earth to do. This is a very delicate balance on how much shall be given and how much shall be withheld in order that the Light and the Truth may continue to shine, to light the path that the student may not stumble in the darkness of the shadows of his own creations.

And so it was said long ago: a wise teacher suffers well the growth pains of his students. My good students, the growth pains are the regiments and the armies that race across the bridges of rapport in order that you may receive the Light and, in so doing, awaken the Light, the Truth which is within you and that which you truly are.

Thank you.

*****

Personality is the door we open for the shadows of the past to enter into the realms of consciousness where they may satisfy their needs and obstruct the divine Law of Goodness, known as Principle.

*****

Man loses the threads of his tapestry of life through the lack of effort, called personal responsibility, to take charge over all his creations and through that lack of effort, personal responsibility, shadows of the past, they gobble them up.

*****

A loan, a loan clearly reveals a denial of the source of your sustenance, the authority of your life. *[Please consider that the teacher may have said "alone" instead of "a loan."]*

*****

When we take credit for anything, we deny the Source which sustains it and, in the denial of the source, are bound by it.

*****

[There can be] no self-glory until man denies the Source.[17]

*****

The plane of purification purifies by the process of a great war: the war between the angelic soldiers of the Light, the living souls, with the dark shadow forms serving the darkness of ignorance. And upon the battlefield, the slaughter takes place: the red blood flowing from the angelic soldiers of Light and Truth and the green blood of the soldiers of the shadows. For the blood of the angelic soldiers of the Light is the living blood of the heart, and the blood of the soldiers of the shadowlands, serving the darkness, is the blood of mental substance, the human mind. And so it is in the planes of purification, we smell the mixture of the green blood of the shadow soldiers and the red blood of the Light soldiers.

*****

When you have a confused mind, you know where you are. You are the recipient of the battles taking place between your heart and your mind. And in that moment, if you will pause, you will hear the trumpet sound of the charge of the Light brigade, representing reason, the light that will transform you.

*****

Now does anyone know how many soldiers there are in the great charge of the Light brigade? Does anyone know? *[After a short pause, the teacher continues.]* In order for reason to transform you, what must take place, does anyone know? *[Again, the teacher pauses.]* Harmony must prevail supreme and the eighty-one soldiers who come in as the Light brigade represent the eighty-one levels of consciousness.

*****

Just a minute. Hold it.

*****

And in so doing, the final victory within your consciousness is won and there is peace, the power of God, unobstructed, flowing freely and you are the fullness of the Divinity.

*****

Demonstrable, the revelations; man in God *is* God.

*****

Of *his* universe.

*****

For the fullness of a thing becomes the thing. Amen.

*****

There are no freeways to truth. It is a single path, winding, twisting, and turning up the mountain to the eternal Light.

*****

Without personality, there is no possibility of self-deception.

*****

Only through communication will you gain understanding that wisdom may cast her light of reason, which will transfigure you and free you from the bondage of self-deception.

JANUARY 23, 1983

Class January 26, 1983

—define the falsifying hand of the copyist in reference to last evening's class?[18]

Yes, sir.

Yes. Because we all have, while attached to the human mind of mental substance, the great need, as tonight's class is revealing, to glorify the self in order that we may continue to serve it, for if we do not, in consciousness, have great value and importance for it, we will not long serve it. Consequently, in the falsifying hand of the copyist or in any job or endeavor that we have, the first thing that we experience, of course, is to make it our own. You have to remember that this process of glorification only takes place when the human mind dictates ownership or possession or reliability.

Now, first you must, in your mind, judge you possess it; you own it; you have the right to it. It, of course, is your security and, therefore, reliable. So, anything that enters the conscious, anything that enters the human mind is filtered and is sifted and dependent upon whatever is already *in* the human mind. Therefore, the tendency of anyone in copying anything is very simple: if it does not fit into what is already existing within mental substance of the individual, then it gets adjusted; it gets changed in order to fit the forms of the shadows of past experiences that we are serving.

So the teaching was given long ago: Put God in it or forget it. Well, we understand that number one: God is Light; number two: God is Love; number three: God is Life. So, God, Light, Truth, design, which is love of God—that is, to design so that it may enter your consciousness and take form and have life; it is dependent upon what is already there, unless you take control of your mind and you create what is known as angelic forms. I hope that's helped with the question.

*****

You ready? *[The teacher asks the recording technician.]*
Yeah.

Ofttimes we attempt to put God in something that we choose to have or to experience. And in our efforts to do so, we create forms in keeping with the censorship of the forms that already exist in mental substance because we do not go through the necessary process that was given last evening.

The experience to the conscious mind is one of confusion and bewilderment as the shadows of the past are being adjusted and taken control over by the eternal being, the soul. After the confusion and the bewilderment, there is a moment of peace and harmony. That is known as a state that is healthy and harmonious, freed from the forms of past experiences. That is how you put God in it and create angelic forms.

*****

The spirit of spontaneity is the joy of life expressed, for wisdom in creation is free from the bondage of the shadows of the past.

*****

The difference between an instruction and an order is instructions have total consideration and orders have total self-motivation.

*****

So a wise man instructs the world as he orders himself.

*****

The spirit of spontaneity is Truth without form, is Light without limit, is Love without bondage, is Life fulfilled.

*****

In the discernment or difference between the spirit of spontaneity and the impulse or compulsion of the human mind, one soon learns that the spirit of spontaneity is spontaneous and does not repeat or hound the consciousness. However, impulses from the mind repeat themselves in ever a torturous seeming way.

*****

—records. Is that ready? *[The teacher again refers to the microcassette recorder.]*

Yes.

All right. Now in speaking of the spirit of spontaneity, we speak of Spirit, one God. So, there is one Light, one Truth, one God, one Life, one Love, which is Truth. There are, throughout the world, many forms of creation. They are dual and they multiply. So, we see that God, the servant, subtracts from itself in its service to all creation, and we see that creation multiplies unto itself in order to support its own illusion.

*****

Man's awakening to whether or not God is in anything in his endeavors is ever dependent upon his own efforts to subtract the thought of his desires before they multiply into the illusion, delusion, deception, which is the bondage of the darkness of all time.

*****

As man gives, he demonstrates the divine principle of subtraction or God or service; and in so doing, the truth crushed to earth within his consciousness awakens, for by subtracting, he demonstrates unto himself the limitless supply which is the divine Principle of God and is never left without.

*****

Now we know the path to be free from lack, want, need, and desire.

*****

The divinity of desire is ever dependent upon the principles just revealed.

*****

A person who wants to be absolutely sure about any effort they're making in any endeavor whatsoever, who insists on being absolutely sure they're doing the right thing and will reap the harvest of what they're after is a person who must be very patient until all the shadow forms of all experiences rise up and finally agree they're all going to get their share from the effort.

*****

That is known as self-reliance.

*****

Adversities, we now know, are nothing more nor less than hidden desires, hidden from the view of our conscious awareness. An adversity (hidden desire) is established in consciousness by whatever we deny, for what we deny, we reject. And by the law of rejecting, guarantee its acceptance through the divine will, which is total, not limited. And man is ever subject to, in the illusion of time and space, to the will of God. Therefore, all rejections, which are denials, become adversities (hidden desires) and are destined to be fulfilled.

*****

[The following teaching may have been given to a very small group of advanced students.]

Whoever is without responsibility, the ability to respond, is void of the beauty and the joy, the love and the goodness to be impressed.

JANUARY 26, 1983

Class January 27, 1983

[The following teachings may have been given to a very small group of advanced students.]

Impression is a change in the molecular structure of consciousness which ever attempts to restore its balance in order that it may continue to flow freely on the river of life.

*****

Hold your lamp high, O Protector, that you may see clearly the obstructions that lie on the ground, that that, the feet of understanding, which moves the soul through creation, may not be a stumbling to the vehicle that must move it throughout the world and lighten the path that the souls may not wander again. For visit they shall and visit they must. It is the Law of Evolution. Visit; do not wander. Learn the wisdom, the great wisdom and strength to pause, not to tarry; to visit, not to wander; to view, not to blind; to free, not to fascinate. He who visits, views; he who tarries, fascinates and is bound. So *be* the viewer; *be* the observer; be not the observed.

*****

[The following teachings were on an undated microcassette; however, written notes taken at the time of this recording suggest that these teachings may have been given on this date.]

The divinity of infinity is the eternity of its expression.

*****

Whoever feels good knows God in the moment of his goodness.

*****

In all our communications, let us never forget to burn our lamp of honesty brightly, for in communication is the birth of understanding. And the wisdom of truth is ever dependent upon the brightness of our lamp of honesty.

*****

In our efforts to improve and perfect, we ofttimes lose the truth.

*****

Mental substance is the letter of the law and spiritual essence is the spirit of the law. So, the letter killeth and the spirit giveth life.

*****

Principle becomes personality when it expresses through form.

JANUARY 27, 1983

Class January 28, 1983

[I have] two questions.
One at a time, please.

*****

Do the to-bes and the have-beens know each other at the time of the soul's incarnation into form?

*****

The question is asked, Do the to-bes or the have-beens know each other at the time of the soul's entrance into form? The only forms existent at the time of the soul's entrance into this form or this planet are the have-beens. Upon the moment of entrance, they view possibility or the to-bes. And in that sense, that's the only time, [the] first time they get to meet.

*****

Your question is, What happens to the have-beens when the to-bes break out of the parameter established by the have-beens? Is that your question?
What happens to each of them?
What happens to each of them? A war goes on. And either the have-beens or the to-bes are victorious. Does that help with your question? *[After a short pause, the teacher continues.]* And it's usually the have-beens.

*****

That's why man has such a struggle in making changes in consciousness or evolving.

*****

When all hell breaks loose, the battle between the have-beens and the to-bes, the best possible process is the light of reason, which is established when you gain some degree of self-control, which grants you an awareness that you are serving forms that are not you. Therefore, one must awaken within their consciousness that they are truth, covered in form, are deceived by judgment, and are bound by their self-deception, the defense of the judgment.

*****

The question—the statement is from the teaching, offer the mind alternatives and it will make a wise choice in time.

Yes, sir.

Whenever you offer to the have-beens and to the to-bes alternative tactics to use in their great battle, what you are doing is granting to them time, that great illusion, opportunity of choice. And from the opportunity of choice that you are granting to the forms you have created, that grants unto them a sense of encouragement. And with that sense of encouragement, they slowly but surely gain a little bit of wisdom of patience. And in their tactics and in their battle and their war within, a wise choice is made, and you don't have to be concerned.

*****

If a little boy wants a match—experience has shown the last time he had it, he burned his bedroom down. And so [if] you tell the little boy, "You can never have matches again," you guarantee and you can be rest assured he'll find a match someplace. But if you tell the little boy that he may have matches, but he can't burn his bedroom down again, but he may burn the woodshed or the garage, then you're going to have a new little boy awakening.

*****

Because, you see, you have to make that choice: whether you have more value for the garage or the bedroom or the woodshed or the bedroom. You make—that's an extreme case. But there's always something that you must give in order to gain. You don't necessarily have to make it your garage or the woodshed. You could make it a little box or something, but that's the principle.

*****

Because we are, through our own lack of effort and through our own ignorance, we are controlled by the have-beens and the to-bes, and because of that, you see, you must offer some tidbit or the hounds of hell will never leave you in peace.

*****

I believe the question is, Do the have-beens accept the to-bes? And if so, then how do they accept them? Well, they do accept the to-bes as long as the to-bes will fit in to what the have-beens are already familiar with. Now there may be a very slight variance, a very slight difference, but if it's more than slight, they just get kicked right out of consciousness. There's no parameter even to be considered for them.

*****

The question is, Do the to-bes contain judgment? All things formed are the effect of design. All design is the effect of decision. Now decisions entering form become limited and in the limitation process of the form lose the total consideration, which is in the design, and gain the limited consideration, still total, but bound by form. And in reference to your question, that is the process and that's what happens.

*****

Well, how to-bes display passive resistance is quite simple: when you want something bad enough and you've banged at the door and you couldn't get in, there's a pretty good chance you'll lie on the porch waiting for someone to open the door. And, I mean, if one way doesn't work, you know, an intelligent being will try all ways, no matter what it takes and no matter what it costs, depending if they want it bad enough. So, one might consider that to be passive resistance. That is part—passive resistance, of course, is part of a tactic, a very intelligent tactic of a great war, any war, passive resistance. Certainly, India exemplified that in recent history. And, certainly, India got what it wanted through passive resistance. And so ofttimes a wise person can get exactly what they want through passive resistance.

*****

However, you must realize and understand that passive resistance takes a degree of self-control that very few people are used to practicing.

*****

[A student asks a question, but he or she is too far from the microcassette recorder to accurately transcribe their words.]

The have-beens and the to-bes are soulless forms. That is correct. That is correct.

*****

We better leave the thing on. *[The teacher refers to the microcassette recorder.]* Yes, they both are. Leave it on. We bought more, more, ah, tapes today anyway. Yes. *[After a short pause, the teacher continues.]* Is there a question that follows that?

The celestial forms, their celestial, spirit forms are not involved in this war?

Oh, they most certainly are, if we permit that. Now here we have the have-beens, created of mental substance. And here we have the to-bes, created of mental substance, dependent, of course, entirely upon their creator for their sustenance, for their life, for their survival, and for their continuity, as all—the source of all form is dependent upon the form that has created it. Therefore, mental forms are dependent upon mental substance, which is the human mind, for their continued existence. However, when man enters his soul consciousness within, he becomes receptive to the divine Source itself. Any and all forms created in that state of consciousness are celestial forms with living soul, for they have received their source of life direct from the Source, not through mental substance.

*****

Now in reference to that, these angelic or celestial forms, we understand, having the eternal soul, which is direct from the Source itself, become the little guardians and servants, which, in others words we have spoken, is your spiritual bank account. That's what the coinage is, is these celestial, eternal forms that [are] brought into being in your universe to serve you in your great times and needs. Through the transgressions of natural, divine law, you need divine grace to free you from a condition, an effect [of your transgressions]. And that's what these celestial forms do. That's their job.

*****

It's too bad we don't create more of them and less of those other ones. That's our problem. Any other questions? Did you have a question—oh, no questions? We can conclude class.

*****

Leave it on. *[The teacher instructs the recording technician.]*
Could you please explain—
The inevitability of the to-bes?
—the inevitability, yes.
I've never met a person in my life in any universe that did not have hope. Now, for example, have-beens are the despair in your consciousness when you want to make a change. They rise up when you decide that you would like to do something and it is not in keeping with the have-beens that you have created in consciousness; they rise up and give you many strange kind[s] of feelings and emotions. One of the first is discouragement, despair. And they bring up all of their ammunition of past

experiences into your consciousness and say, "Oh, what the hell, that won't work. Didn't work before." And they offer you all the doubts. They offer you all the fear. For the have-beens are despair and discouragement. The to-bes are hope and possibility. And the inevitability of the to-bes is man is never left without the thought of possibility. And man is never left without the thought, no matter how small a thought, of hope. That answer your question?

Thank you.

Yes, now we have questions. [Student V], please.

Can you tell me how we become, how we may become a little more receptive to our guardian angel?

Well, the only way I know of that you're going to become more receptive to a guardian angel is to free yourself from the have-beens. And, of course, there are many ways of doing that. The thing is, the have-beens have no effect upon you, you have no awareness of them, and they have no control over you whenever you gain control over self, where they live. For that's what self is. Now if you have a need for glory, then you have to accept all of the regiments and the armies of the have-beens [and] there's no possible way to enter the divine neutrality of guardian angels or that which will free you.

So, as long as you permit them to tell you that you have want, need, and desire, then you must accept the inevitability of service to them, for that is what they offer as their ammunition to your consciousness. Does that help with your question?

But remember, man is never left without the to-bes: the possibility. So as the have-beens tell you, "That's never going to work. Da, da, da, da, da, da" and they give you all the excuses, all the justifications, which we all know is the first line of defense for self-deception, judgment, and go down the list, as they offer that to you, you can counteract them in the creation of to-bes to enter your consciousness. But, oh, watch the battle go on.

The wiser path is to say, "O God, now what is this great need, this thing called self, this, this glory, this charge I get within my consciousness when I think how great I am?" And go on down the list.

It's just like saying, "Thank you, God, I accept the possibility of something better." The have-beens all rise up and said, "Yeah, ha, ha! Ha! Keep it on, kid. Keep it on." Because here's all these armies looking at your to-be. That poor, pathetic thing that you've just created in consciousness. [It's] hardly got a damn chance at all. One soldier? To face a hundred thousand? [That] help with your question? Uh-huh.

What did the Old Man often [say]? He said about—what is the effect of self-control?

Freedom. [Different students speak.]

Responsibility.

Freedom.

Freedom! Well, now you know, perhaps a few years later, the effect of self-control, well, of course, you're freed from having to serve all those soldiers ever marching in your consciousness.

Someone else had a question? [Student M], please. And then [Student A].

For each thought of hope or possibility, you create a celestial form?

No! You absolutely do not because you are creating in mental substance. You do, however, create a little bit of balance. And it's going to take an awful lot of thought. Say that you got, oh, maybe, say you only got 500,000 that say, "No, no, no, that'll never work." And you start creating hope. "Ah, to God all things are possible." And here comes, if you're fortunate and you're not listening to the have-beens who give you all that negative garbage, here comes a dinky, little, stumbling private, buck private across the field. He looks at that huge regiment—ahhhh. *[The teacher sighs dramatically and many students laugh.]* He backs off and tries to find a tree to hide behind. Well, look at your own thoughts and you'll see what the armies are like.

Thank you.

Does that help with your question?

Yes.

Uh-huh. The best path is the divine path: control of the self and, in so doing, enter freedom. However, if there are times, from your emotions, that you feel that you cannot enter that degree or a sufficient degree of self-control, then create new soldiers. Remember, when you create soldiers of to-bes, don't dictate. For example, say that you want an orange. And you dictate and create a to-be to bring you an orange. That's personality. That is not going to give you the winning in the war, the battle that's going on. Say that you just want to eat some fruit; well, then there's all kinds of fruit for you to eat. Don't be specific and in so doing, be bound in that respect. That help with your question?

Thank you.

Yes. Now [Student A] had a question.

I was wondering, when you do have those armies of have-beens—

Excuse me. When you do have? I've never seen a person in this planet without them. Thank you, [Student A]. Go on. *[After a short pause, the teacher continues.]* We always have them.

I know.

Awake or asleep. Not when. It would be so nice if there was only a when. Thank you, [Student A]. Go ahead.

OK. How can we help ourselves to stay in the consciousness of the now, instead of the to-bes or the have-beens?

Ah, now you're getting some awakening. We just got through talking about it. Freedom doesn't exist in the future or the past. Eternity isn't tomorrow or yesterday. It's the moment of now. You just answered your own question. Does it help that you answered your question, [Student A]? *[After a short pause, the teacher continues.]* Pardon?

Yes. Thank you.

OK. Now [Student D2] was next and then [Student L]. Yes.

Do the have-beens and the to-bes, are they the way in which the sense functions and the soul faculties are expressed in creation?

In reference to your question of the faculties of the soul and the functions of the senses, of which we are well aware there are eighty. All are sustained by one divine, intelligent Power. Therefore, there are eighty-one. Well, there are armies in all functions and there are armies in all faculties. Now we're talking about, this evening, the mental substance in which we are constantly moving on the river of consciousness, creating various thoughts, which are forms, which grow up and become soldiers to defend their right to survival.

Now some soldiers are satisfied with survival. Many soldiers are not satisfied with survival. And the ones in consciousness who are not satisfied with survival, they rise up and they can never get enough. No matter what you do or no matter what you don't do, it's never enough. Those are the soldiers who have really grown up in consciousness. And sooner or later, some people call those things addictions. Does that help with your question? *[After a short pause, the teacher continues.]* It should because we're dealing with this particular area of consciousness of mental substance and how to get free from it. Then we could move on to a greater war: faculties and functions. Yes.

Yes. For those grown-up soldiers that we create, the to-bes and the have-beens, by what process would we find the motive, their motives?

Thank you very much. By what process can we use to find out their true motives?

Yes, sir.

Well, first of all, you [have] got to understand have-beens are the only soldiers that are grown-up. To-bes, the poor things, you're trying to create them. Now that takes a great deal of effort. And someday, when they're victorious, they'll be grown-up. And hopefully they will balance it out for you. How—was the question do you—what was the question again?

By what process do we find their—

Their true motive?

Yes.

Well, very simple: they are created by self. I mean, it's our thought that has created them. It wasn't someone else's thought. Would you not agree?

Yes.

[It] exists within our consciousness. So, we know immediately by where they live, where they were born, and where they continue to express that they are self-motivated, for they were born in self and they are destined to serve self. So, if you have a thought, then you create a form. And that form grows from your very life force to be a soldier someday. And it doesn't take too long, believe me.

Now, it's created in your self-interest. So, if your self-interest is to go and do something and you don't go and do it, that soldier you created, he starts to get upset because you didn't do what you created him to do. You changed your mind. And so you find difficulty with people in changing their mind. First, it's this; then, it's that. And then the next thing you know, they don't know where they are.

Say, for example, that you're told that you will have a job to do on a certain day at a certain time. Fine, you accept that. In that acceptance, if you are in self and you're not aware, you create a soldier, a to-be one, that you're going to do something at a certain time on a certain date. Now if you have accepted that in consciousness, that means your have-been soldiers have agreed and have laid out their battle plan on the battlefield. The day comes and the time comes and a change has been made. You're furious. You're emotional and you're all upset because they were created to serve your selfish motive. And they did not get to serve your selfish motive because *you* changed your mind. Or somebody else changed their mind and you couldn't do anything about it. And then the whole damn regiment rises up. Do you understand?

Yes.

And so, the process of this academy has always been a constant process of change. A person's on a job [and] they're pulled off the job without notice of any kind. They're put on to another job. They're on that job for a short time [and] they're put on to another job. They are not told exactly what jobs they will do when they come here because, otherwise, there is no way to help them to free themselves to take a look at their own armies, which have formed their parameters, have formed their judgments, have established their tactics for the battle within. Does that help you?

Yes.

And we experience around here belligerence, forces, and everything else that the functions have to offer, which is nothing more than the have-been soldiers demanding their right to their way.

Anyone else had a question? [Student L] was waiting on a question, please.

We've been taught in the past that like attracts like, and that the armies multiply. What about the to-bes? Do they multiply while they're still young and little or do they have to wait . . .

They multiply if the have-beens will let them in. If the have-beens will let them in. If they don't, they stay out in the cold. And staying out in the cold, man calls that wishful thinking, a dream so beautiful: no substance and no reality. It's the great delusion.

Any more questions? Yes.

Can . . .

Yes?

Can—you said earlier that the have-beens, they have battle plans when the to-bes are being created. Can the have-beens capture the to-bes? Is that process [how] the to-bes become have-beens?

Can the have-beens capture the to-bes and make them have-beens?

Uh-huh.

They annihilate them. Because, you see, if they haven't even let them in, that means the to-be was not able to make the necessary adjustments within his own little mind to be accepted by the have-beens. So, they just cut his head off. Yes, they behead them. Yes, [Student L].

Now when we bow the ego, does that—I mean, literally bow the ego, when you really try to be humble and change your attitude toward something, can you make the armies lie down at that time or do they just become more furious?

Well, the question is in reference [to] bow the ego so the soldiers lie down. What we have to understand is quite simple: humility, the soul faculty, which brings peace on the battlefield, a stillness in consciousness, is known as humiliation to the human ego. Now the human ego, depending upon our attachment to it, depending upon how uneducated it is—and the more attached we are to it, the less educated it is—will not bear that degree of humiliation, which is the soul faculty of humility, in order to bring peace on the battlefield. There are some, in certain areas of consciousness, where, of course, these have-been soldiers and to-bes in, or trying to get in, where we will express the soul faculty of humility to varying degrees of humiliation to the human ego because of our lesser attachment to the human ego, which means not as great a pride in certain areas of consciousness. Then we have peace on the battlefield. Yes. At least momentarily.

Any other questions? Who—I'm sorry. Yes, [Student U].

Is there any way, any process which these have-beens can be returned to the mental substance from which they were created? [As Student U spoke, the teacher addressed a comment to the recording technician, but that comment is difficult to transcribe.]

Is there any process through which the have-beens can be returned to the mental substance from which they were created? Yes, of course. You starve them out. You [have] got to remember they survive only on energy directed by you to them. And when that energy no longer flows to them, they slowly, screaming, raving, ranting all the way, they slowly return to the substance from which they were created. As our bodies return to Mother Earth, so do the forms in mental substance return to its source, you see. Because we are the director of the Divine Power to them. They are totally, wholly, and completely dependent upon us. We are their god. We have created them. And they look to us for their continued sustenance and life.

And now, perhaps, you can understand how difficult it is for man to truly change a thought or a judgment, especially when it's of long duration and much energy has been directed to it over a long period of time: the soldiers are very strong, very great, and there are many. That help with your question?

Yes.

Any other questions? Yes, [Student V].

The faculty of honesty, can you explain how that works with what we've been talking about?

Yes, of course. Honesty, the lamp of honesty will lead us through all creation. When we—go ahead, change the [tape]. *[The microcassette tape is turned to record on Side B.]*

*****

Whenever we carry the lamp of honesty into the battlefield of creation, wherever form is, and that's what it is, the battlefield of creation, then what happens [is] the light of reason is cast upon all forms. Now the light of reason is the great power: the wisdom of understanding *is* the light of reason. That is what transfigures us and all about us. Now what happens, it transfigures our own being; our own ignorance is illumined. And when that is illumined, you understand, all that we have created, that we are in charge of, by divine right, it is transformed for us.

But how often do we cast the light of reason upon an issue, a soldier of the shadows? Of course, it's always possible. That takes self-control. That takes a bowing of the will, which we obviously have been and are directing to the self-glory, known as the crown, the pride. For pride is the crown of self-glory, total reliance upon the self. And to the degree of that reliance upon self is how great our crown really is. Hope that's helped with your question.

Anyone else have a question? [Student G].

I speak my word forth into the universe, knowing that it will not return to me void— [Student G speaks an affirmation of these teachings.]

Uh-huh. Knowing that it—

—but accomplish what I'm sending it to do. [Student G continues to speak as the teacher spoke. Her version of the affirmation is not entirely accurate. Please see the appendix for the correct version.]

That's correct.

What are—what forms shall we create?

The forms of your choice. That depends on how controlled you are by the have-beens. Many people speak their word forth into the universe; it does not return to them void, but it does not seem to accomplish that which they send it to do. Because they think they sent it to do such and such, a to-be army. It turned out to be a have-been because they didn't know who was controlling them when they spoke their word. A house divided cannot stand. So, we speak our word controlled by have-beens while we *think* we are creating a change. And we awaken one day and say, "Oh my God, it's just the same as it was before. Why, there's no difference at all. And I was feeling so great when I did that. Look at this disaster." Well, all you [have] got to do is be honest with yourself. Carry your little lamp of honesty into your consciousness, where reason will light the way and the wisdom of understanding will transform you. Because that's what reason is. Does that help with your question? Yes, go ahead.

But may I ask one more? If you desired a house, for example...

Uh-huh.

...how do you send this out without dictating what that house is going to look [like] or be?

By control of self. Absolute control of self. Because without control of self, you do not have the flow of Divine Principle; you have person, personality, or form. Then you are subject to the have-beens in consciousness and some of the to-bes. That means, no judgments. That means, the divinity of decision.

Any more questions? Yes, [Student S], please.

You spoke of starving out the have-beens by cutting off their energy.

Uh-huh.

I'd like to ask, Is any review of the have-beens feeding—

Absolutely.

—them energy.

Absolutely and positively. As long as the thought affects the emotions, one can be rest assured that the have-beens are very active in the water center. Yes?

And I'd also like to know—

We have—just a moment. We have someone sleeping. Shut it off. *[The teacher instructs the recording technician to stop recording.]*

*****

The difference between design and device is the divinity in design is lost in device. Now design is the essence, the forming, without motivation, without self-interest and, therefore, is pure, is good, no matter the design. It is when design is taken by need into mental substance, formed, and having need—because self does not recognize, nor accept, the source of its sustenance—when it is formed in mental substance, device is established in order to attain or fill its need.

*****

The convenience of truth is the falsehood of man.

*****

[The following teachings were given to a very small group of advanced students.]
Good feelings are strange sensations to one who feels more than they sense.

*****

Because you are consciousness and use a body, you are not limited by the body which you use, unless, from error, you have abused the body and, therefore, are limited and bound by the body. Your consciousness, its ability to respond must ever be in all areas of your domain. Therefore, if your body is one place, your consciousness must never be limited to that place. Your consciousness is there, and it is also somewhere else, if somewhere else is within the domain of your responsibility.

*****

If, through ignorance, we have abused the body—and we know if we have abused it if we find our self, our consciousness bound by it—we must honestly look at the very patterns established concerning our body. And we see that through those patterns we have abused the body and are therefore bound by it. We must broaden or expand those patterns, for it is in the contraction of the consciousness, not in the expansion of the consciousness, that we are bound. So, expand or broaden whatever patterns you find that have bound you by abuse. And in that expansion, shall you begin to broaden the consciousness in the area in which you have, from abuse, bound yourself. And after the expansion, in any particular pattern, which has revealed abuse or bondage, then one moves throughout all patterns, realizing they have been trapped and bound. And that is the process of freedom from the error of ignorance known as bondage.

*****

Fear not the bondage of abuse. In the broadening of use shall the chains that bind weaken, break; and greater horizons of the consciousness lighten the path throughout your entire being. That's when man no longer is has-been, no longer is to-be; that's when man *be* in charge of all creation within the divine right of his domain.

*****

One shall never free themselves from bondage or abuse of anything by stopping the use. The bondage only increases through the contraction process. Only through expanded use do we free our self from abuse and, therefore, are no longer bound in the ignorance of the past.

*****

One wishes to be freed from what they are bound to. One does not step from bondage to freedom. One steps from bondage to the next step to freedom. And the next step, the step in between bondage and freedom, is the broadening of the horizons. Still a little, not as much, in a different perspective and broadening of consciousness.

*****

He who loves pride is in truth so grateful for bondage.

*****

It is never what one is that is a problem. It is what one *thinks* they are that is the problem.

*****

To justify the reason why anyone does anything to us reveals, in our consciousness, our reliance upon and need for the deception of self.

*****

It's on. [The recording technician announces.]

Truth is individually perceived and it is perceived individually because it is dependent upon our receptivity to it, which, in turn, may or may not be obstructed by the self-interest shadows of past events and experiences.

*****

Bladder-blue days, like the morning after, always find someone to blame.

*****

When our emotions cloud our light of reason, we have the days of bladder-blue treason.

*****

The perfect balance of unity is not only strength but the harmony that is necessary for the restoration of perfect health, the fullness of life, of which the eagle is an eternal symbol and represents its ascent to heavenly heights.

*****

In the great battle in the war of mental substance, the soldiers of the shadows of has-beens in their battle of the soldiers formed in substance of to-bes is the difference between the army of despair and the army of hope. And so, my children, listen and prepare. The soul perceiving the principles involved prepares itself as the great observer in watching this battle in mental substance, the armies of despair and the armies of hope. Because there are, by far, greater number in any area of the battlefield in consciousness, greater by far are the numbers and strengths of the soldiers of have-beens and fewer in number are the soldiers of to-bes, man, in this great perception and awareness, makes great effort to establish the soldiers of to-be, which are the direct opposites of the soldiers of have-beens.

And so it is, for example, if you have eaten an apple because of your great desire and you have, upon eating the apple and its completion, found a strange sensation taking place, perhaps from the eating of the apple, an awareness, the timing of eating was not in the best interest, you feel and believe, and you end up with a stomachache, an affect upon your emotions and affections and feelings, you think, you cast the apple aside, never to eat an apple again.

And yet time passes and once again you have a great desire to eat an apple; and your have-beens, looking at the apple, do not permit you to eat the apple, not the same apple, possibly a different apple. But something inside of you doesn't want just an apple. Therefore, the have-beens working in your water center, fire centers, earth centers, air centers, the lower portion thereof, they rise up with great will. Naturally, of course, they are the will, the power, which has given them birth within your consciousness. Those are the have-been soldiers.

And now you can no longer endure, for change has taken place within consciousness and the have-beens that have you in control in consciousness begin to rise in fear, horrible fear, for to-bes, somehow, are coming across the mountain, over the horizon, though few in number, great and strong are their new soldiers. The have-beens, though very few, the great armies of have-beens fear the new to-be soldiers. And so a great battle about to begin in consciousness causes a great fear to rise, a great uncertainty and, yea, confusion begins to set in. Despair, rising with all its dark glory, takes over the consciousness with great clouds of a forthcoming, horrible storm.

And yet wisdom dictates create in consciousness the contrary. Create it; nourish it; feed it that soldiers of hope, who will bring balance between despair and hope—the battle will free you; that you, your eternal being, may enter the great awareness under the light of reason, be.

And so you begin to be. You never stop hope, for those are the soldiers that bring the great balance. And as the battle rages and as you feel you're losing the battle, the battle of the soldiers of despair, create, with the divine will flowing through your being, create the soldiers of hope.

And from this great battle as you remain and be, that which is left when the battle is over is neutralized and balanced. And great soldiers of living soul in the goodness of God, for being is in the goodness of God, lift your soul to heavenly heights, beyond despair, beyond hope. You are the eternity, the love, the fullness of truth. Your angel soldiers of living soul, eternal beings, shall ever lift you to heavenly heights.

Balance is the law of the universe. No soul can be filled, no being fulfilled, without the balance in mental substance between despair and hope.

So, children, *be* in God for that is the goodness that you are. Free your minds from concern, for those are nothing more than the messages that are sent from the shadow soldiers of despair. Free your mind from suspicion, for those are messages sent from the soldiers of hope; as the soldiers of despair respond to hope, you become suspicious and all the functions rise up to dictate. Parameters are made. Judgments are formed. And bound, your eternal being.

Be not so foolish, my children. Be not so weak in your faith in God, for God, the Goodness, is dependent within your consciousness upon your faith in the goodness that God will never fail you. Concern not. Free yourselves and be, moment to moment, just be and all of life shall love you and me, for then the Light shall shine; the angels walk upon your Earth.

Good day.

JANUARY 28, 1983

Class January 29, 1983

[The following teachings may have been given to a very small group of advanced students.]

Lilacs, the beautiful and ancient symbol of friendship, for friendship is use. Friendship is understanding. And with the use of understanding we have the awakening of consciousness, universal and applicable that we awaken to who we truly are. And so, principle is not without its finer vibrations; beyond and above need, want, and desire, principle *is*. Its use in friendship is understanding, and consciousness beyond the human imagination is the greatness of God, the glory of the eternal Infinite Being. Enter the lilac of understanding and know friendship which is truth.

*****

Note the many flowers in the cluster of the lilac's expression. Each flower is similar, though different. And in all of their similarities and differences, they all stem from the same trunk and the same root. They all give forth equal, the scent of the beauty of life to the atmosphere in which they live and breathe. And so it is with friendship, respecting the many differences and similarities. They are in truth the one principle from the same trunk and the same root; knowing that, they have understanding, true friendship, and consciousness.

*****

Peace is a feeling . . .
Absent of need.
. . . absent of need.

*****

And that is why it is the path to fulfillment.

*****

The wise use of understanding is the peace that passeth. The effect of that wise use, being the peace that is above and beyond it, is in truth the fullness of life.

*****

Concern not how God or Goodness works and, in not being concerned, experience the benefit thereof.

*****

He who is peaceful is never concerned about being patient and, therefore, is the living demonstration of wisdom, which lives therein.

*****

The divinity of decency is the purity of its love.

*****

Which is total consideration.

*****

Which in view is the absence of self-motivation. Therefore, freed from limits, freed from has-beens and to-bes, freed from parameters and judgments, there is the fullness of life, and that is decency.

*****

When a language loses its meaning, it loses its decency. And so many things in creation have lost their decency, but time shall pass and decency shall return.

*****

Perceive the awareness of reason.

JANUARY 29, 1983

Class January 30, 1983

[The following teachings may have been given to a very small group of advanced students.]

Imprint in spiritual consciousness is sensation in physical substance.

*****

And direction by a mental world.

*****

Mental substance is directed by self-will or divine will.

*****

Those who have a great fear of responsibility live with the have-beens or the to-bes, for with the have-beens and the to-bes, they do not have to make the effort and face that life is ever as they make it and just the way they take it.

*****

The reason that responsibility does not exist in the consciousness of eternity when it is directed to yesterday or to tomorrow simply reveals that man can justify and therefore deceive himself in what has been. He can justify and therefore deceive in what is to be. But [with] what *is*, the Light of Truth Eternal, which is in the moment of now, there is no justification, and therefore no self-deception.

*****

Truth and freedom exist in eternity which is ever the moment of your conscious awareness. Falsehood and bondage are the domain of past events and events yet to be.

*****

The stillness of the mind is the expression of infinity, which is the truth, the awareness, and the freedom moment by moment, never past and never future. Man is full in the moment of now.

*****

Though distraction may be beneficial and is beneficial only when it is under conscious control and distraction—only when it is under conscious control of the will to distract. Otherwise, distraction is simply a device used by the have-beens or the to-bes to pull you from the truth you are in the moment of your conscious awareness.

*****

[The following teachings may have been given to a larger group of students.]

And in putting it in very earthly terms, like a child without a father, known to man as a bastard, so decency, without divinity, is an orphan. And many things are orphaned. In other words, that which is an orphan is not cared for, is not loved because it is not considered. And that which is not considered is indeed an orphan. And so we're an orphan in life in many ways because in many ways we don't consider. And in not considering, we become very indecent: indecent to other people's rights, to other people's feelings, to other people's responsibilities. And the reason that we do that is only an error in our own awakening process in considering a limited amount of our own personal desires; [so,] that's all we offer to the world.

*****

I don't think you need—

*****

The have-beens and the to-bes, though in consciousness the thought is in the air center, that thought, that seed, must descend into the water center in order that it may have birth. And so you find all your have-beens and all your to-bes struggling in your water center for their survival, and you call that, in your conscious awareness, emotion, frustration, and forces. And how properly named—forces—because from the water center and the great magnet, they are indeed quite a force.

*****

We clearly see and experience that all things are louder or stronger in the reverse gear than in the forward gear. And therefore, we have a stronger tendency to listen to and pay attention to all that is in reverse gear, known as past events. For it takes more energy and effort to put the gear of our consciousness into forward motion, which is the inevitable Law of Evolution. And yet, if we would push the gear to neutral, we would be freed from concern, freed from reverse, freed from forward, and we would evolve peacefully, graciously in the eternal be.

*****

A new moment is never new until we make it so through our own conscious effort.

*****

The alchemy of the alchemist was nothing more nor nothing less than the beautiful, pure light of reason, which reason is the wise use of understanding or wisdom.

*****

And so the alchemist transformed the base, gross metals of Earth into the beautiful, pure gold of Earth. Revealing to man the ability to transform all the flesh in which he is presently residing into the pure spiritual essence through the truth that has just been revealed.

*****

One of the indispensable ingredients for the chemical transformation in consciousness is the absolute and total removal of the delusion of need.

*****

For as you well know, need is a demonstration and an expression of the Law of Denial.

*****

We note in life that all minds seek with insatiable need, of all the metals and offerings of creation, they seek with a great insatiable need the gold of Earth, for they want that which they know is enduring and, they know, represents the very power which sustains them.

*****

And so we see, of everything the planet has to offer in creation, gold is that which is indestructible throughout the eternity of form.

*****

And so, children, fire centers for sex, air centers for gold, and water centers for need. Use the alchemy of the gold of heaven and be freed from all of it in creation, never a part thereof. With all things, yet, ever separate. That is truth. That is love. That is life. And that is freedom.

*****

Whoever seeks with the mind truth, the power of God, must live forever and a day and burn in the fire center or suffocate in the air center and experience trauma, the illusion, delusion, deception of self, until the day dawns, they awaken and rise in consciousness to be, not to have been and not to be.

*****

Be of good cheer, children, for when the heart rules, your little boat sails upon the river of life harmoniously past the many centers of consciousness and does not become adrift and, therefore, unable to move in the clear, cool winds of harmony and the rhythm, which is the pulsation of eternal life.

*****

Whoever is in the be, that is, the eternal moment of consciousness, is in God. And *being* in God, all good is their experience.

*****

Well, in reference to our efforts to meditate and free our self from mental substance, long ago it was recommended that we visualize a rose and the petals unfolding. And so it is with the human mind as it unfolds, as it gives forth that which it thinks it contains, we move to that, the essence, the power which sustains the metal—mental substance, which is also the gross metal that is in great need, for need is all it knows. And reason, wisdom, reason transforms it as you pass through the great mist of human mental substance and you enter the essence which is the expression of infinity, known as eternity, that which you are, the I, not that which you think you are, the thought, the form. Therefore, when you *be*, you are. And when you are, truth, the Light is life, is love, is eternal.

*****

All father god or electric religions throughout the ages are aggressive and warlike. All mother god or magnetic religions throughout the ages are passive and peaceful.

*****

And now we have, once again, in your world the religion, the philosophy, the Living Light, the God of neutrality, which is the God of freedom.

*****

For father gods are victors and mother gods are victims. Neither can offer the truth that frees.

*****

Whenever we deceive our self, it is forever and a day at the cost of the Light of Truth.

*****

And because you have entered the Light of the academy and [for you] to bring [these] great shadows of self-deception into the light of the academy, great energy must be utilized to keep the Light shining. As the clouds get darker and darker, they dim the humble Light of Truth: the very thing you come for, and certainly the only thing that will ever bring you joy.

*****

Therefore, students, your needs for creation must forever and a day remain in creation. And greater effort must be made to separate truth from creation. Here, come with your heart. Leave creation to the jungle for your pleasures. Bring here, to the Light, your heart; and in so doing, you will receive all that you have come for.

*****

Whoever loves form more than God shall not know truth, but suffer falsehood, deception, and disaster, for that is the destiny they insist upon following.

*****

Truth has no appearance and no seemingness. Truth just is. That which seems to be, that which appears to be is nothing but the effect of the curtain of illusion, called delusion, deception, and disaster.

*****

And so only by appearances can we ever be deceived.

*****

It is wiser in life to be tempted and strengthened than tempted not and weak, the hot-house flower in the storms of creation.

*****

Ever in keeping where one places their consciousness, either in truth or in creation, is dependent upon how they will receive their sustenance and their vital energy for their own health and their own welfare. If, [for] our sustenance, we depend upon the vehicle through which truth may flow, then, when that Light of truth is dimmed in the atmosphere in which we live and breathe and move, then we have less sustenance and less vitality. If our sustenance and our energy, our receptivity to the Divine Source, is dependent upon the vehicles of creation through which the energy also flows, then creation we must have for our health and our welfare.

*****

Pride is the only thing that binds us. It binds us because it is the crown of self, which is the great throne of denial.

*****

[The following teachings may have been given to a very small group of advanced students.]

Man is in truth the rhythm of eternity in the heartbeat of infinity. And that pulsation is formation or form.

*****

Affection, the word means, to affect a desired result through the process of imprinting, pulsating, and manifesting.

*****

Our form is ever dependent, in eternity, upon directed energy through the Law of Identity. And so as we identify, do we be the instruments of the great power to support the illusion or illusions of our choice.

*****

Upside down is, of course, dependent upon duality, which is dependent upon seeming opposites, which is dependent upon the split, the division, the multiplication, the greatest of all great illusions called deception.

*****

No forms, no creation shall keep you from that which is justly yours. Not that which *is* yours, for that which we believe is ours is dependent upon the illusion. But that which is justly ours is only dependent upon the truth that we are.

*****

Time, the expression of the great illusion, is ever dependent upon reference. And so, the expression of illusion and the meeting of reference strikes at what you call the midnight [and] noon hour. Twice in your illusion does it strike: in the high noon of the light and in the deepness of the dark. Revealing to you without opposites, there's no attraction; without attraction, the magnet does not meet that that it is destined (the electric pole) to meet. Beyond the illusion is that which sustains it. And beyond the illusion is the truth you are. That, my friends, is the awakening consciousness for in the subtraction from itself is the manifestation of the forms, until, layer by layer, they're peeled away, and in consciousness you awaken to that which you are.

O home of infinity, on eternity I am bound, returning to the Formless that which I am.

And so in your world of illusion of time and reference, of form and bondage, be of good cheer, for the Light is near. It's ever near, waiting for your view, waiting for your stillness, waiting for your acceptance, for in the stillness, the acceptance, the void of eternity, the home of the soul.

*****

When one meets the form of oneself and, in so doing, has difficulty in acceptance, it only reveals the difficulty one has within oneself of the form they believe that they are.

*****

He who is tempted without form or reference of desire fulfills the law that leads to the Light within. And in so doing, the freedom of the principle is therefore the manifestation and the inevitability of the goodness that is being served.

JANUARY 30, 1983

Class January 31, 1983

[The following teachings may have been given to a small group of advanced students.]

The determination of need is known as tooth and nail.

*****

In all our needs for rising, let it be the rising of our humor.

*****

Now in reference to your question on the illusion of time, the so-called hands of your clock of illusion meet twice in your twenty-four-hour counting. It is at those meetings, when the curtain, the veil of illusion, is the thinnest. And therefore, at those times are you able to pierce the veil at its weakest point: 12 o'clock noon, the brighter Light, and 12 o'clock midnight for the lesser light. As illusion is represented by time and delusion is represented by space, for having no reference man does not have illusion and delusion; and without reference, of course, there is no deception. And without deception, of course, there is no self. There is, however, being. And being, of course, is truth.

In your efforts to understand and to apply your freedom from the veil of illusion, it is important indeed to separate the thoughts of your mind from the I that you are, to gradually, slowly but surely become the awakening in consciousness that you are not the have-beens or to-bes. They are in truth the illusion that you and you alone are using or being used by.

And so we gave to you, so long ago, be ever the observer, not the observed. That is, be; do not to be or become; do not have been. Be. That is when you are the observer; that is when you see life for what it is, not for what you thought it was or think it will be. There and there alone, we have said, and say, in so many ways, is your fullness and your joy of life.

And now I know there are questions within the consciousness. And I will pause that you may form them, for it is necessary to identify. And in identification, to form; and in forming, to create; and in creating, to express; and in expression, to satisfy; and in satisfaction, to awaken the senses of the vehicle in which you presently, frequently respond to. And, of course, in keeping with the law of the ability to respond or personal responsibility, it is natural and understanding. But, my good children, remember, the ability to respond or personal responsibility has never been limited to one form, one vehicle, when in truth you are expressing through many forms and vehicles. And because you may not be presently aware of the other vehicles does not exempt you from your responsibility to them.

*****

Gravity, like identity, is dependent on reference. Without it, there is no pull; there is no bondage.

*****

Children, when you see who is observing you, you will quickly become the observed. *[The teacher may have intended to say "observer."]*

*****

Sharpen your blade of personal responsibility with the light of reason by your care for something greater that will fulfill your life beyond the limit and bondage of form.

JANUARY 31, 1983

Class February 1, 1983

[The following teachings may have been given to a very small group of advanced students.]

Infared is the principle of the infinity of action.[19]

*****

The human mind cannot form what it cannot conceive. And the infinity of action is beyond the conceivability of the human mind.

*****

The phenomenon of form is the ability to conceive it.

*****

For it is finite and conceived by mental substance, the great illusion.

*****

What exists for one exists for another in keeping with the Law of Consumption and ever dependent upon the blindness of desire.

*****

Whoever shall take pride in their accomplishments must enjoy pain in their changes of evolution.

*****

The call of creation is loudest after the Light of Truth has been received.

*****

A day in eternity is but one suit from the closet of infinity. And one day in eternity is one life in one suit in one place through the curtain of illusion. Now many suits already you have worn. And many suits await you to wear. So be prepared through your perception. Pierce the veil of illusion and know what you are, not what you've been or going to be.

*****

Seeming disasters are transformed into divine directions when we begin to practice what we preach.

*****

Is it here?
Right by the microphone.
The peace of being in God is known as enthusiasm. Where's the stop button?
That's it. The big one.

*****

The fullness of life is ever in the serving, not the receiving, and that is revealed in the great, demonstrable truth that God is the greatest servant of all.

*****

Of what benefit is survival, if it's the survival of something you cannot control.

*****

[The following teachings may have been given to a larger group of students.]
The call of creation is loudest after the Light of Truth has been received.[20]

*****

No one is indispensable in the service of a soul to God; however, a friend may, at times, be useful in the principle of friendship, which is use, and not the personality, which is abuse.

*****

Through the bondage of attachment, we are destined to discern the living of the Light and the loving of the lie.

*****

When man smiles, the angels sing. When he grins, deception is satisfied.

*****

In the act of illusion, when time meets itself, we see what we be and be what we see.

*****

When man smiles, the angels sing. When man grins, deception is satisfied. Learn to discern between a smile and a grin that truth may free your soul.

*****

—your definition.

*****

Did you receive the class on confusion and bewilderment?
I think I did, yes.
All right, then what did it say?
I'll have to go back and look [at my notes].
OK. We'll wait.

*****

When we feel confused and bewildered, it is simply an experience within our consciousness of our efforts to adjust our have-beens and our to-bes to put them under the control of our will in order that we may have the clarity of mind, commonly known as the control of self.

*****

Now you understand what is meant by the statement, "When man doesn't know, God gets in."

*****

The curtain of illusion is known to man as time and space. Therefore, reference or form are indispensable to man's identification with and attachment thereto, the curtain of illusion. In your world, the hands of the clock, which represent a part of this curtain of illusion to which you have attached yourselves to, the hands of action in illusion meet twice in keeping with the Law of Creation. They meet at the high noon and the midnight. That is the two opportunities in your curtain at which the curtain, in its meeting, is at its weakest point, and you may perceive the truth that lies behind it. Your efforts in that perception, of course, will reveal at the high noon, the brighter Light; at the midnight, the lesser light.

*****

As we understand the number of infinity, a horizontal eight, a wise man chooses the timing of his daily meditation in keeping with infinite, infallible law and never dependent upon finite laws of creation. Therefore, by viewing the brighter Light, the greater Light, man adjusts, in keeping with that law, to be receptive to the Infinite, the Formless, and the Free.

*****

Check it's recorded. *[The teacher instructs the recording technician.]*

This evening's discussion, the Law of Health, its restoration and its loss.

As man is ever dependent upon the divine, intelligent Energy for his health, for his being, for his sustenance, the Law of Harmony, the rhythmic flow thereof, he must, in keeping with laws established, ever be receptive to. For example, one who has, through laws of mental substance, created forms through which the infinite, intelligent Power may flow, must make effort to permit himself to be receptive to the forms of his creation in order that the intelligent Energy may harmoniously, rhythmically flow through his being for the sustenance and continuity of so-called good health. There are, in keeping with man is a law unto himself, many forms that the minds of man create through which he may continue to experience the benefits of harmony or perfect health. There are also those who have few, if any, forms of mental substance through which they permit the intelligent Energy to flow. And there are those who have no forms or vehicles created in mental substance through which the Energy may flow.

It is when, in a law established, when great effort is made throughout life to receive and value, as the highest priority, the love of truth that man indeed must be cautious, must be careful where he lives, the atmosphere he breathes, and the consciousness in which he permits himself to move. For those who are dependent upon, as we all are, the intelligent Energy, and those who are dependent upon its flow without the forms or vehicles of creation and mental substance must have an atmosphere that is formless and, therefore, free in order to be receptive to the intelligent Energy which is the perfect health. Therefore, whenever one whose highest priority is the love of truth exposes themselves to an atmosphere contaminated and polluted by a multitude of forms through which the Energy may flow and has not established that law of form in mental substance, there is a rapid and sure decrease, to that soul, in available energies which are necessary for the vital body and good health.

The alternative to such an exposure is to remove the soul from the contaminated atmosphere and place them where the forms no longer, in consciousness, for them, exist. As man is responsible unto himself and to all his creations, he is responsible, by divine law, to receive the energy necessary for his sustenance through whatever forms he has made priority in his consciousness. If there are no forms, then, of course, there is the responsibility to live and breathe and be in an atmosphere where forms are nonexistent.

*****

Now in reference to forms, everyone in life experiences, at some time, good or goodness. In the moment of that receptivity is when they know God. Everyone, all life, must know God in order to be. Some people feel good when they see a certain movie. God, Goodness, they are receptive to through the mental form they have created within their consciousness. Some people feel good, therefore know God, when they watch a football game. Others feel good (know God) when they go to an opera or a symphony. Other people feel good when they serve other forms which stand between them, the truth they are, and the Truth, the Source that is. Therefore, man, in his struggles in so-called creation, reveals unto himself his lack of effort to separate truth, that which he is, [from] creation, the illusion he believes he is. It is not the I, which is truth, but the thought of I, the vehicle, the illusion, that is man's great struggle. For truth *is*; therefore, man *is*; therefore, God *is*.

And it is ever in keeping with our own efforts to control the many forms that we have created in mental substance that through our own efforts that we awaken to the truth that we are, that in so doing we expand our consciousness, we broaden the forms of our own creation through which God flows. The broadening of the forms of our creation, of course, is the movement from personality, forms we believe we are, limits, parameters, and judgments that we believe we are, the illusion, the self-deception. Man cannot move from the deception of self until man, through his own choice, through his own will, chooses between truth and creation to recognize and, therefore, to accept the divine will that he is, no longer dependent upon created forms in mental substance that through his own delusion, which he has accepted the illusion, made the delusion, and become the deception and believes it is self.

*****

When they're finished with their papers.

*****

No, when they're finished with their papers.

*****

In the bondage of attachment, we are destined to discern the living of the Light and the loving of the lie.

*****

To believe that your God or Goodness is dependent upon any form or forms is the greatest lie you will ever do unto yourself.

*****

Deceiver, deceive and die, for death is the destiny of falsehood.

*****

And truth, honesty is the life eternal.

*****

Truth is a living light that must be carried in the lamp of honesty.

*****

Long ago you received, "Dreamer, dream a life of beauty before your dream starts dreaming you." And so, you dream and the illusion *is*, and you believe you are the dream. And the more you believe you are the dream, the more you believe you are the form and the forms; do [until] you find, in time, you are not the form. You are simply that which is serving the forms of mental substance. Until the day in eternity you cry throughout infinity for freedom from your bondage, which becomes unbearable.

*****

The destroyed always know their destroyer.

*****

One day in illusion is one thousand years in truth.

*****

Eternity has no time. Infinity has no space.

*****

Of course, that truth is inconceivable to the human mind, for the human mind is finite with limits, forms, and boundaries. Infinity, *there,* does not exist. Truth, *there,* does not exist. Only what exists is the forms created from the illusion of the substance.

*****

Ask yourself the question, Do you lose truth if you cut off the hand? Do you lose truth if you cut off the foot? What is it that you have lost? What is it? Then you shall know.

*****

Children, if you must, in consciousness, have something to rise, then let it be reason.

*****

So we clearly see that the will of man is just like an Alka-Seltzer.

*****

It fizzles for a time.

*****

Words don't make values. Demonstrations do.

*****

The awakening of truth is dependent upon the control of self.

*****

And the gift thereof to God.

*****

Man's pride in his attainment is the payment of his loss.

*****

When you understand the principle of infrared, you will know the Law of Infinity.

*****

That that comes from a thing, by the law of its coming, is destined to return unto the thing. And truth, like a circle, cannot be pointed or controlled.

*****

Now we'll get it correct. The closet of infinity is where we go to pick the suit we're going to wear for a time. The closet is the illusion.

*****

Without beauty, there is no harmony. Without harmony, there is no rhythm. Without rhythm and harmony, there is no Light, there is no truth; there's only discord and disease.

*****

The cloud that deceives you from the Light that frees you is your insatiable need, want, desire, and so-called love of form, the great shadow.

*****

Truth frees us from all judgments; truth frees us from all bondage because truth frees us from all forms, and that is certainly freedom.

*****

Stop loving the lie and start living the Light and never again will you fear the night.

*****

The determination of desire is known as holding on tooth and nail.

*****

The Divine Spirit issues instructions, known as commands. A wise man follows instructions explicitly and never feels ordered about.

*****

So, a captain commands and the crew responds. That's known as the ability to respond or responsibility.

*****

So, take charge over all your creations, for that is the command of God.

*****

Or the wisdom that brings goodness.

*****

And so, children, good night: God in darkness, Light in heaven.

*****

The defense of deception is the denial of truth.

*****

At any and all costs.

*****

Deceiver, you are deceived. Truth you cannot stand against.

*****

Light, you cannot live without. Blind yourself in satisfaction, for you live not in the Light, the Love, and the Life of God.

*****

What shadow can survive when the Light of God shines the brightest?

*****

Truth *is* encouragement. It is not dependent upon thought or form.

*****

[The following teachings were likely given to a very small group of advanced students.]

That which is enjoyable is the expression in finite mental substance of the formless, divine Spirit known as joy.

*****

[The cadence and rhythm of the teacher suggests that stanzas may be a more appropriate type of formatting, but it may also be helpful to read these teachings as though they were formatted as text.]

>Be of good cheer, for God is ever near.
>Ever near, no need to fear.
>Be, O children. Be good cheer.

*****

>O children of illusion, grow up, grow up.
>You be.
>Children of illusion, awaken, awaken
>That you see.

Children, children, children of illusion
You are one, you are two, you are three.
O children, children of illusion
Whatever was
What's to be
O children, children of illusion
All of that is you and me.

*****

The dog, the cat, the mouse, the tree
Everything, my child, be.
Rip aside the veil.
Do not fear, do not be pale
For your God, you are within.
The Light, the lamp, your ship.
Do you not see?
The storm that rages
Can never be your heart, your soul,
Your form you see
You are not, can never be
The things that pass along the sea.

*****

The seed of the saint is the joy of his being
And the joy of his being is the servant of his love.
And the servant of his love is the light that shines to thee.
So be the saint and plant the seed.
Be not concerned for what you see.
All illusion melts into the depths
From whence it rises, only to-be.
And that to-be has-been, you see.
You're not those things, O child, so free.
So listen not to echoes hollow,
But open eyes that you may follow.

And in so doing
Rise above all creation, you seem to love.
For that is only what you see.
It never was, nor can it be,
The truth you are, the joy you free.

*****

Awaken soul, you're here on Earth.
Be patient, wise, for another birth.
Look out across the universe.
There I am, a suit of clay.
In illusion I'm formed for another day.
And so it be forever the eternity.
The I will find what need to be.
So sadden not your heart with weight.
We come again. We'll see, you wait.
Patiently, oh patiently, the bells of freedom toll.
Your ship arrives and shall unload
The suit you've waited so long to see.

*****

Waiting, waiting, O souls so free.
Waiting, waiting, when what you see
Are suits so many impatiently
Calling for their being be
Choose wisely, soul, for you are free
And suits are many
And sometimes see you be their servant
You be their crew.
Not the captain that you are true.
Patience, patience, souls so free
Your day is destined for you to be.

*****

O run, run, run river free
For I am I and thou art thee
Over the cliff, the waterfall
There you wait until I fall
Oh no, you river, run, run, run
I am the one you serve, to be
Run, remember that I am I
You'll ever be what you be
For I am I, you cannot see
So run, river, run
Run from me 'til you learn the day
To serve unto me.

*****

Across the wide horizon
My ship, it sailed on time
Across the wide horizon
I looked and watched and waited to see
Across the wide horizon,
Security, security
Across the wide horizon,
O land so firm, where do you be?
My little ship, it sailed across the sea.
It sailed and sailed. It wanted to be
Free as a bird, fly in the sky.
But no, but no,
The ship I be.
Sail, O sail, with winds so free
Sail a horizon that's yet to be
For there, across and far away
The land you want is waiting to be
Sail, O ship, sail so free
The day will dawn you'll fly with me
And when, little ship, you are to be

Your sail shall turn to wings so free
Soar above the eagle I am
And that I am, can never have been
For now from ships to sail so free
The eagle soars for heaven to see
And soaring high across the land
Above the skies to other planes
Yes, the eagle shall ever be
That which soars to heaven to see
But soaring, soaring shall descend
For want shall call the eagle to see
There's other forms and places be
The eagle looks and cannot see
That which blinds the eagle to be
The eagle destined ever free
Must fly and soar to heaven to see
So let it be, O let it be,
Eagle great and eagle free
Do not want the blind to see
For you are eagle and you are me.

*****

O day of Life
O day of Light
O night of love
O night, O night
Awaken, awaken your destiny
Awaits, awaits commands from thee
Awake, awake your soul it be
Soaring over the land you see
Many there are, many to be
But you, but you, O destiny
Awake, awake, your soul to see
Captain, captain call your crew

They must know what it is you see
They must know, O captain be,
You are the ship, you are the sea
They are the crew for you and me
Captain, captain, pause and be
Captain, captain, all is thee
O captain, captain, view eternity
Captain, captain infinity you are
You are the captain of the life, the sea.

FEBRUARY 1, 1983

Class February 2, 1983

[The teachings given on this date were on six different microcassette tapes. Some teachings were on multiple tapes; other teachings were only on one. Although considerable effort was made to determine the correct order of these teachings, including consulting the personal notes of different students who were present, given the nature of the surviving tapes, the order of teachings in this transcription may not be the order in which these teachings were given.]

Pardon?

Right now, I feel I have an incredible opportunity. [Student O remarks.]

Yes, well, then you feel that you've got an incredible opportunity.

Yes, sir.

Right now. Outside of that, what else do you feel that you—or think that you got? *[After a short pause, the teacher continues.]* Do you think you got [Student O] and everything that [Student O] represents? And if so, what does [Student O] represent?

I feel I'm a wanderer.

A wanderer. So, you got wandering, right?

Yes.

Well now, when you give what you got (that's all that you think that you are) you'll get what you need, but not always what you want. So, when you understand that we *think* we got da-da-da-da-da, all these different things: we got so-and-so; we are identified with this and identified with that. And that's called the great package of self. So, when you give self, you get what you need: you get truth. But self represents, to each individual, many different things, and those many different things are in a constant process of change. So, at one time we think we got this. At another time we think we got that. So, it's all that we think we got, when we give that, which has already been given in our teachings, when we give the gift of self, we get what we need: that's known as truth. That's the awakening to the truth that we are. That is not always what we want. Did that help with your question?

Yes, sir.

Good.

Thank you.

*****

In fact, it's very rarely what we want (what we need). *[A few students laugh.]*

*****

Remember to smile and never to grin; then you won't have to worry about being in sin.

*****

When you give what you got, you'll give—you'll get what you need, not always what you want.

*****

Now when you give what you got, that's all that you think that you are. Well, because you *think* that you are, it's the illusion, the thought of I, that you're giving to God. That thing and all that it represents, that pride controls, the illusion, you give that to God. Now you get back from God the awakening of the truth that you are, but that's rarely what you really want.

*****

In other words, the birth or awakening of truth is ever at the expense of the death of illusion at any given moment.

*****

That which seems or appears to be is a light so dim we cannot see, known as self-deception.

*****

Why don't you wait for the Spirit to decide? *[The teacher speaks quietly, perhaps to the recording technician.]*

Now we've already had that wonderful teaching that to God all things are possible and that God is within us. So, we are presented, through the Law of Presence, which is solicitation, with the truth that frees us. But when that enters our consciousness, the have-beens, who do not have the truth to free us—if they did, we'd already have the truth awakened; we'd already be free!

So, we now know, of course, surely, we all agree, that the have-beens can only offer us what we have already experienced. They can offer us the repetition thereof. And if there is sufficient repetition, in time in eternity—repetition is the law through which change is made possible—because finally we wear out from without ([from] the experiences); we start to go within. And when that happens, we face the have-beens, who we're tired of serving, and we try to introduce the to-bes, for to us, to God within us, all things are possible. And then we experience these seeming contradictions in our consciousness because what is being introduced is not in keeping and is not in accord to what is already in control.

*****

Contradiction in consciousness is an experience of irritation through which our soul awakens.

*****

[The question[21]] must be asked. How are the has-beens, the forms in mental substance that we have created, how are they sustained? Does anyone know? What keeps them alive? *[After a short pause, the teacher continues.]* The question is being asked. Yes.

Energy. Where we—

How does the energy get to them?

Thoughts.

You mean that, for example, you had a thought two years ago and two years later you entertained that thought in consciousness and that's how they get it? Is that what you mean to say?

Uh-huh.

No, that's not what happens. Someone else know how the has-beens get their energy? Yes.

Me?

Yes.

It's a constant replaying of that thought or tape.

What calls them up to replay them?

Experiences which remind us of that.

That's one way, but that doesn't call them all up. It may call up a few.

Judgments that we have that we constantly bring forth.

Well, judgments are the parameters in which any possible to-bes are placed inside of to grow with their rations according to the has-beens. That's not the way. A very simple process. And we do it constantly. Yes.

I think we magnetically pull them in, if they have an emotion . . . and if we . . . [It is difficult to transcribe several words.]

You're absolutely on the right track. It's the Law of Magnet or Magnetism. Now just how is that set into motion? You should know that, if you want to be freed from them. Yes.

Do we just have to compute need and have this unfulfilled desire?

Well, there is need registered in consciousness; that is instrumental in establishing the law through which they are sustained, yes. But does anyone know what that need is? *[After a short pause, the teacher continues.]* It's the need of one word. Yes.

Is it attention?

No. *[The teacher responds and then calls upon a different student.]* Yes.

Survival?

No.

Self.

No. What is the one thing we need more than anything?

Oh, energy? [Different students respond.]

Well, we need energy, yes, but that's not what it is. Energy flows through the form of the need, that is true, but that is not what it is. Yes. One word.

Enthusiasm.

No. Well, I guess we'd better—shut it off for a minute. *[The teacher refers to the microcassette recorder.]* Give them a chance to think what the one thing is—

*****

No form survives without God and God is love.

*****

And so all of the has-beens, they survive, as we survive, by love. Now how do the has-beens get this Love, this God that sustains us? Well, they don't get it directly because they know if they got it directly, they'd soon be annihilated, considering what they do down there. This God or the Love flowing through us [when it is] directed to the thought of I, known as the self, [is] taken by and glorified in the throne of our experiences: we take pride. And pride gets our love and rations it out to all the has-beens that serve the throne of pride.

*****

Why would they be annihilated if they attempted to get their sustenance directly? That's the question.

*****

It's your pride that annihilates the has-beens when they attempt to run to the table, take all their sustenance, and leave when they have yet to be called to dinner.

*****

You ready?
Uh-huh.
Is the thing on? *[The teacher refers to the microcassette recorder.]*
Yeah.
Hmm. The love of self is the call to the realms of has-beens to come to dinner.

*****

—is it? What is it within our consciousness, in our sincere and honest effort to ask an honest question, that rises up as a line of defense to protect something we cherish with all our being? What is it we cherish so much? Well, it's quite obvious. We cherish so much our image, which is the slave of our own pride. And we do not want to tarnish our image, what we judge our image to be, that we present to people. And consequently, from that great need of delusion, we create the soldiers of deception, the first line of defense in the honesty that we are. Now in doing that, we do serve the crown called the pride.

*****

The closet's where we find honesty and truth because no one can see our image.

*****

As we love our self, we glorify our thoughts, expand our pride, and become what we think is god.

*****

That which has power over a thing is god to the thing and is therefore the final authority. Consequently, all your judgments, all your has-beens, knowing that your pride is their god, they are subject to their god and will do whatever their god bids them to do in keeping with the law of their own birth and design.

*****

Light is the great electric power of God. Love is the magnet that pulls unto itself all things throughout eternity.[22]

*****

The has-beens in their working in your field of consciousness, doing the job that you have originally designed and formed them to do, return, after a weary day, for their sustenance. They view the table before them and all the food that you have placed upon it. And in that viewing, they rejoice. They're about to eat. Now their expression of that rejoicing is a glorification of yourself and it is an expansion of the consciousness of your—

*****

What are experiences?

*****

Ready?
It's ready.
Experiences are the effects of the labor of the has-beens doing the work that they have been designed and formed to do by your consciousness. They return from the fields of labor and in their return, they view the table, the feast that is set, waiting for them. They experience, in that viewing, a great enjoyment of the possibility of feeding their hunger. It is that enjoyment and that rejoicing that is in truth the glory of the throne of self. And so, through that, the crown of self, known as pride, expands itself, and in that expansion process becomes more receptive to a greater flow of Love, of God.

*****

And so in keeping with the truth, Goodness or God is not a luxury, but a necessity, is not limited to a few forms, is applicable to all forms, including the form known as pride.

*****

One must not attempt to annihilate or to destroy the human pride. However, a wise man directs the pride. And the only thing that will benefit man is the direction of the pride to the truth, which is personal responsibility.

*****

Now, of course, the direction of pride is subject to and dependent upon those who serve and, therefore, help to sustain it in a world of creation in a world of forms. Therefore, man cannot say, "I choose to direct my pride, now, to personal responsibility," for the armies of has-beens, designed in form to serve other things besides personal responsibility, will not make that change. It is necessary with the lamp of honesty and the light of reason to transform the many forms that are serving the house of self and its crown, called pride.

*****

Let me know when you're ready. *[The teacher may be addressing the recording technician.]*
It's ready.
Not yet.

*****

That which serves us without the lamp of honesty and the light of reason, we are destined by the divine law to serve in time.

*****

We ofttimes, in the forming of a question, have such a line of defense in front of the question that we have to first clear away the justifications for asking the question in the first place; so, we get right to the root of the problem.

And it appears that the Law of Decency has, through your efforts, created a state of confusion or contradiction, [to] more properly put it. Because you said you felt contrary. What do you understand that contrary is? What causes the mind to go into a state of consciousness known as contrary? Do you know what takes place in your mind?

Would there be conflicting, two thoughts about something?

Yes. Do we understand that thoughts are forms?

And it would be a judgment . . .

So, we have the plurals at work already, right? So, we understand that thoughts are forms. And we already have been given the classes and the teachings about the have-beens and the to-bes. So, one faces the possibility of something entering into the consciousness that is not in keeping with the have-beens who are already in control. And so, they go to war. The war goes on and we feel, within our consciousness, contradiction, emotional upset, and everything else as we try to root out the to-bes who have entered our consciousness.

*****

Why is the problem a root and not a leaf? We at least should question that. What is it that nourishes the tree? Without a root, there is no tree. And the tree is the life.

*****

—read the last two lines. Don't, don't do that.

*****

[The following teachings were likely given to a very small group of advanced students.]

Pain is the reflection of the illusion as it impinges upon the consciousness.

*****

The day? No! Oh, short the night and great the day for he who knows the Light and way.

*****

Counterpart. Counterpart. The counter of the part! Without it, there's no balance. For nine is five and five is nine. And seven, oh seven, where you be, you don't, you don't, you cannot see. But take the two and five you be. Counterpart, counterpart, blind to two; awake to five. There you'll be. There you'll see. You are the pivot. You are the Light. You are the balance. You are the right. So take, oh, five, and look at two and be the seven through and through. For truth, the honesty will take you to the nine to be.

And seven, nine you shall return. And seven soar to planes, you see. Oh, yes, oh, seven, do not despair for what you see and what you be. Seven, seven days, they number. Not below and not above. Seven, seven, yes, you be. And let the nine follow thee. For all everywhere you'll always be true to seven, true to see. Ever sincere in honesty.

*****
[Clouds²³]
Soldiers, soldiers, soldiers, marching on the sea
Soldiers, soldiers, soldiers, what could you possibly see?
Marching, marching, marching, across the great blue sea.
Soldiers, soldiers, soldiers, where's your ship to be?
Soldiers, soldiers, soldiers, drown you not in sea.
Soldiers, soldiers, soldiers, wings is what I see
The feet that were to march on land
Has sprouted wings to fly on sea.
Soldiers, soldiers, soldiers, marching, flying be
You are the soldiers, courage, strength
Great in power, great in truth, great in love,
   and great in life.
Marching, marching, marching, far across the sea.
Ever, ever marching, soldiers you must be.

FEBRUARY 2, 1983

Class February 4, 1983

[The following teachings may have been given to a very small group of advanced students.]
Yes.

From the closet of infinity, I stepped into eternity. Waiting, waiting patiently for what has been or yet to be. Look not without; illusion see and lose the Light, Divinity.

*****

Has-beens may serve a useful purpose: when the light of reason places them on the plane of objectivity, they become directions to awakening and filling the cup of eternity.

*****

The furnace of creation is necessary for the warmth, the security, and the enjoyment of the forms to be. But remember, the forms to be are coals upon the fires of infinity.

*****

O closet of infinity, you wait to trap me in the sea of living, loving, hoping, being, trapping, trapping in the sea. O closet of infinity, what e'er I thought, what e'er I be, you cannot trap the sea I be. O closet of infinity, let Light of Truth shine upon thee as I go along the sea. The life I live, the life I be is not the trap eternity. For I am thee; thou are not me. I am the closet beyond the sea.

*****

A protector is a friend who speaks the truth when illusions call to trap his friend into the fall. He holds the lamp high in the night when demons come to tear and fright. His lamp, it guides the ship to be into a port where light can see that all of life and all of joy, all of good is waiting for the be.

*****

Rhyme is the child of rhythm, and rhythm the wife of harmony.

*****

Infatuation, your need to bind,
Reveals the truth: you're so unkind.
Grant me, God, the love divine
That shares from heart instead of mind.

*****

The fruit of the tree is not the tree, but the reflection thereof and, therefore, is illusion. Whoever seeks the fruit of the tree must remember the illusion to be.

*****

[Please see the addendum for this teaching.]

*****

The thought of I, through which the will flows, is the instrument controlling mental substance until that which it controls begins to control it.

*****

Closer.
How about—how about that?
Perhaps now you understand why man is not only upside down, backwards, but in reverse, sadly, in his eternity on the planet Earth.

*****

Spin and retrospin. We spin and pull unto ourselves with the great power of love. We retrospin and send out from our universe the great force of belief.

*****

Manifestation of illusion is man's experience with action and reaction, is what he believes is form or action. It is actually the duality in its spin and retrospin that he views as stationary and therefore form. Beyond love, beyond belief, illusion disappears and man, the truth, be.

*****

Love, the great magnet, attracts unto itself. Belief, the great power, makes it so. When the spin and retrospin, when the electric and the magnetic are balanced, then you know, beyond movement, for you are the stillness. That which you call the peace that passeth all understanding is that which you are. No movement is the frequency balance of all movement. And then you be.

*****

For whoever knows the birth of illusion stands on the principle to control it and may enter or leave it at their choice at any time in any way in any world.

*****

O rainbow of my soul, the clouds of mental substance no longer can block your view for you are the Light that's true. I am the soul with you. No longer can you hide from me my just and honest due. O rainbow of my soul, so true. No longer dark and dreary is creation old and weary, for I have awakened: captain, once again. My ship, it sails to new and broader horizons. The ports of call I chart by choice, no longer am I the victim of things. Have been to return. Have been again. No longer shall have-beens be my to-bes, for I have gained control over all things I see and know. I am captain once again.

*****

All these suits of clay so dele—so de—No! All these suits of clay, so deceiving, standing in my way. O suit, O suit, O suit of clay, you crack and crumble and return to that which formed you. Once again to rise to crack and crumble. Always rising, always falling, suit of clay, you're in my way. But I shall rise beyond your clay and take control once again. You shall do what I form you to do and not crack, nor decay, 'til I choose you do. Listen to me, suit of clay. Without me, you are no way a form that lives, a form that breathes. Subject to my rule, you be. O suit of clay, you listen, listen, listen to me, you suit of clay. I rise you from the dust of Earth. I send you back; that is your birth. Remember who I am, O suit of clay. Don't ever again tempt my way.

*****

As rhyme's the child of rhythm, and rhythm the wife of harmony, so harmony is the manifestation of unity. And unity, the awakening of the soul united. One God. One Power. One Light. One Truth. That, in harmony, we ever be.

*****

I'm so happy just to be, for then I see, I see, I see the ocean of my eternity. Captain of the ship I be. Crew aboard; they wait for me to instruct and chart the course on to greater lands to see. All creation waits for me to instruct, Divinity.

*****

When opposite your suits of clay, you struggle, suffer for brighter day. And yet the struggle never ends as long as suits are end to end. And so, the suits opposite be; the pain, the pleasure return to thee. But now the day, the brighter light, they neutralize and therefore be. There's something greater than suits of clay. There is the Light that is the day. And that, my friend, you come to know where e'er you be, where e'er you go; the suits shall neutralize the way, for that's the Light, the brighter day. The mist has gone and dawn has be. Yes, indeed, you wait to see. Beyond the forms is where you live. Beyond illusion, the Spirit free. That's what you are, you and me.

*****

[The following teachings were given to a larger group of students.]

See the divinity in direc—the divinity of direction that is contained within disaster is your own awakening to the God or Good that is within it: telling you to make necessary changes and showing you how to make them. All disasters offer us that divine direction, if we carry with us the lamp of honesty in the realization of the disaster.

*****

The hands of the clock, in reference to the hands of the clock and one's opportunity, their greatest opportunity to pierce the veil of illusion: the twelve-noon was given, which is the highest or brightest light, and the twelve-midnight, which, of course, we all know is the night or lesser light. Now the hands of the clock meet every so often other than those two most important times. If you look at your illusion, you will see that it does meet at other times also. However, because time is the great illusion, dependent upon space, the illusion which supports time, and because without reference or form for the illusion, the illusion does not exist. Therefore, in piercing the veil of illusion, the twelve-noon or high noon is when all levels of consciousness are united, and in that unity, see clearly beyond the veil, beyond form and have the awakening to who they are (truth) and what it (the veil) is, illusion or creation. Does that help with your question?

OK. Thank you.

*****

I do feel that that was given just a few minutes ago in reference to carrying the lamp of honesty, which would cast the light of reason over any particular thought, which is in truth a form. Now if you, who are in truth the creator of the form—therefore, the form is responsible to you and you are not responsible to it. If you don't carry the lamp of honesty, which reveals the light of reason that you may clearly see the child you have created and, in clearly seeing, use the faculty, the soul faculty of respect and discipline—because without respect, there is no discipline; without discipline, there's no respect. So, respect and discipline are inseparable. People who have unruly children are people who do not have respect. And not having respect, they do not have self-respect; they do not have self-discipline. And a child grows up without self-discipline, has little or no self-respect, and consequently stumbles in the dark. Do you understand that?

Yes, sir.

Thank you. Does that help with your question?

Yes, that helps.

OK.

*****

In reference to when a wise man is in the moment of now and what the dialogue would be reveals, in the question, to which a wise man is expected to respond, that the greater and brighter truth would be the silence he maintains.

*****

What do you understand is the difference between horizontal and vertical?

Horizontal is a flat plane and . . . [Several words are difficult to transcribe.]

The recorder doesn't tape your motions by hand.

No. I know.

Yes.

It would be like the east and west instead of the north and south.

What's the difference between north and south, and east and west, in your consciousness, if any?

Well, the east and west—east is where the sun rises and west is where it sets. So—

Does it move north to south and round about?

No.

South and north? *[After a short pause, the teacher continues.]* Then I think you have answered your question, don't you?

I have.

Where does the Light move?

Thank you.

What is infinity?

Thank you.

*****

Truth is always beautiful. It is ignorance that's ugly because it is discordant. And that which is discordant is diseased and to the consciousness appears as ugly.

*****

Because it is not harmonious to the universe of which we are an inseparable part.

*****

—question. In living in a realm of illusion, which we, fortunately, seem to have grown to that awakening, how can we best have the illusion, known as time, serve us instead of us serving it? Without the first illusion, the second, third, and all thereafter are nonexistent. And so a wise man removes the first illusion. And what, to the questioner, do you believe the first illusion is?

*****

Of all the gifts, of all the gifts you have to give to God to be free, what is the greatest gift you have to give?

The gift of self.

And what is the gift of self? What is self? What does self grow out of?

[It is difficult to transcribe the student's answer.]

No, [Student A]. The gift of self is born from the thought of I. So, you clearly see the first illusion is not the I that you are, but it is the thought of the I that is the illusion. So, if you want time to serve you, time being an illusion, then you've got to take control of the first of illusion and put it where it belongs: in the realm of illusion. And once again be the captain of your ship, and time will begin to serve you.

*****

Well, in reference to the question, the process is asked for, in how we make divine choice. Is that correct?

Yes, sir.

That that is Divine, and therefore offering choice, is beyond the realm of illusion. So, whenever we have the thought of I, we are not in a realm of truth where divine choice is established. So, to make divine choice, we must free our self from the first illusion, which is the thought of I, and make the choice with the I that we are, which is truth.

*****

When everything fails, be grateful. There's only one thing left, and man calls that truth.

*****

Why is the payment greater in the Light than it is in darkness? Because the Light is truth, and therefore we are aware of the payment. Darkness is illusion. We stumble and do not see the payment. And as we stumble, we blame the one on both sides [and] in back of us, because we can't possibly see anyone in front of us. How would that be possible and still maintain the illusion created by the thought of I?

*****

Try to understand: in a world of creation, man follows what's behind him and thinks it's in front of him.

*****

That's called experiences have sure ways of repeating themselves.

*****

Isn't it nice to know that we're not only upside down and backwards but we're even in reverse?

*****

Now perhaps you understand why only a fool chases a ball uphill.

*****

—brain. Now you think about the Law of Gravity and perhaps you'll understand.

*****

Eternity is a ladder with many rungs. And the ladder begins and ends in what man calls infinity.

*****

Reason is the light that shines from the lamp of honesty. So hold your lamp high that you may see the forms in the way of your feet, known as your understanding.

*****

Well, in reference to the description of the center where truth is, also, its temperature, which is the illusion thereof, as all temperature is, the question is, What then, therefore, [do] the North and South Poles represent? The farther we get from truth, like a circle, we return unto it. And so whether we go north to freeze or we go south to freeze, we still freeze in this great illusion. But what is it that freezes? The only thing that freezes is the illusion known as the senses. Now it's the senses that sustain and support the illusion. So let the senses freeze and awaken to the truth.

*****

Absolutely, reason is cold. Why shouldn't it be? It doesn't have the senses of emotion to warm it up. It doesn't have the fires of lust to keep it warm. Thank you.

*****

That that appeals is like that that seems or that that appears. It's known in this philosophy as self-deception.

*****

Appeal not, seem not, and appear not, and you won't have to be concerned about truth.

*****

In the closet of, in the closet of infinity, there are many images, garments on the coat hangers of your eternal life. You choose them—unfortunately, you think you choose them when in truth they're constantly choosing you.

*****

A person has someone scheduled to come to dinner. They work all day cleaning their house because the image hanging in their closet says to them, "Clean up this place around me so I can shine my brightest. There's something that I want." So you work all day. You're all frazzled and hazzled and in terrible vibrations. You put on your best bib and tucker, that is, the one that chose to wear you; you didn't choose to wear it. And you think you have a good evening until they're all gone and you're totally exhausted. I see no good in total exhaustion.

*****

It's like a woman who colors her hair because the image in her closet tells her that by coloring her hair, she will look her best, feel good, and, therefore, experience God. It's sad when God, the Divine Power, is already coloring the hair, changing the hair, in keeping with the goodness the soul within it has established in the laws of evolution.

*****

Try to remember that all illusion not only thinks but believes that it can improve on the Power that sustains it. And this is why people do so many different things in the delusion that they are improving on the Divine.

*****

An ego, uneducated, is not in harmony with the Divine and, therefore, insists on improving the job the Divine has done.

*****

It's like the daisy looking at the pansy. Seeing it has color, more than the poor daisy has, the daisy decides to go borrow a paint brush and paint itself with many colors that it may *appear* to look like the pansy, which it [the daisy] believes is quite beautiful considering it [the pansy] has more than it [the daisy] has. But it is not in the having or the gathering that we find peace or harmony or truth.

*****

You cannot paint and change the temple of God and expect the Light within it to shine brightly and clearly through it.

*****

Of course, that takes an educated ego. It takes a person accepting and dependent upon the source and sustenance of their life and that that eternal, infinite, intelligent Energy knows more about goodness than all the improvements illusion could possibly create.

*****

A person does certain things. They paint and prim and prance. And they go out into the jungle and someone tells them how good they look, how great they look. When that registers within their consciousness, they feel good. In those moments they know God. Therefore, illusion has them trapped, when they could feel good at the moment of their choice with no need to primp and prance and strut around like peacocks.

*****

Wrinkles are no longer the character marks of dignity. They're no longer the course we have charted in our evolution. And so we cover them up and deceive our self and, in so doing, grant that deception to the world.

*****

It's like charting a course on a river for your boat, which is taking your little soul to its final destination. Someone comes along with a giant eraser and erases all the charts that you've labored so long to make.

*****

There is a plane known as the plane of objectivity. When man stands upon the principle on which that plane rests, man views what has been and is no longer it; he views what is to be and is no longer it. He is the observer. He is no longer the observed. He is no longer that which things which have been are observing to see how they can use him best, for he is no longer there. He has now separated truth from creation [and] is in a position to use creation for the purpose which *he* and he alone designs it. Therefore, if a form, which is a vehicle through which the energy from God, flowing through him to the form of his creation, if that form no longer is useful to his consciousness, then he brings with him the lamp of honesty and casts the light of reason upon the form that has been created. It is transformed into a being where the design, he fits the mold thereof, and it becomes an angel for his service.

*****

That's called separating truth from creation. That's being *with* the forms that have been created and never again a part *of* the forms. It means, he uses *them*, for which he has already designed them; they no longer use him.

*****

In reference to your example of frying a potato, of course, within the consciousness the form rises, "This is the way I've always fried a potato." Man becomes aware whether or not that form of his creation is serving him or he is serving it. That awareness comes in the divine blessing known as change.

*****

The degree of man's own victimization is revealed to man at the opportunity called change, which is indispensable to evolution; it is revealed to him to the degree and the extent of any emotional upset or trauma at the change.

*****

And also, his own ability to harmoniously direct the forms of the change to fry the potatoes.

*****

The victimization of a person by the forms of their creation is easily revealed in their ability to follow instructions.

*****

And their graciousness in the application thereof.

*****

[After most of the students had left the temple for the evening, for a very small number of advanced students the teachings continued.]

The reaction of a magnet to an electric charge is in keeping with the charge of the electricity that the magnet is receptive to.

*****

Let your heart be round that nothing may enter but all may be, for in the being all shall see you're whole, complete. You're part of me. And me, what is the me? I am, I am, I am the be.

*****

Pointed hearts piss on what they cannot control.

*****

Pointed hearts, like toilets, must be frequently flushed.

*****

Be a pumpkin-head and your seeds will grow in fertile soil. Your life will fill your cup to overflowing.

*****

For pumpkin-heads are rounded hearts, and rounded hearts are filled with joy.

FEBRUARY 4, 1983

Class February 5, 1983

[The following teachings were given to a very small group of advanced students.]

Record. *[The teacher instructs the recording technician.]*

Neutralization is the process through which created forms return to the essence of their substance and are then available for new design, new formation, new labor, new harvest, and the benefit thereof.

*****

Two poles equal in power and force. Two poles, identical forms neutralize through amalgamation, return to their essence.

*****

The poles contained within the form attract the poles of like kind and, in so doing, neutralize within themselves.

*****

For example, the neutralization of ice to water or its transformation is the light or heat or sun. Now the ice is the water; yet, it is formed. And through the light, through neutralization of that which is contained within the ice to make it the form of ice, returns to its essence, the water, the living substance.

*****

Learn to be a student of the physics of infinity.

*****

The life force needed for the neutralization of forms is absorbed by the greedy and selfish has-beens who absolutely refuse to let go of their sustenance.

*****

A river without rocks is a life without obstruction. A mountain without snow is an island without a tree. And an island without a tree is like a boy who cannot see.

*****

The eagle's one and, yet, is two. He walks on land and flies so true. And yet his walk, his flight you see to be as two is one, is you.

*****

Why do we love obstruction more than we love Light? What is the great temptation that keeps us in the night? Why do we see the path so clear and turn around to what's ever near? Why, oh, why, the question be? Why, oh, why, can we not see? Why, oh, why, doubt and fear? Why, oh, why, with God so near?

*****

As the spider spins her web and represents a symbol of supply, so the wheat of natural growth brings harvest to the laborer, brings bread to all of life. Without the weaving of the web, the harvest is pure, the wheat is golden, virgin in the sustenance of the life it's designed to serve.

*****

Seventy-two, the number of power over creation. Seventy-two, nothing escapes the power. O creation, bow your head for seven has come and there to blend that you may know there's beginning and there's end. But seven, the power shall ever be amalgamated with two; thou art the be.

*****

Power over creation is totality, king of illusion, servant of the master. Take charge over your creations and the vehicle through which it flows, for it is yours to be captain of and it is yours to serve you well. Therefore, use it wisely that its service may return the good unto you.

*****

He who declares the truth and becomes king over creation shall, in the moment of his kingship, be freed from the slave and the bondage of creation, for he has declared the truth, the right to his throne. The king has once again risen.

*****

Blue, silver and duty calls. *[As this teaching is given, a telephone at the temple rings.]*

*****

Reason lights the way for a brighter, glorious day for she reveals the truth: wisdom and her use, understanding, not abuse, dignity and strength, character and courage, the glory of the Light is the life it gives to love.

*****

Greater is the victory of understanding than *all* the victories of desire.

*****

Remember, that which casts the shadow is not the shadow. The shadow is an illusion; therefore, it is a cast. Remember, it is never the thing. It is the cast of the thing, the illusion.

*****

Seventy-two, the power over creation. The number of the planet, five. For the multiplication of seven by two is fourteen, the God of foundation and the purpose of your journey on Earth. The planet of faith grants you the power over creation, your destiny, my child, on Earth.

*****

Whoever uses wisely the understanding already earned in evolution steps up to the power over that that he has already earned and from that broadens his horizons and has power over that which is in creation to be.

*****

Will is greater than desire for it is the power that moves desire. As desire is the expression of the Divine, so will is the being, the source that sends it forth.

*****

So learn to will what e'er you desire. Learn to will it without effort, for will is effortless. Power is not effort. Power is movement. Power is direction. Power is the instrument through which, and without which, design, desire, form are not possible. So will, O instrument of good. You are the will. All desire, all design, all form, all manifestations, all creations are subject and dependent upon you, O will. O will, O will of Good, you are the Light and the Truth, for Truth, the Light is the will of Good. It is God. No expression of God can ever be greater than the will of God.

FEBRUARY 5, 1983

Class February 6, 1983

If you do not apply what you receive, then you are a house divided, wanting and not doing. Being a house divided, you are in discord and disease. You are not in unity, and not being in unity, you are not in harmony. Not being in harmony, you are not in rhythm, for without harmony, there is no rhythm. Not being in harmony and rhythm, you are not in the divine flow, which is harmony and rhythm. Therefore, you end up, after receiving, through the lack of application, why, you end up discordant, in want; you end up in need; you end up in lack, for you have transgressed the demonstrable Law of the Divine Flow of Goodness, which is harmony and rhythm. Now I think, hopefully, we all understand that.

Do you want to save the tape? Or have we checked to see if this is recording properly? *[The teacher addresses the recording technician.]*

Shall we check?

Let's do that.

*****

Yes.

The last Sunday you were speaking about the Law of Decency.

Yes.

And you said that when a language loses its meaning it loses its decency.

You hold it. *[The teacher speaks quietly, as an aside, addressing another student. He may be referring to the microcassette recorder.]*

And I was wondering, does this refer to the limitations that we have imposed on words? Do we understand certain words in a very limited way? Does that relate to that?

Yes, a very good question in reference to the Law of Decency and especially in reference to the law as it applies to a language.

We have taken words and lost the meaning of the words by our ignorant abuses of the words. Now through abuse of anything, whether it's a word, a person, an animal, a plant, or a tree, by taking something for granted, we establish the Law of Abuse. By taking something for granted, we lose the love of God; we lose total consideration. Now when we lose goodness, the love of goodness, which is God, we establish the Law of Abuse. We no longer consider the object of our choice, for we have become the victim of the object of our choice. By taking it for granted, we have lost the goodness in our consciousness that it contains. Now this, of course, is an abuse of the Law of Decency. This, of course, establishes within our consciousness a bondage. We are the slave, the slave of taking for granted.

Now the only thing within us that takes anything for granted is the thing that has no value for anything that it thinks it does not have full control over. When we take something for granted, we establish that law in mental substance and we become the victim of that thing, person, or place, object of our choice, director of our desire, and suffer the consequences as the illusion becomes the delusion, and we enter the realms of deception, become obsessed, possessed in self-deceit, and darkness descends and the light of reason goes out. I hope that helps with your question.

Thank you very much.

*****

Yes, in reference to the teaching the divinity contained within the form of disaster, all disasters, like all problems, as a problem contains its own solution, disaster contains its own direction: direction to go within and awaken and make the changes necessary in the direction of divine Energy to the forms of your choice. For example, disaster reveals to us, that is, the goodness that it contains, the God within it, reveals to us—say that we have a shovel. And we use the shovel and the shovel serves us well for the purpose and the design which the shovel had been given birth in mental substance, formed of physical substance. And we use the shovel and one day we awaken in disaster that the shovel we need, at the moment we need it, is broken and does no longer serve the purpose for which it was designed and for which it had been formed.

The shovel is broken because we took the shovel for granted. And what we take for granted, we abuse through the lack of total consideration, for that which does not have total consideration does not have the divine faculty of care or kindness. And the little shovel, the tool that served us so well in our time of greatest need, no longer serves us at all, for it is broken and cannot fulfill the purpose of its birth.

Therefore, in all disaster God's little light shines humbly but bright to one who pauses and accepts the wonderful, demonstrable truth of the ability to personally respond to all experiences and awaken in that response. Does that help with your question?

Thank you very much.

*****

—in enthusiasm. Could you please explain that to us, if that's correct?

It is correct. Absolutely it is correct because it is demonstrable. That which is demonstrable reveals the truth, and the truth, of course, is correct.

Now pride can and does, to an awakened person, serve a very constructive and good use. For without pride, we are not encouraged to do a job. Without pride, we are not enthused in order to establish the Law of Continuity, which reaps success and abundant good and its potential, [that is,] without pride, wisely used under the light of reason.

Now as reason, its light, which is the humble lamp of honesty—see, honesty casts the light that is reason, and the light which honesty casts returns on the great circle and is reason. So, honesty and reason are inseparable. Without honesty awakened within one's conscience, there is no light of reason to transfigure the many experiences and forms of one's own creation.

And so, as we take our humble lamp of honesty into the very throne of the house of self, it casts its light over the crown and reveals to man that it is an instrument to be used in a constructive way for the greater good of oneself. For unless man uses the various functions to restore balance in his universe, which, in turn, neutralizes—and by neutralization, man frees himself in the Light of Truth—Goodness, God, he cannot experience. Therefore, the light of reason transforms the function known as pride. Man becomes encouraged, enthused, enters the realms of principle, the essence of truth, and Goodness or God lights the path before him and he stumbles not on the pebbles and the rocks of the judgments of the has-beens and the hopes-to-bes. I hope that helps with your question.

*****

Do you know what the vowels are?
A-O-U. [Student Q responds.]
They're A-O-U?
A-E-I-O-U. [A different student speaks.]
Oh, A-E-I-O-U. [Student Q responds again.]
OK, take a moment and write down the vowels. A—

*****

—[E]-I-O-U. *[After a short pause, the teacher continues.]* Now say all vowels together.
Aiou.
That's what "ah" is. That's for your ears only.
Now you are proficient in singing. What do the vowels do? What do you understand about vowels and voice?

Well, air goes up the throat. [Student Q responds.]
And what does the throat represent spiritually?
Yeah, resentment.
It represents resentment.
Uh-huh.

And do we resent anything unless a judgment has been established in consciousness? Is it possible to resent without a judgment? *[After a short pause, the teacher continues.]* Because resentment is the servant of judgments. OK.

Now you've asked the question why the Spirit uses, on occasion, the sound "ah." You have received the answer. For what is happening, my friends, is a freedom of the throat from resentments, judgments, parameters, and limitations. Many times, the Spirit has corrected students from saying "Ah" because they don't know what they're doing and they are abusing a spiritual law of untold ages ago that man used for very great good in a world of this planet. That's the reason. And that's the reason it's not to go beyond this group. That help with your question?[24]

Yes. Thank you.
OK.

*****

—and the—
No, I believe we've mentioned that Eve was created from the rib of Adam.
I'm sorry. Adam.
And, of course, we have various understandings of what Adam represents, I'm sure of that, according, of course, to our own ignorance. Yes.

I'd like to ask—you mentioned that, possibly, at a later time we could understand what the rib was.

Yes, indeed, you may ask. And it's *very* important. When the students no longer need what the rib of Adam represents to the exclusion of truth that frees the soul, then we shall indeed be happy to give the meaning of the rib of Adam. Thank you.

*****

Yes, discouragement is the queen of the functions. Now most people don't seem to realize the king, called God, and the queen, called Mother Nature. Mother Nature represents form, creation, pain, and pleasure. King, the King of Kings, is Light, is Truth, and sustains all form. Without the Light, there is no form. Without the form, Light is not known. Because Light is only known in darkness; and therefore, the shadow of form is necessary for the Light to be known.

In a world of identity, there is no awareness without duality. So, the darker the night, of course, the brighter the light. That is, our awareness of it.

Now discouragement, prince of the mother of form. Discouragement is the instrument through which man descends to serve creation. As man becomes more discouraged, the call of creation is greater. And so in keeping with the truth, as it is received in consciousness, man becomes discouraged that he hasn't made greater efforts. But what he little realizes is that's the prince of the queen of creation and her defense to make you serve, yea, even more by going, yea, even deeper in your descent to be a better servant of her needs. I hope that's helped with your question.

Thank you.

*****

—would you?

The moment you permit your mind to rise supreme in consciousness—and that, of course, happens whenever you *think* of the I and are no longer the I, for in the thought of I, you enter the illusion. Whenever you permit the thought of I, instead of the I—that is the to-be or the has-been; that is what the thought of I is. Now the thought of I is known as reference. Without reference, there's no thought of I. Without reference, there's no has-been. Without reference, there's no possibility of to-be. Therefore, the thought of I, instead of the I, opens the door of illusion, and you enter therein.

Now, without reference, there is no time. Without time, there is no space. Without the illusion of time and space, no reference, no thought of I. However, you have opened the door of illusion by the thought of I. And as you entertain in consciousness, [even] a split second, for there is no time to truth, in the thought of I, eternity, *you* enter the closet of infinity. There, in the closet of infinity, you view the many clothes on the hangers of your evolution. And there, in the thought of I, one of those suits come[s] off the hanger and drape[s] itself over you. The one that does that, of course, is the one, the suit that there are the most of. Those are created in the realm of illusion by what you call past experiences.

Now a wise man, awakening to illusion, makes a choice and he says, "I am." The "I am" is the Light, the Truth that you are. Not the "I am" because you think you are, but the I that you are. Many philosophies teach "I am because I think I am." Yes, indeed, you are now the illusion. You have left the Light of Truth and you have entered the mist. You're already on your way to the closet of infinity through what you call eternity, time, infinity, what you call space. And you're in the closet of infinity, but you don't have to enter that a victim.

You may, through your own efforts in awakening, step from the Light that you are, know where you're going through time, which is eternity, know that you're entering the closet called infinity, just space, and with that awakening, *you* choose the suit, the image in illusion, that *you* are going to wear. You know what you're choosing. You choose it with the light within you called reason. You know how long you're going to wear it. You know when you hang it up, it's not going to pop out and grab you, for you now are the captain of your ship and you now are the master of your destiny.

That great teaching has been given to you for years known as, "Be in the world and not a part of the world. Be with a person, place, or thing and never a part of a person, place, or thing." For in the illusion, if you do not stay aware, awake, and alert, then you become the victim of it and live in the realms of pain and pleasure, instead of the clean, clear atmosphere of the eternal moment which you are, called joy. I hope that's helped with your question.

Thank you.

*****

—and I'd appreciate it if you could discuss that.

The difference between daydream and reality is the power of will. Now we just got through explaining that, but I will explain it once again, about the closet of infinity. The difference between a daydream and a reality is the power of will. You enter the closet of infinity and are cloaked with the suit of your conscious choice, and you call that a daydream. Now you call that a daydream, and people, they daydream all the time. Some people, when they're really daydreaming, they're known, when they're bound by it, it's called fascination. You can't stop it. The images keep appearing. Well, it started with a daydream.

Through your lack of directed will, your reality was not granting unto you the satisfaction of any particular desire. And so you entered another dimension and you fulfilled that desire because it took less effort or will to do it that way. For you, in that realm of consciousness, you found there to be less obstructions. You could, what you thought, create in your mind these fantasies, these daydreams, and they would satisfy to some degree. But always lacking was the reality, the physical world, in which you are conscious.

Are we out of tape?

Almost.

Well then, shut it off and flip it over.

Go to side B. [The recording technician verbally documents the end of the recording on side A.]

*****

Reality. Are you ready?
Side B. Sunday night class February 6, 1983. [Again, the recording technician labels the recording.]
And—are you ready?
Yes. [The recording technician replies.]
And so we clearly see the difference between daydream and reality is how much will we choose to direct. Of course, it takes more will power to move a physical mountain than it does to move a mountain in a realm of consciousness that we are used to controlling, called daydreaming. But, my children, the dangers of daydreams is, through abuse, you become the slave and victim of them.

Now these images, you think, are exclusively, perhaps, yours, that you direct the power of God to create in realm of illusion; someday, children, they finally filter through the atmosphere into physical substance and you call that "circumstances." I hope that's helped with your question.
Thank you very much.

*****

—imagination, the doorway to the realms of spirit. Well, that's a very important question. All illusion is image. What illusion is—it is image, of course. Illusion is the image in the mirror that we choose to view. Illusion is the image in the mirror that *we* choose to view. That's what illusion is.

Now imagine, imagination is a conscious and, therefore, controlled direction of the power of God, called will, to create from the substance of which illusion is, to create from it images of one's conscious choice. And in so consciously creating, the light of reason flows unobstructed, keeping man, the truth, separate from form, creation, the falsehood. Therefore, man, at any moment in the illusion, has the ability, the awakening, the will, the strength, and the Light, to pierce the curtain, the veil of illusion, and enter the realms of Light, called the world of spirit. I hope that's helped with your question.

*****

And I believe that—
Want to know about a sigh?
Yes.
All right. I have asked my students for years—I have told them repeatedly that a sigh is taking away your very life. What does a sigh mean? It's quite simple. It is an expression and a revelation of man's absolute and total resignation to the illusion that, at the moment, he is serving. Sigh not and you will awaken. Resign not and you shall be free. Deny not and joy will be your life. That help with your question?
Very much.

*****

It's the swallowing of one's own resentment. That's called personal responsibility. The effect of personal responsibility is freedom. So I have taught my students for years don't sigh; don't yawn. Just swallow and you'll be free. Would it be so easy that all man had to do was go around swallowing to accept and, therefore, face personal responsibility; but it is a humble crawl.

*****

[Mighty oaks] from the smallest acorns grow.[25]

*****

The snow melts in the high noon of the Light of eternal truth. So does illusion melt when you love the truth more than what you *think* is satisfaction. Do not be so deceived that satisfaction is fulfillment. Satisfaction is a monster that haunts you in the night, in the night of your own consciousness, regardless of the hour. Satisfaction is a greedy substance: a monster that can never be fed, for it has a hollow belly. Which, of course, we all know what the belly represents: affection, emotion, need, need, need. And, finally, an awakening to what man calls greed. Seek, then, through the light of reason, the lamp of honesty, the fullness of life that is your birthright, that waits within your consciousness for you to lift the little lamp and stand guard at the bow of your ship that you may see, finally, in the night of your sail, what lies ahead, that you don't have to question and will never again be discouraged, for no man who sees where he's going is ever discouraged because in the seeing with the lamp of honesty he can steer his boat in the direction of goodness.

*****

—through the narrow, narrow channels of the demons of the deep. His boat will sail to the ocean of peace and eternal joy. Not tomorrow. That shall never be. Today. The moment in which you are aware.

*****

So, sail on to broader horizons. Sail on, for the island that waits [for] your arrival is the island you call harmony, which is heaven, the fullness of life, that which you are, not what you thought you be.

*****

[The] reason that truth is, by far, more easily received in the form or cloak of entertainment, which is the appeal to the senses, is because the senses, which are controlled by the garments or suits of has-beens and hopes-to-bes are very busy with their pleasures, and the Light slips right on through.

Shut it—

*****

And down into the nothingness from whence they rise shall they descend. Formless you shall then be and free. Now where were we? Oh, yes, we were on ancient religions, weren't we?

Yes.

Is that thing on? *[The teacher asks the recording technician about the microcassette recorder.]*

Yes, it is.

I see. Well now, ofttimes we look with repulsion at the great, wonderful truths of ancient pagan religions when they took their virgin maidens up to the alter to sacrifice to their God. You know, what's so sad is we don't realize that these souls entering these forms, and these virgin maidens, they were prepared from the time of their entrance into this form of illusion to give the greatest thing they had to give to God: the vehicle known as self. And so they willingly—of course, they understood what they were doing. And the priests who did the work, they knew very well what they were doing. They were rising the senses of the masses to its highest peak in order that the greatest truth may be revealed to the followers.

We look back because we do not understand, and we think that wasn't even civilized. They were so far advanced to what we think is civilized it's pathetic. We're real cannibals in comparison. We still kill. We still slaughter. And we do that not only physically, we do it mentally to others because we do it to our self. And I think that's very sad when we study ancient religions and rituals that all we can see is repulsion and horror because we are so ignorant in the darkness of self in which we live today.

*****

[Some religions[26]] have all these statues that they pray to. Why, why do they have to have a thing to pray to?

Because their faith is in self, they must have an image, as self is an image, in order to relate to. They have no reference of Truth, formless and free. Because their reliance is upon the illusion, which is substance or form, they must have form to reach their God. Now they will tell you, "I have a picture of a saint in order to help me think of God." And they are telling you the truth: they need the crutch. Because of their total reliance upon image, upon illusion, they can only find their way through to their God through image or through self.

This is why you find intolerance to other religions who have other ways of finding God because other religions have found different paths through the veil of illusion. That's the reason. So, any religion that teaches and demonstrates the passage through illusion or form to find God is a religion that is destined to bind, to cripple, and to restrict the freedom, the Truth that man is.

But a little religion, though a winding path through the realms of illusion, is better than no religion at all to return to God within consciousness, where we truly are. But you'll always find they lack the first soul faculty: duty, gratitude, and tolerance for difference.

Thank you.

You're welcome.

*****

—find—you'll always find them in great need to convert another because of their lack of security in what they *think* they have, but know they have it not.

*****

Because to recognize that demonstrable truth would be a great earthquake on the crown of self. That something different in form, than themselves, could possibly have eternal life. Therefore, because their path is winding through the realms of illusion to finally enter truth, that which differs from their form cannot possibly have the same value, such as an eternal soul.

Thank you.

*****

[All you] have to do is to look at animals, at people in animal instinct, what they will do to anyone whose form differs, whose acts and thoughts and beliefs differ. And show me where understanding or tolerance is.

*****

That's known as prejudice or prejudgment. Without judgment, illusion will disintegrate before your view. For without judgment, there's the light of reason; there's the lamp of honesty; there is understanding, the wise use thereof, called wisdom. There's principle, and where principle is personality is nonexistent. Where principle is, formless and free is the reign. Where personality is, form, illusion, delusion, deception, and self-deception is the reign.

*****

Whatever determination rests upon should be considered its foundation and security. So ask wisely the question, "What is, O God, the foundation of my determination?"

*****

—know what the gums represent? The one word? *[After a short pause, the teacher continues.]* Do you understand? Do you?

I'm not sure. Would it be motive?

Oh, my good friends, if you will take a look at what was just given, it is demonstrably revealed that it is reliance. On what does our determination rely? On what is it dependent? *[After a short pause, the teacher continues.]* Hmm. What is that dependent upon? Truth or illusion. No problem. Truth or illusion. How many times have I been to the dentist and he says, "Your gums are like a child." Has he not, [Student S]?

Uh-huh.

Well, with all my teeth problems, with all my determination, one has to go to work. Especially when they know what these things mean. Now finally—you've asked the question many times. Now you have received the answer. Yes.

Thank you. Since you've continued sitting, what did [Student R] say? And then you said it's untrue.

Yes, that's because of his lack of discernment. He was corrected.

OK. I am—

Yes.

—to understand that gums are reliance?

They are reliance. Yes, that was just revealed.

OK. May I ask for a clarification, years ago—

Yes, I know years ago.

Oh, is there more than one?

Why, of course. Do you think that a soul faculty, being triune to the sense function, is singular? Hmm? Was it ever taught that a sense function, the balance of a soul faculty, was singular? Well, children, you have not been studying your own teachings that you have received. I have given you several soul faculties and taught you they are triune. Whatever possibly caused you to make a judgment that a sense function was singular? Hmm? Don't you think that's a good thing for you to start considering?

I wanted to make sure that what I had in there—

Oh, you're making—

—was correct.

What you have originally is very correct.

OK. Thank you.

It's a triune function.

OK. Thank you.

How can you have balance with a triune function—with a triune faculty if all you have is a singular function. Does that make sense to you, [Student G]? *[After a short pause, the teacher continues.]* Does that make any kind of reason to anyone? I think you've answered your question, [Student S].

Thank you.

All sense functions are triune, the perfect balance to the corresponding triune soul faculty. Yes, did you have a question? *[After a short pause, the teacher continues.]* I see. Do you remember the rest of that triune function? *[The teacher addresses Student S.]*

One of them—

The gums—you remember one.

Uh-huh.

Well, it's not quite a triangle, is it?

No. I think I only had the one.

Perhaps that's all you did get.

Now I have the two, though. I'm grateful for two.

Duality is better than nothing, as we're moving through illusion. What did you think the other one you have is? I have it upstairs.

Should I say it?

Well, yes, you may; you opened the door.

Experience.

Uh-huh. My God, now you've opened the door. Isn't that wonderful? And what in hell do we rely on, children, with our determination? What do we rely on but the has-beens called experience.

O little mind, you do not see, that's all. You're not designed to see. You're designed to blindness.

Yes, some of you advanced students who worked with me so many years, [the] word was given, the meaning of the gums. Like you. *[The teacher addresses an advanced student.]*

But if you had been thinking deeply, you would have said to yourself, "The gums are now reliance. They used to be experience. Just a minute this doesn't make sense. The teeth are determination. They're resting in the gums. They're resting *on* the gums." We understand there's a bone down there, too, you know. We all understand that. We don't have to be dentists. And you would have questioned. You would have asked your soul, your spirit. "This doesn't make sense. I'm a bit confused. Experience. Reliance. Determination. What is my determination resting on?" Then you would have said, "Well, it's resting on experience; I was taught years ago. And now it's resting on reliance I'm taught today, this moment. What does this mean? My determination relies upon my experiences. My experiences, I now know, are what has been that controls my life." And you would have had the truth awaken from within your own being. That's why you're here in classes of dialogue and discourse. That's how truth is taught. But you should have asked yourself that question. However, not having asked yourself that question, you have been an instrument through which all of them have benefited.

*****

—fortunate for you because it reveals to you the difficulty of awakening to what your determination is resting upon: relying upon experience, which is the has-beens. And where do the has-beens—where were they born? And where do they live? And where do they do their duty that you have created them to do? In what center of consciousness? Now that you've opened the door. What center of consciousness do they live in?

The water.

Yes, indeed. And what does the water—where do affections and emotions live?

In the stomach.

Yes. And what center is that? Child, you know where the fire center is. Where's—what's the next center? *[After a short pause, the teacher continues.]* Hopefully, you're going up!

The water.

Yes, the water center. Yes?

So, the stomach's in the water center, is that what you're saying?

Why, certainly. Isn't it your stomach that bothers you when your has-beens are running wild?

Yes, it is.

Isn't it your stomach that bothers you when your determination rests and relies upon your experiences in life? It's not your toes that bother you, is it? It's your stomach, isn't it?

Uh-huh.

Isn't that what gives you all the volcanic eruptions and uproar? Well, there's your answer. It does the same thing to everyone else. [The] water center in all forms is in the stomach. That's where your affections live. That's where your emotions thrive. Cast the light of reason upon it and you will see calmer days and greater good. What has been has been, and he who chooses to live therein must enjoy the pain thereof. The law is demonstrable.

Pleasure is the satisfaction of the has-beens who are now floating in the ocean of your consciousness called emotion.

*****

One question and class is concluded.

*****

May I ask where judgments are located?

Of course, you may ask. Judgments, limits, and parameters are born and thrive in the southern portion of your air center. That's the half below the bridge.

And so, in concluding this class this evening, remember, understand, perceive, and wisely use "Bladder beware."

*****

As we were saying, the "would" of the "would-be" is the fuel on a fire that is self-consuming, for it lacks the light of reason, is controlled wholly and completely by what has been. It activates and feeds, through directed energy, hollow forms without soul, for it has placed the curtain of illusion before the Light of Truth and is dependent and reliant upon the illusion for its sustenance. And whoever depends upon the illusion for its sustenance must ever suffer, must ever move from pain and pleasure, the emptiness of satisfaction under the guise of the divine Spirit of fulfillment. For that which fills is everlasting and enduring, freed from lack, want, and need, for there is no end and no beginning to that which is Life, Light, Love.

Love is not dependent upon such foolishness as mental substance. Life is not dependent upon such stupidity as the judgment of mental substance. Light is not dependent upon the forms of man's creations.

So awaken within your consciousness and stop the childishness. In the playpen of creation make the effort to separate truth from it, to use it and not abuse it, for in your abuses thereof are you the victim and destined to bondage, the bondage of possession and obsession, for that is what illusion, delusion, deception, and self-deception have to offer all souls until they awaken.

Until the need that you direct God's energy to disintegrates into the nothingness from whence you gave it birth, until God moves into that place in consciousness, until that day, suffering, struggle, disaster, and strife is the payment of such ignorance. For you have risen in mental substance supreme: telling God, the Truth that frees you, that which you truly are, what *you* shall be dependent upon for the Good or God in your life. Therefore, through the suffering of the senses the soul is freed. And that indeed is a great blessing for all.

Thank you. Good night.

*****

[The following teachings may have been given to a very small group of advanced students, perhaps after the majority of students had left the temple for the evening.]

Illusion is an image in the mirror we choose to view.

*****

To be or not to be, that is the question. Not to be the has-beens of yesterday. Not to be the to-bes of tomorrow. And so it is to be or not to be. To be the I of eternity. Not to be is the thought, the illusion of the be, but is not the be. So truth be. Illusion, to be, has been. *[Please consider the possibility that a more appropriate transcription could be "To be the eye of eternity."]*

*****

Bladder beware and the be you'll ever be. No concern, nor need, shall you see when bladder beware awakens the Light you are.

*****

The bladder is where the river flows through the torturous realms of purification where the demons live and where the demons control the small passage of your boat through the great cliffs. Study and understand the golden fleece.

*****

Which is, golden fleece, the wisdom of strength.

*****

For the golden fleece is the hair on Samson's head.

*****

Remember, with his great strength he stood between the pillars of the temple.

*****

And remember, she cut off his strength and weakened him, but he rose, like truth, again.

*****

[Please see the addendum for this teaching.]

*****

We cry with the pain of the cracking of the walls of judgment. We scream with the torture of their crumbling. And we're discouraged and saddened with the dust that's left, until we pause and see the freedom that we have entered.

*****

Infinite happiness is the joy of eternity.

*****

Now, soul, each soul in form has its counterpart, for soul, individualized, is formed, a covering of the free Spirit in truth we are. Form is only possible through a division, for form divides of itself and conquers all within its domain. For it creates and, by the Law of Creation, has charge over its creations. And the charge over creation is the conquest and the return and service to that which has created it. And so when that which has been divided is united, the power of truth flows whole and complete. And that flow of truth, whole and complete, man knows as the fullness of life, which is the joy of being. And the joy of being is the destiny of return to the source within, which it is. For in unity, there is strength. In strength, there is God. That is where courage reigns supreme. For courage is the open door through which God's ministering angels flow and cast their great Light upon the dimness and darkness of creation that man may conquer that which he has created, that in his conquest, the forms of creation he has created shall serve him, and he not serve them.

*****

The law clearly reveals that opposites attract. And yet man, not awakening to the many bodies through which his soul is expressing, attracting with one body does not in any way guarantee the attraction in all bodies, for man's evolution is wearing the suit of different bodies in different dimensions; and therefore, only when man awakens to the dimension where the bodies are opposite is the attraction solidified. In unity and in time, in eternity, he will, he shall awaken that the attraction of opposites is in principle the electromagnetic, which inseparably he is.

FEBRUARY 6, 1983

Class February 7, 1983

The lamp of honesty is a humble lamp. And it is humble because it must forever bow to the glory of the pride of man.

*****

Man is ever as honest as his pride will ever permit.

*****

Neutrality, the Divinity, God is the perfect balance between opposites.

*****

Now we know what peace is.

*****

Record.
Now does—you have been given the meaning of the fingers. You've also been given the meaning of the fingernails. Now—yes, you have been given that, but not directly, but truth is taught through indirection. Now what are you placing on your throat?

*****

Leave it on. You got enough tape? Leave it on. Spent over a hundred some dollars on tape today. What are you placing on your resentment or your throat? This is very important for you, [Student Q].

Perception and—

*****

Now how do we become aware of what we perceive? What is it that perceives?

The soul perceives.

The soul perceives. So, you are placing your awareness in soul perception on the resentment that you have at any given moment.

*****

Because resentment is a mental substance and because identity is in the illusion known as mental substance, awareness is only awareness of the illusion. Therefore, you must identify with that which pierces the veil of illusion, and that which pierces the veil of illusion is the perception of your true being, known as your soul.

*****

—questions in reference to the vowels, to the exercise, to what is taking place. There is—now is the time to speak it. Because you especially, [Student Q], as a singer, should be very, very aware of the use of the full vowels of the "Ah," although I guess it is not taught in singing. But become very aware with those, the thumb and that finger of what takes place in this area of your throat. Because that's what tightens through resentment for everyone. So when there's a tightening of the throat, you may feel it down here. It's taking place up here. This is where it's taking place.

Now does anyone know what that is? Does anyone know about the glands or anything? Is anyone familiar with the glands? How they swell. Hmm?

Is the thyroid in there?

[Student G]. The glands. These are glands. Don't you feel those lumps, like eggs—

Uh-huh. [Several students respond.]

One on each side. Aren't you aware of a soreness up here, when your throat is sore or you have a cold?

Uh-huh. [Again, several students respond.]

This is what swells and tightens.

Uh-huh.

And doesn't your nose all stuff up? And isn't your throat raspy? Because your glands have swollen, revealing the truth to you: the cause of your own cold, so-called.

*****

Now you take a person that's getting ready to sing and something passes within their mental substance that, beneath their conscious awareness, causes a judgment to rise, a rejection to express, a resentment affects the throat and there is a[n] actual swelling and a tightening of the glands which control this whole area.

*****

They don't need a cold for that to happen.

*****

Go ahead. *[The teacher may be instructing the technician to begin recording.]*

As long as you insist on believing that you are the emotion, that you, through your own ignorance, permit yourself to identify with, there is no way possible that you can be aware and perceive the fullness of truth that you are, let alone the freedom thereof. There is no possible way until you separate the truth which you are from the illusion which you believe you are. Now you cannot believe the illusion until you identify with the thought of I, which is the illusion, the step that you go down into that illusion. You first must permit the mind to identify with the thought of I, which takes you from the truth of the I that you are. Unless the conscious, daily effort is made you will not yank yourself free from the curtain and veil of illusion. Thank you.

Now perhaps we'll go on with the other. And we'll save—

*****

No vowels, no voice.

*****

In reference to the fullness of all vowels, "Ah," and the freedom of the throat of resentment, which rises from judgments, limitations, and parameters, let it be clearly understood that the throat of the atmosphere is indispensable to the receptivity of clear communication. Ofttimes during communication the has-beens rise. Usually they rise immediately after, but at times they rise during the broadcast.

*****

The reason for treason is need.

*****

—you best pause and give your understanding of what the word *reference* means to you.

*****

We can go on with this. It will be on tape for you.

You are the I of eternity, Truth, that, you are. In the being, you review, refer, look again at your eternal evolution. And in so doing, you enter what is known as the thought of I, which is the substance of illusion from whence all forms are created. It is when you, the eternity, in the truth of infinity direct the intelligent Energy, which you are, to events, experiences that have passed, you return; you enter the closet. And in so doing, the garments or vehicles on the hangers of unfulfilled desires cloak you with the form, the image of that illusion. Whoever identifies directs their being to that which has been becomes the victim of and bondage to unfulfilled desires. *[Please consider the possibility that a more appropriate transcription could be "You are the eye of eternity."]*

*****

Are you ready?

Yes. [The recording technician responds.]

When the eye of eternity blinks, it sheds a tear, the very substance known as illusion from whence all forms are created. Whenever you establish rapport with anyone, you go with them or they go with you to the closet of infinity. There, you are draped from one of the many hangers of unfulfilled desires with the vehicle in which you are bound by the illusion and become the servant of delusion, deception, and self-deception.

*****

So bladder beware what closet you enter moment by moment by moment.

*****

For a closet is a closed space in illusion in which your light is dimmed 'til you can no longer see.

*****

A new garment in your closet of infinity is fashioned from the honey of the bee, containing divine consideration, divine acceptance, and the purity of the light of reason.

*****

All people have an inner knowing, an awareness, and always feel Good or God with new threads on their being.

*****

Perhaps now you understand and will be wise in your choice in life.

*****

To you.

*****

The honey bee is a worker. What else is the honey bee?

*****

What else?
Creator.

*****

He is a creator.

*****

What else is the honey bee?

He's organized.

He's certainly organized. What else is the honey bee?

Produces food.

The honey bee is a producer. What else is the honey bee?

He serves.

He serves! And what does the honey bee serve in his labor?

The whole.

The what?

The whole or the hive.

He serves the hive, but the honey bee serves something even greater than the hive.

And nature.

What nature?

Mother Nature.

Does he serve the leaf, the root, the branch? What does he serve?

No, the flowers. [The student speaks simultaneously to the teacher's last question.]

He serves the flower. And what part of the flower of God does the honey bee serve?

The stamen. [The] center. [Several students respond.]

And what is there?

Nectar.

Nectar!

*****

The nectar of nature is the wine of the goddesses of creation.

*****

And so, when those in control, that is, the gods and goddesses of nature, when they are drunk with the wine, the worker comes and makes his honey, and man awakens, and we use the suit that serves his soul the best.

*****

For when those in charge of illusion are no longer, though temporarily, capable of charge, then the Light may take what is justly its.

*****

Unfulfilled desires, like used clothing, are best served when given to someone who will use them.

*****

The thought of I is the blink of truth, the essence of illusion, the substance of self, known as form.

*****

Look back, dream ahead, and you'll never know where you are.

FEBRUARY 7, 1983

Class February 8, 1983

[The following teachings may have been given to a very small group of advanced students.]

Survival is for the fools who don't know how to live, for living is the spirit of joy.

*****

The bee of the sea is the bee to be for the nectar of the gods lies within it to be. *[The beginning of this sentence could also be transcribed as "The be of the see" or other alternate combinations of those words. Without additional guidance from the teacher, who, at the time of publication, is unavailable to us, it is difficult to determine the correct transcription.]*

*****

The life-giving waters and the salt of earth remain the secret for a newer birth.

*****

Obstructions within the temple are easily removed when saltwater you take; there's freedom from the obstructions and growth and decay.

*****

Saltwater, in very small amount, releases the tension, the bowels they count. And man is freed from what he views as obstruction. But what he views is only the outward effect, and the outward effect, once removed, helps man to awaken and harmoniously move.

*****

Sensation is in truth the positive actions impinging upon the senses and the magnetic reaction of absorption thereto.

*****

The duration of happiness which always follows the impingement upon the senses is dependent upon the ability to control the shadows that rush in.

*****

A wise person uses the tools of the divine design for the purpose of good everlasting, not for the abuses of pleasant moments of pain and pleasure.

*****

If you must be busy, then, O busy, be a bee.

*****

Gather the nectar and make your honey.

*****

From the gods and goddesses of nature, we see the work of the honey bee. To the flower, the bee descends and, on the stamen, works to gather, to return into the hive. And there for all the world to enjoy the goodness and the sweetness of its effect: the honey. From the gods and goddesses, it has taken; and to the gods and goddesses, returns the nectar, the wine, in which they drink and drink and drink. Until they've drank themself into a stupor. And in the stupor, the forms, they sleep. And in their sleep, the soul moves on to heavenly heights.

Remember, all rivers flow into the source from whence they came. And it is the flowing of the river that is the sensations of creation. Ah, but the essence of the river—the rhythm, the harmony, and the rhyme—that, you are.

*****

In a world of so-called form or creation, you have imbalance, for you have need and, therefore, direct intelligent Energy to one end of the pole at the sacrifice and imbalance of the other end of the pole. That's not neutrality. That's not balance. That's not truth. That's not freedom. That's not joy and certainly not the heaven of ecstasy. It is, however, bondage, suffering, pain, grief, disaster, and destruction.

*****

Look for the unicorn, the purity of white, the golden hoofs of wisdom with the awareness, the eyes of understanding and the nostrils that breathe the harmony of heaven. For the unicorn, that unicorn, is the angel that has descended into a world of creation to guide you, to protect you, to bring you to that goodness that you are. That unicorn will take you home in ways your minds could never dream.

FEBRUARY 8, 1983

Class February 9, 1983

[The following teachings were given to a very small group of advanced students.]

In the garden of paradise is the flower and the nectar of life.

*****

The wise use of understanding is the joy of life, the step and the wonderful light to heaven above.

*****

Be not wasteful in your consciousness for all thought is effect of energy. All feeling is effect of energy. Energy is needed for build, to build the stairway to your home, your heaven, which is ever above you.

*****

The imbalance of salt in the temple of God is the major problem for the chemical balance and free flow of the river of life.

*****

—too little. The truth revealed is that old salts contain wisdom. And so wise is the captain who's an old salt on his ship of destiny.

*****

Faith in the divine Law of Return is the freedom and the joy from the lack of concern.

*****

A person who says, "I do not see. I cannot understand," is a person whose mind is protecting what they do see, what they can understand. It's known as self-defense, self-deception: the line that protects the darkness and shadows from the light, peace, and the harmony of freedom.

*****

[The following teachings were given to a larger group of students.]

Faith in the divine Law of Return is freedom from all concern.

*****

When you give what you got, you will get what you need, not always what you want.[27]

*****

It seems to me that concern seems to be the problem. And we might have faith in the negative, but when we start directing it or trying to direct it to something good, all of a sudden, those levels rise and fear sets in and concern. And we dictate how the return should be.

And it is not divine.

Yes. How can we be free? What should we do? What can we do to be free from concern?

Well, faith in the divine Law of Return, of course, is freedom, freedom from creation, which is bondage. So, if we, in our faith in the divine Law of Return, wish to keep the law divine, which means good or goodness, God, then there can be no mental interference with the law that is divine, or it no longer is divine. You can't have faith in the divine Law of Return and then tell God what the return is because then the law is separate from the law that truly precedes it, which clearly says when you give what you got, you get what you need; it's not always what you want.

But faith in the divine Law of Return frees you from any and all concern because you know that whatever you need you get through the divine Law of Return, though it may not be what you want. But it *is* what we need because it awakens us that we may see what we are doing in life, not what we *think* we are doing. There's a great difference between what we're doing and what we think we're doing.

*****

See, ofttimes we think by doing such and such we will attain or gain such and such. Now, that is not the way the divine Law of Return works. The divine Law of Return is subject to the Law of Motive. Therefore, we do get what we need, not always what we want, but the motivation, the initial step . . . [re]vealed to us in that divine Law of Return.

[Based upon the recording, the ellipsis in the above sentence identifies a point in the tape that may have been recorded over and two words inserted that, perhaps, were not in the teaching as it was originally given. The words that may have been recorded over the original teaching are "that we." The personal notes of a student present at this class record the sentence as, "Therefore, we do get what we need, not always what we want, but the motivation, the initial step is revealed to us in that divine Law of Return."]

*****

Sometimes the return is pleasant, we think. And sometimes the return is painful, we think. But that is only our limited view, which is dependent upon our judgments, which are the parameters in which our to-bes have been locked in by our has-beens.

*****

Let us try to remember, friends, that shortcuts to truth are detours to deception.

*****

It's on. [The recording technician refers to the microcassette recorder.]

When we think we know what we want and we receive what we think we did not want, our has-beens are furious. When we think we know what we want and we get what we think we know what we want, our has-beens are satisfied, and we are bound on the karmic wheel of the continuity of past experiences. Therefore, awaken soul; let irritation serve her purpose.

*****

—motive? Well, you be patient and let me ask someone who should be pure enough to know, we hope.

*****

In reference to your question, How do we establish pure motive? it is clear; it is demonstrable that when man in consciousness, through personal responsibility, through the continuity of effort to place the Light which he is the highest priority, he's freed from need, and therefore all motivation is pure, the Light itself.

*****

In reference to your question, reliance on God or faith in God, does it play any part in the Law of Return? The Law of Return, the divine Law of Return is not dependent upon the fluctuating and changing mental substance of which the human mind is composed. It is not dependent upon the thought of man. It is wholly, completely dependent upon the motivation, which is the law, the divine law that shall return like unto its kind.

*****

Mental games are spiritual disasters. And in time, man wearies of the games of life and awakens to a realm of consciousness where he is freed from them.

*****

In reference to your question—Is motivation a soul faculty?—motivation is the Divine Principle. The perfect balance between soul faculties and sense functions is the neutralization of being, which is the awakening in totality of the Light, which is Truth, which you are. The effect thereof is harmony, known to man as a state of consciousness called heaven.

*****

You're ready? *[The teacher asks the recording technician.]* Uh-huh.

Harmony is inseparable from the Law of Unity. And that which is harmonious is united. That which is united and harmonious *is* the peace passing all understanding.

*****

Motivation is movement. Movement is Light. Light is Truth. And Truth is God. Therefore, you, Truth, Light, God can never die, for death is that which no longer moves.

*****

In the great battle between the has-beens and the to-bes, in time, in that great illusion, there is a neutralization when both armies have spent their last drop of energy. And that neutralization awakens the Light within you, and you be the eternity that you are in the great illusion called space, known as infinity.

*****

When your hopes in life equal your despairs, you will rest in truth and the joy of life. You will go beyond survival, which is only for the fools, and awaken to life which is the spirit of joy.

*****

[The following teachings may have been given to a very small group of advanced students.]

The mystical power of the unicorn is the horn of unicorn. It is the touch of the horn to any form of creation that instantly brings forth the obedience to his command. The unicorn, ever searching for pureness or virginity of any form—all form—is greatly disturbed whenever he is deceived by the pretenders. And when so deceived, he annihilates them. The golden hoofs of the unicorn are the symbols of wisdom in his understanding (his feet). The wise use of his understanding is the great power he uses in his golden horn to command all creation.

FEBRUARY 9, 1983

Class February 11, 1983

[The following teachings were given during the afternoon to a very small group of advanced students.]

The starvation of the senses is destined, in time, to sacrifice the Light, the brighter Light that waits for the soul's expression. And so man with the understanding that God, Truth, that which he is, is neutralization, the pulsation of being neutralizing all things within which it comes [in] contact, brings harmony, health, rhythm, and the rhyme, which is the joy of life and its purpose of being.

*****

In reference to your question, comes into contact, being is what you know as spiritual, universal, mental, physical, many bodies, you, being express through. It is, at the moment of contact, the Law of Flow of the Divinity is established. Therefore, one should consider all bodies, all forms that it comes in contact with. To contact with one body at the sacrifice of another is not harmony, for it is not fullness. Therefore, it is not rhythm and cannot be rhyme, the joy, the flow, the purpose of being, which is life. For being is life; its expression is joy. So be. In be is be-ing and be-ing *is* what you are.

*****

Saturday, the day of Saturn, is the day of the dawn of understanding.

*****

OK.

And the day which follows the dawn of understanding is the Sunday of the fullness of wisdom.

*****

For the day of sun or Sunday is the day of Light, which all things are accepted into awareness.

*****

Thursday, the day of drama, the day of the height of sensation, the day of the flow of emotion, the day of the feeling of fullness. Thursday, the day of Thor.

*****

Jupiter—Thursday.
Wednesday—Mercury.

*****

Wednesday, Wednesday, a day of balance. Mercury, the guiding light, balances the temperatures of creation.

*****

Mercury is that which holds the poles together, North and South, that the gyro may spin and retrospin. Mercury. Study the planet and you will understand.

*****

Mythology, the science of myth, is beyond the control, the conception of mental substance. And that which is beyond the control and the conception of mental substance is the Light of Truth. It wears the garment of appearance, the garment of seeming, the garment of appeal, for that's when the Light shines the brightest.

*****

That's what it is. *[The teacher speaks very quietly, but in his next sentence, he speaks much louder.]* The divinity of infinity is the neutralization called affinity.

*****

When you lose the purpose of design, become the thing and then are blind, that which you are, the joy divine, you lose to that which bin to be.[28] You lost the Life. You lost the Light. You lost the Love. You forgot the design; it is divine.

*****

From your fingers up your arm over your head until the other side go down. There you see the anchor be. Straight and sure your body be. The center line. Then hold to me.

*****

Stand up straight. Down your arms. Down. Ah—now you see you are the anchor. That you be. You are the anchor of the soul that holds the ship of destiny. You are the anchor, whole and free. You are the anchor when you be.

*****

The lifeline attaches to the anchor. Without the anchor, without the lifeline to the ship, man has no port of call, man has no goal, man has no destiny. So, attach well the lifeline to the anchor that you may see clearly the goal, may chart your course, may raise and lower your anchor at the ports of call on your chart of destiny to reach your final port and rest in the harbor of harmony.

*****

O my child, without the thought of I, there is no rib of Adam.

*****

For without the thought, there is no entrance into illusion. Without the entrance into illusion, there is no want, for there is no need. Man *is* whole and complete. There is no thing missing within man that *is*. However, man that is, is not separate from the Being, the Truth, and the Light. He is united; therefore, whole. However, man is not aware in form until he enters form. Therefore, man knows something in form is missing and that something is the rib of that bow of his ship that has departed and left the stern ashore.

*****

The bow of a ship is the great electric power that moves it ever onward. The stern of the ship is the stability that holds it together.

*****

The stern is the magnet that holds. The bow is the power that moves.

*****

As the bow is direction; so the stern is detour. And the power that moves the bow is in the stern. Therefore, detour and direction must unite for destiny to be.

*****

Ofttimes no is God's direction and man calls that detour.

*****

Man's detours in life are known as deception. God's direction in life, man calls detours. Forgetting that, when we give what we got, we get what we need, not always what we want. The ship and the sail thereon must never tell the captain, "We don't like the way the wind blows." For in so doing, the sail no longer serves the purpose of its design: to carry the ship to the port of call that it is destined to its own fulfillment.

*****

The unicorn is whole and complete. It has no mate because it does not enter the curtain of illusion until it has pity for what it views. Creation is the pity of the unicorn, its weakness, its bondage, and its treason unto itself. So awaken that which you [are], whole and complete. Awaken. The unicorn knows the way.

*****

The unicorn pities what it views in the illusion that it enters. The pity is the awakening of the has-beens of its own evolution. And then it descends to the depths from whence it has risen so many times. Unicorn, truth crushes itself to earth from the illusion which it remembers in the moment of its pity.

*****

The thought of I is the blink of the eye of eternity as it enters the closet of infinity.

*****

For it cannot enter the closet with the I of the Light that it is. *[Please consider the possibility that a more appropriate transcription of this teaching is "with the eye of the Light that it is."]*

*****

And so, in the closet of infinity, as the garments, worn and tattered, pull off themselves from the hangers of unfulfilled desires and cloak the being, the tear is shed for all creation.

*****

The tear is known as the sorrow and the sadness, the struggle and the grief, the pleasure and the pain of survival.

*****

That which is even is equal. That which is equal is balance. That which is balance is free. That's known to man as "uni." That's known in truth as unity. And so the power that is, called "uni," is you and I free.

*****

I will not give you a stone for your head to rest upon, when there's a cloud made from the substance of God. It's called the love that you are shall return and comfort your journey in years in your stay on Earth.

*****

The anchor to heaven is the rocket of man.

*****

For the rocket of man is the will of God.

*****

The purpose of life, the joy of being.

*****

Sail on, little ship. Your anchor's on deck. The sun is shining. The dawn is bright. We have a day of greater Light. Prepare for when the dusk shall come. Anchor well the night of terror and you shall sleep in the arms . . . The action of the Living Light, the substance of a brighter night. *[The teacher speaks very softly and a couple of words are difficult to transcribe.]*

*****

—you see, O forms to be. You are the Light when you respond to me. When you serve my destiny, when you know I am . . . the captain of the ship you're allowed to be. *[It is difficult to transcribe one or two words.]* To serve me well, my destiny, return to God that all may see. You are, then, the angels true. You are soul and substance sure. You bring to me. You are to be. You serve me well. You are, you see living beings yet to be. Not those fools who desire and know. They think they are in charge. No. No. You are the to-bes in the light of day. You work your job. You rest and play when you remember to obey.

*****

Hope, form to be. You are eternal, but truth you see when you obey the me that be.

*****

The curse of the has-beens, and cursed they are, is the blessing of the to-bes who carry the light of obedience to me.

*****

No man is an empty vessel until he views the vessel and sees them filled with has-beens. Then he knows how void his life seems to be.

*****

So empty your vessel and fill it free with hope and cheer of what's to be. Obedient, loyal, and duty be those to-bes who obey thee free.

*****

Build anew your ship to be. Safe secure from storms you see. Build it strong and build it free. Build it with the angels free. Build it in their obedience for they are designed to serve thee. Build your ship for any storm. Build it strong for any port. Build your ship. Hoist the sail. Let it sail and heaven see.

*****

Builder, build your ship to be that it may sail and ever be free from the reefs that tempt to shore and ground you as it has before. Builder, build your ship to see that you may sail and ever be.

*****

The eternity of hope is the light of reason. The light of reason is the duty of service. And the duty of service is the obedience of the law, which is the Light, the Love, and the Life.

*****

Transgression of the Law of Obedience is known to man as discouragement, the loss of hope.

*****

For transgression of the Law of Obedience is in truth interruption and failure in the Law of Continuity.

*****

Which, my children, you clearly see is the lack in faith and joy of duty.

*****

The equator of creation, the way in, the way out. Remember the veil of illusion. The equator or equalization of creation, the neutralization, the fullness is the freedom.

*****

The design, divine, becomes the form. And the form must be filled for the design that is divine to free the form designed to serve.

*****

How does one educate it? How does one educate a desire if they feel they cannot fulfill it? Think and think and think more deeply. Design divine must be fulfilled. Design divine is movement, and therefore man moves design in principle; he fills the form and serves the design, which is divine. So think and think and think more deeply that your design may be to be, not has been, not what you see, but design divinity.

*****

[The following teachings were given to a larger group of students.]

Truth, like air, is difficult to hold. So remember, what you think you hold is far from truth, but it is falsehood.

*****

So bladder beware of tooth and nail.

*****

For that's how you hold on.

*****

To desire unfulfilled.

*****

The divinity of d—the divinity of desire is the disaster of its release.

*****

Man calls that freedom.

*****

It takes place in hell.

*****

And sends us joyously to heaven.

*****

A fool is satisfied with has-beens and is hopeful with to-bes. A wise man is filled with the bes of being.

*****

When the change of your pocket becomes the change of your head, you'll have the coinage to purchase what you desire.

*****

Whatever you have to do in life, be the director, not the dictator, and you will not experience the struggle of survival.

*****

Reason is a director and regret, a dictator.

*****

So that which has been regrets the being, but that which is to be can be directed by the light of reason.

*****

Which has no need.

*****

Yes, Truth is Light. And Light is Life. And Life is Love. And that moves, for it is being. Death is that which holds [and] destroys itself for it consumes its own being.

*****

Just hold a thought and see how much you are consumed.

*****

Whoever holds a thought and descends knows the place of its birth.

*****

Therefore, ideas that fly to heaven are far more precious than thoughts descending to hell.

*****

For the law reveals that all things return to their source of origin.

*****

It's called the awakening of personal responsibility.

*****

There are three panes of glass to the lamp of honesty. They are care, kindness, and consideration.

*****

Known as spirit, soul, and body.

*****

Half-truths are more detrimental than no truths, for they are cloaked in the light. And being so cloaked, they easily deceive.

*****

So be not fooled in the rush of illusion called time and do your duty halfway. And you know what I mean.

*****

In man's need to improve, he sees no reason to repeat what he already knows and, in that delusion, breaks the back of the Law of Continuity, which leads him to victory and freedom from bondage.

*****

So do your duty and don't despair for death is waiting if you don't care.

*****

So, students, what's the opposite of despair? *[After a short pause, the teacher continues.]* Someone answer.

Joy.

Hope. [Multiple students respond.]

Hope! Hope: the opposite of despair. And how does one sustain hope?

[A student responds but it is difficult to transcribe his response.]

*****

The sustenance of hope is the freedom from what has been or the thought of what is to be. It's called the be-ing, Truth, you are.

*****

[The following teachings were given to a very small group of advanced students.]

Rounded hearts go round and round. They can't descend and go on down.

*****

The pleasure of a job is dependent on the motive of the duty.

*****

The past is buggy and wormy from our need and failure to control it. It is beautiful for those who gave it to God. It returns from God with all its joy and beauty to begin anew in the joy of life.

FEBRUARY 11, 1983

Class February 13, 1983

[The following teachings were given to a small group of advanced students.]

One does not fear what they will become when they know what they already are.

*****

Illusion fears what it cannot control.

*****

The word, the word *identified* in truth means indentured by.

*****

Identification, the process of i-denting or indenting, imprinting upon consciousness design, becomes indentured in the limit of mental substance in formation of the fulfillment of the imprint within consciousness. Therefore, man's identification, through error, has become indentured.

*****

The heartbeat of a being is the reflection of the pulsation of the being, the imprint in consciousness, the entrance into the substance of illusion. Therefore, when the heartbeat, the reflection, is too fast or too slow, it is out of harmony with the original purpose of the imprint in the substance of illusion. One then should take heed, become aware of their reflection or reaction of the imprint in illusion to thought substance, so-called circumstances and conditions that they have permitted themselves to enter in consciousness. The pulsation must remain harmonious to its original imprint, for that lack of harmony, in time, brings about release from the substance, the curtain of illusion.

*****

When what we should do is contrary to what we do do, then we experience discord for we are separated from what we be. And what we be is a harmonious flow of impulsation of the being in accord with the be.

*****

Infinite Intelligence, the perfect balance of electromagnetic power, moves or impulses; that is known as motivation or movement. This electric power impinging upon the essence of design, which is magnetic force, becomes the magnet which attracts from the substance of illusion and cloaks or forms itself as thought form. Thought form, being a magnetic force, attracts and pulls like kind unto itself. It's known as retrospin. This process is known to man as experiences of life. To bring about a neutralization requires a return to the source of origin and to spin this electric power in equal proportion to the magnetic form in order that man may free himself from the bondage of the forms that have captured him.

*****

Take heed, instead of need, and you'll find your way to heaven.

*****

In a mental world of illusion, the forms we create to serve us, we're destined in time to destroy in order that they may save us.

*****

The forms, my friends, the barricades, they're known as judgments. We believe our judgments for they are the children we have formed from the substance of illusion to serve us in our days of ignorance. That's how we experience the intelligent Energy called God. And time, the illusion, marches on. And those barricades, those judgments, we work, through pain and suffering, to destroy. For as we evolve, their destruction is our salvation.

*****

Between the rungs of the ladder of eternity is what you call space. Empty and void. Be of good cheer, the next rung of the ladder you shall step upon.

*****

He who identifies with the difficulties of change, the Law of Evolution, indentures himself to the struggle and strife of life and, in so doing, loses the goodness of joy.

*****

[The following teachings were given to a larger group of students who regularly volunteered at the temple Sunday nights.]

—that, that reliance is reliance on experience. That determination relies on experience, past experience. And I wonder if you could tell us a little more on how to really rely on God.

Well, in reference to your question and statement, there, that we had said that reliance is dependent upon past experience, there is no set law that everyone's reliance is on past experience. That's dependent on your need. Now, I spoke a little while ago in reference to ... that ... *[The teacher pauses for several seconds.]* Shut it off. *[The teacher refers to the microcassette recorder.]*

*****

You see, all things are dependent upon motive. Motive is movement. And that's what consciousness is, the river of life in its movement. So, all things are dependent upon motive. So, you must ask yourself what is the motive for desiring to rely on God rather than past experiences. What is the motive? Now if, in honesty in our conscience, we see, "Now, my motive here, to rely upon what I understand or call God, is to return to the source of good that I may have the experiences thereof," [then that is one motive.] "Or is my motive to be freed from the lessons of transgressions that I have established in my evolution?"

*****

Now if your answer, with your little lamp of honesty, is the latter, then the continuity of experiences are guaranteed. If your answer is the former, then there is, of course, no experience to be concerned with, for your faith is now on the great circle of the divine Law of Return, for that's where you now be.

*****

—been using the term divine Infinite Intelligence. *And I'd like to know if that should be, like, divine Eternal Intelligence since we now understand infinity to be in the closet of illusion?*

Well, infinity is not the closet; infinity is infinity. Man creates a closet in infinity. But the closet is certainly not infinity.

*****

And in reference to your question on Divinity, Divinity is ultimate or final authority. That's what Divinity is: ultimate authority of Goodness. That's what's Divine.

*****

Questions are short and answers are long to those in truth who know no wrong. We ask a question. It rises from our consciousness, is censored by all our judgments and has-beens, and we present, with the life-giving energy of the spoken word, a form to support, of course, the censorship that has risen in the presentation of the form created. Not the form designed, but the form created. And so we find a house divided against itself, spiritual and mental. Therefore, answers to those in truth must be long, for they must share and cast the Light upon the many forms that have censored the truth that has risen within the consciousness of the questioner. So bladder beware. Deception is ever with us.

*****

It is impossible to experience reliance separate from motivation.

*****

Nothing in life is difficult until we think about it. And when we think about it, oh blessed is the brain and pride of the thought of I.

*****

The true meaning of the word *identification* is indentured. We are indentured to whatever we identify with.

*****

In the thought and consideration of identification, one must pause and think more deeply. The I that you are dents itself into the illusion you become, and you are then aware of the illusion; you are then form. Therefore, without the pause to awaken, you become the blink of the eye of eternity and in the blink, the darkness, the form, the obligation.

*****

The depth of your thought is the degree of light you cast in the closet of infinity.

*****

So fathom well what you think, that your thoughts be not hollow from hell.

*****

For hollow thoughts lack the substance of the spiritual design and do not serve their true intent.

*****

So now you know. Full thoughts containing consideration are in truth ideas.

*****

Forms which contain their original design are worthy of use. Forms which have lost, by error, their original design are worthy of where all rubbish should go.

*****

In reference to your question, How much more time do they have? And you're speaking now of the shadows of the past?
Of the senses.
Well, in reference to your question, How much more time in truth anything has? is dependent entirely upon our love of and bondage to illusion, delusion, deception, and self-deception, which the question, of course, reveals.

*****

All the preceding may be summed up, as we clearly see, in what is called the thought of I.

*****

Irritation, the process through which the eternal divine soul is awakened in consciousness, actually is the upheaval of all the has-beens and to-bes as they are taken by the light of reason, grabbed by the feet, and shaken until they lie down and take a rest.

*****

As a question rises in consciousness, all the has-beens and all the to-bes rush in to use it for their benefit. If the has-beens win in the battle as the question rises, then the question reveals a need of supporting, of course, what has been. If, on the other hand, the to-bes manage to win out as the question rises, then they want to know how much longer will it be.

*****

Has-beens use discouragement as their line of defense. To-bes use encouragement for theirs. So remember how great and good it used to be and feed the has-beens the feast of a lifetime.

*****

The difference between resigning and designing is the light of reason.

*****

But that takes effort.

*****

Has-beens offer satisfaction and sleep. To-bes, the dream of tomorrow. So a wise man, looking at the dream of tomorrow and the sleep of yesterday, becomes very irritated.

*****

When the magnetism of sleep (yesterday) and the electric power of dreaming (tomorrow) balance themselves, we awaken and be in God enthused.

*****

An abundant good no longer is concern.

*****

He who gives up everything gets what he needs, not what he wants.

*****

How much of anything we have depends, of course, on how big and how uneducated our ego really is.

*****

Bladder beware is soul prepare.

*****

An uneducated ego is the king of deception.

*****

For it is constantly conceiving.

*****

Its need is so great for it's empty and void, not aware of its purpose of being.

*****

Study the goose and you'll know what it's like.

*****

Only a fool would follow a goose.

*****

Loose as a goose is the love of self.

*****

Don't put on a shelf whatever in life has served its purpose.

*****

For by so doing, you are indentured to decay.

*****

Indentures, like teeth, are very determined.

*****

Their bills are always due.

*****

And that is known as the debt of ignorance.

*****

Pride, like brass, is in constant need of polish.

*****

For brass is the deceiver of gold, the wisdom of life.

*****

You note that brass appears to be what it is not.

*****

And so pride, like the goose, you're not worthy of following.

*****

Pride, like brass, is in constant need of polish. Otherwise, pathetic thing, it will show its true color.

*****

People who do not show their feelings are petrified of tarnishing their brass.

*****

And so are people who fear honesty.

*****

Motion, once directed to the thought of I, becomes emotion.

*****

The cause of a forked-tongue is the has-beens and the to-bes. This is why it is said God's greatest work is done in silence.

*****

And so, of course, silence is golden or gold. It is not the brass that is polished by the forked-tongue of has-beens and to-bes.

*****

We face the light of opportunity with all our to-bes, only to turn our back and serve our has-beens.

*****

Until the day we awaken and carry the banner of personal responsibility.

*****

The declaration of divinity is the acceptance of the authority of Good.

*****

The only thing that denies us our right of Good, the Divinity, the authority thereof, is our has-beens and to-bes.

*****

The very first step in gaining control is personal responsibility: the ability to personally respond to whatever we choose.

*****

The golden fleece is the strength of wisdom.

*****

Reason flows freely through communication.

*****

Leave them confused in the arms of God; they'll begin to think more deeply.

*****

When a person doesn't know what you're going to do, their defenses have no value.

*****

It's known as keeping them off-guard.

*****

Off-guard, on God; sail to brighter shores.

*****

The degree of fear, of course, is dependent upon the reliance of our mind.

*****

Sadness is when the has-beens lay down in defeat.

*****

Gladness is when the to-bes awaken for breakfast.

*****

Joy is when we no longer think of self.

*****

Don't be a turkey and gobble for Thanksgiving. *[Some students laugh.]*

*****

The difference between a turkey and a goose is the turkey prepares for his day of sacrifice, but the goose shares constantly.

FEBRUARY 13, 1983

Class February 14, 1983

When the love and need of Good or God is dependent upon the thought of man, we're destined to enter the realms of hell.

*****

Man enters the state of consciousness known as heaven when, through the power of his will, he removes from mental substance the thought of need.

*****

The question, then, must be asked, How does man remove from his consciousness the thought of need? My children, it's so simple: your love of God removes all thought of need.

*****

[The following teachings may have been given to a very small group of advanced students.]

I am I and thou art thee. Because I am, I be; I be freed from all insanity. Because I am, I be, I be. No need, no want, desire to be. Because I am, I am the be. Because I am free, I'm free. Freed from all insanity. Because I am, I be; I see the Life, the Love. I am, I be. I be. I be.

*****

Record, please. Record, please.
Round hearts roll to heaven. Pointed hearts drive to hell.

*****

The pain of the mind is the joy of the soul, for the pain of the mind is the starvation of the has-beens.

*****

Caution is the servant of discernment.

*****

Careful means the fullness of care.

*****

Dreams are dens of despair, lacking action. Then let your soul act and let your mind be. And know the peace and learn to see.

*****

There is no discernment when dictate is the rule.

*****

Do not seek for something greater when you tenaciously refuse to give up what you think you have.

*****

Whoever tempts to control the river of life shall be drowned by it.

FEBRUARY 14, 1983

Class February 15, 1983

The meaning of identification (i-dent) is to imprint upon consciousness; indenture; obligated to. Choose wisely what you identify with, for your obligations shall return as debts to be paid. It's known as transgressions of divine Law of Motive.

*****

The I that you are dents the veil of illusion, and that is called the thought of I. That indenture man knows as identification. He is now in the realm of illusion. He is identified. He is the thought of I. Therefore, he now is the illusion called form. He now has entered the bondage of self where he must serve his creations 'til he declares his divinity. And the declaration of divinity is acceptance of the authority of Good, which is the I that you are and not what you believe you are.

*****

—words on your paper. "I declare my divine right: the acceptance of the authority of Good now." Period. Write—flood your consciousness with that declaration and write down the five things that enter into your being.

*****

Now stop and think. The first thing you have written is subject to the deception, the first line of defense of deception, called justification. Read on, and see the excuses that your mind has [on] why you have not the good yet.

*****

Born in the darkness of deception, they only serve to deceive. Therefore, they justify when the Light of Truth shines.

*****

They will play this back later for all of you.[29]

Application of the Living Light Philosophy appears to be difficult for most people because in the effort to apply the truth they have received and in keeping with the teachings you have already been given, as your mind records the truth, the has-beens, those forms without soul that you serve each time you permit yourself to enter the illusion—and you cannot enter it without the thought of I. You cannot sustain the illusion and become the delusion and the deception without the belief that you are the thought of I, instead of the I. So, each time you enter, you deceive yourself by serving what has been. And what has been will not permit what is to be (in plain words, change in your consciousness) unless what is to be is in harmony with the design and form of what has already been in any area of your life. Therefore, when you go to apply the truth, you must understand and realize, when you go to make a change within your consciousness, the process of what is really taking place.

How do you overcome that? Well, you must pause and think. What does your mind say to you when you choose to have something better in your life? It tells you it is not possible without certain things taking place, which are subject to something beyond your control. Therefore, those forms leave you hopeless and leave you discouraged; and they continue to be your masters.

Now, that is one of the things they tell you.

Say, for example, you want to make a change. You're not sure whether that change is going to be as good as what you think you already have; yet, what you think you already have, you already want to change from. But then, you're not sure whether or not, if you make [that] change, if it's going to be better than what you have. Then, what you think you have rises up to tell you how good what you have already is; therefore, there is no need, there is no reason for you to make any change. There is no reason in any way, shape, or form unless someone you truly believe in has already paved the way, has already proven to the satisfaction of your mind, of your own has-beens, that somehow they can accept those to-bes that you are considering in making a change and they can twist them around to fit the parameters that they are going to allow these potential to-bes to live in.

Now that takes place with you all the time. Therefore, when you face the possibility of changing a job, the possibility of buying a new pair of shoes, the possibility of getting a new coat, the possibility of changing your heating system, and go on down the list, you have to become aware of all those forms that you have been serving and you are indentured or obligated to, for you gave them birth in your own illusion.

Now if you are willing to place your faith in something that is greater, in an authority that is demonstrably good, that is sustaining, without personality or partiality, the very blade of grass that grows, the lily in the field, the breath that you breathe, that sustains every single thought you choose to make, whether it be one of ignorance or wisdom, if you, in your pause to think more deeply, will direct your sight to the Power that is demonstrable, that without the Power even your own has-beens would not live, if you are willing to direct your view, your attention, your energy to that demonstrable truth that is your very breath of life, then there is the possibility that you can gain control over the crew that's running your own ship, your boat of your soul, aground.

But only you can do that through application of constant effort.

You face changes many times a day. If they are in keeping with what you already believe—because your belief is indispensable to the has-beens controlling your soul. If you really believe that it is possible for you to make a change and that change, you are aware within your consciousness, is causing you doubt, fear, turmoil, justification that the change absolutely and positively could not be beneficial—How could it be? You have yet to experience it—then, if you're willing and ready and able—and you are always able depending on how you direct your will. Your will is ever directed by your own belief. Now your will is the will and the power of God. You are not absent of it. You are not lacking in it. You are using it constantly. Unfortunately, [you are] using it without conscious awareness, where the light of reason truly flows.

Now if you are willing to use your will through the form of belief—for that is how will flows—if you're willing and ready to do that, then all of life, the goodness therein, is yours waiting to be when you *be* what you truly are: the Light of Truth and not the things you believe you are.

*****

So close to Valentine's Day. Round hearts roll to heaven. Pointed hearts, they dive to hell.

*****

While pointed hearts demand control, round hearts keep on, keep on roll.

*****

Remember the words of has-beens: "No need to change." "I'm not sure it's going to work." "Things weren't so bad in the good old days." "I was doing all right. Had no problems." *[Several students laugh.]* "I might lose." "What do I have to gain for sure?" Listen to the has-beens, and you'll become aware of your own self-deception. Thank you.

*****

"And what the heck, why should I take a chance anyway?"

*****

"I've tried for years. I don't see any benefit. Why should I change? I've already tried for years." Well, if you had really tried, you'd already know the change, for God's sakes.

*****

"I don't think I'm growing at all." Of course not. The has-beens aren't in charge.

*****

Has-beens don't see any change at all. You feel the same way you always felt.

*****

They're telling you who's still in charge. That's what they're telling you.

*****

Now you know why self-pity is the most destructive force in the universe: it is giving your lifeblood to soulless creatures.

*****

We are often foolish and seldom wise.

*****

We all know the lazy man's way to the hope of truth: it's called convenience.

*****

The spirit of spontaneity is the unobstructed flow while the has-beens are sleeping, taking their nap from their great feast.

*****

Why is the bridge to understanding the unexpected? *[After a short pause, the teacher continues.]* You can leave it on. *[The teacher refers to the microcassette tape recorder.]* Why? Does anybody know why the bridge to understanding—Yes.

The mind doesn't have a chance to control it. Doesn't know what is coming; so, it can't control it.

That's right. When the has-beens don't know, God gets through. Now you understand what he means when he says when you don't know, the good gets in. Keep the senses busy while the truth flows unobstructed. *[The "he" the teacher refers to is the Wise One.]*

*****

Because when the senses are busy, the turkeys and the goose are gobbling.

*****

And while they gobble, your little soul has a chance.

*****

Now you know when you do what your has-beens want you to do, you feel so good. Because they're eating up a storm and your little soul is sliding on to God.

*****

We don't recommend such license. We recommend self-control, a better way.

*****

Show me the person who says they don't feel good when they're doing what they think they want to do, little knowing they're serving all the things that used to be.

*****

Then we wonder about change, the Law of Evolution. And wonder why we're not growing harmoniously or aware thereof.

*****

—form.
That's right.
The little soul is sliding up to God.
That's right. They're all busy. That's right, [Student Q]. Tell me the moment you do what you want to do you don't feel good. [Student Q]? *[After a short pause, the teacher continues.]* What you really want to do. Now when you do what you want to do, you feel good. Right?
Right.
In that moment you know God, which is goodness. Right?
Oh, OK.
So, the has-beens are eating up their storm; they're out of the way and you feel good.

*****

—we do recommend, which has already been given: a much better way. Declare the truth. Let them rise up and say, "Listen. No, I have a right to good. That is *my* divinity. *You* go back to sleep with all your deception, with all your lies, with all your cheating, with all your delusion. I will feed you when I want to feed you. And I will feel good, know God, when I consciously choose to feel good and know God, and I am no longer dependent on your dictates."

*****

That's called self-control.

*****

The effect of which is known as freedom. And now we know freedom from what.

*****

This is the application: the way to apply it intelligently. You already have the truth. Now you got the bridge to understanding is the unexpected. Now you know the good gets in when you don't expect it. Because the only thing that expects anything is not you. It's those has-beens on guard duty right around the clock to kick out anything that doesn't fit in with them.

*****

—must stop believing you are the things that were designed to serve a purpose long ago. They're old and weary, but still as tenacious as your will. Because it's your will power flowing through your belief that sustains them. It's your power. And it's your right to use it the way you consciously choose to use it. But you [are] going to have to learn how to create belief!

*****

—been given to you years ago. Use the process of visualization. Know beyond a shadow of any doubt by consciously directing your will power!

That's it. *[The teacher may be addressing the recording technician.]*

*****

Good Lord, you want a yellow rose? There's the yellow rose. If you can't see it, you don't know how to direct your will yet, for God's sakes. You don't know how to create. Only in realms that are eating up all of your energy, the power you need to create your being to be. That's sad. That is not only sad, it is pathetic because you refuse to step upon the plateau of objectivity that you may see who you are, not what you *think* you are, which in truth is what has already been.

*****

You can't be great, until you believe in greatness and then your divine right to it. You can't be good, 'til you believe in goodness and your divine right to it. You cannot be the abundance which, the truth is, you are, until you believe you are. So start believing and then start knowing.

*****

And don't ever believe in the Law of Transgression that interferes with the beliefs and the rights of another eternal soul.

*****

God gave you charge over all creation. All of *your* creation. You do not create an eternal soul. You create forms by the millions, numbers beyond belief. But eternal souls, you cannot create and, therefore, have no right to take charge over.

*****

Because you have already received the creative principle and because application in the light of reason clearly reveals the process of visualization in creation, then it would be [a] transgression to deny you the opportunity of effort and application.

*****

In other words, I would have to pay for you when I got enough to pay for myself.

*****

I am basically a conservative person.

*****

He who is not receptive to broadening is certainly in bondage to his has-beens.

*****

So, broaden your horizons and put your has-beens in the cellblock number nine, where they belong. That means all of them.

*****

That's one thing about hell: it's ever in need of company. *[Many students laugh.]*

*****

Eyes, designed for awareness, are subject to what the has-beens will permit us to view, and then they interpret to serve their purpose.

*****

Has-beens demonstrate constantly the absolute continuity of the Law of Dedication. They're dead to anything they don't want. And they only want what they're born to get.

*****

The best way to be freed from has-beens is constant change: the unexpected.

*****

And after they rise, expose them. The irritation of them wakes the soul beautifully.

*****

What the has-been tells us, what they tell us after we've had exposure and our little soul is freed, they tell us, "Huh! I won't do that again!"[30] *[Many students laugh.]*

*****

Has-beens have a lot of hope that they can get their way. So, they just keep right on trying, 'til someday they finally lie down to rest.

*****

It's called the tenacity of tooth and nail.

*****

Of course, we clearly see the reason man experiences hope for many things and wakes up to the disaster and failure thereof is because his little to-bes got strangled by the throat with all his has-beens.

*****

Has-beens, like dirt, hide in corners because they feel secure when they're with their familiarity.

*****

Like little children, they always hide in corners.

*****

Because they fear what they cannot see. And if there's a wall protecting them, behind them, to the left, and to the right, then they don't have as much fear because now they can see if anything comes.

*****

Has-beens are very insecure for they know you just might change your mind.

*****

It is the insecurity of the has-beens that cause you the experience known as fear when you go to do anything new or different.

*****

Fear is faith in mental substance (has-beens) and the absolute conviction (belief) in what they have to offer, even though you know it's the same old, ah, stuff.

*****

In this sense, *dent* means to impinge or imprint upon. So when you *i-dent-i-fy*, you indenture yourself (are obligated to) what you imprint upon. For example, you imprint upon the illusion and form the thought which you believe that you are; therefore, are ident—ident—indentured to the form of the, of the thought, which is the illusion you have impinged or imprinted upon.

*****

Has-beens are the greatest losers of all time. They lose anything and everything that they don't already have. And what they already have is what has already been.

*****

[The following teachings may have been given to a very small group of advanced students.]

We have listened attentively to your explanation and wish to share understanding on the need of the boat to be so long in the fire center, for it needs great power to send it all the way up the river to celestial realms of consciousness.

*****

All has-beens are orphans, bastards. They live in the water center, created in the magnetic field. Their fathers (electric) are back in the light of reason. And they stay away from their father because they know if the light shines, they [have] got to grow or go.

*****

Has-beens, like snowflakes in the sunlight, melt and become rivers of life that flow into the ocean of joy.

*****

The value of freedom is the diligence of effort. Freedom is the expression of truth. And truth is revealed in the continuity of reason.

*****

In the place where there are no shadows, there you be. The fullness of life, called joy, is the be in the Light that you are. So, in the be, joy, the fullness of life, is your awakening.

FEBRUARY 15, 1983

Class February 16, 1983

[The following teachings may have been given to a very small group of advanced students.]

The pillars of understanding rest on the foundation of wisdom, the beauty and loyalty, the royalty of the purple pillars rest on the humble goal of the foundation. And as they rise into the heavens, the Light of Truth, reflecting from the wisdom, gives a glow of greatness to the beauty of the pillars of understanding.

*****

All who enter must wear the robes of white. Purity is total acceptance. No shadow is in the way of the will of God.

*****

And so, life flows abundantly in the Academy of Truth. No judgments. No shadows. No yesterday. No tomorrow. Love is the Light. And Light, its expression is Life.

*****

So let the thirst of your soul bathe in the waters of life, as a newborn babe is washed in the spring waters at the morning dew.

*****

Remember the fountain exercise. Remember the beautiful colors. Vibrations are ever dependent on your own effort to still the mind and be in the moment you be. For joy, which is the fullness of life, is expressed when there are no thoughts, no have-beens, just bes. For in the be, your consciousness, the river flow is unobstructed. No concern. No expectation. The be of fullness is the joy of all expression.

*****

As the river flows, forms, has-beens rush, rush to the shore from the depths of the jungle to lap up, with their insatiable thirst, the flowing river. And that needed for fullness, man indeed is short of.

*****

That need not be, if his consciousness be in the moment it be. No thought of yesterday. No thought of tomorrow. No forms to lap the river and leave him short of his divinity.

*****

Get out of concern and you'll never waste again.

*****

[The teacher left no instructions regarding the formatting of the teachings. So, it may be prudent to read the stanzas below as though they had been formatted as text.]

    Temple of Truth, O Temple of Light
    Temple of Good, O Temple of Right.
    All purple and gold, you shine in the night.
    O Temple of Truth, O Temple of Light
    O Temple of gold, O purple so bright.
    Temple of Truth, Temple of Light
    Many are called to awaken here
    Freed from sorrow, freed from fear.
    Temple of Truth, Temple of Light
    Pure is your gold,
    Right as the pillars that shine in the night.
    O Temple of Truth, O Temple of Light
    May you enter and be; there you will see
    Life filled with love. Joy you be.
    Names you forget, places you've been
    Arrive and enter. Be therein.

O Temple of Truth, O Temple of Light
You are the Love. You are the Light.
O Temple of Truth, O Temple of Light
You are my armor in darkness the night.
O Temple of Truth, O Temple of Light
Wise, your understanding. Just, your right.
Temple of Truth, O Temple of Light
Shine on forever, your love is so bright.

*****

One in the Light. Two in the night.
Be Temple of Truth. Be one and be right.
Shine on forever, throughout infinity.
Temple O Temple, be, O be, O be.

*****

When you speak the truth "O be," you establish the law: Obey the authority of good. Obey means "O be."

FEBRUARY 16, 1983

Class February 17, 1983

[The following teachings may have been given to a very small group of advanced students.]

Healing is in truth a feeling of good when the river flows unobstructed.

*****

A wise man uses "O be" before the has-beens get to see.

*****

They have destroyed the pillars of the temple of truth, and in so doing, they crawl upon the floor like snakes that crawl and not coiled for wisdom.

*****

Crawling snakes, deceiving ways, they lost the spring of the coil to heaven.

*****

A river turns as it flows. Open your eyes that you may know.

*****

You must look *through* the water, not *to* the water, to see the coil of the power that is.

*****

You see the manifestation and not its triune faculty: atom, electron, molecule. Movement. Turning, turning, turning!

*****

Record.

One must learn to move when the river flows. And when the river flows, the soul moves. And when the soul moves, the soul evolves. And as it evolves, the Light is brighter. And as the Light is brighter, heaven is closer and man shall be the ecstasy.

*****

Go ahead.
    You are the river. You are the flow.
    And when you are, you will, you shall know.

*****

Oooooo beeeeee[31] and you will place the Light of Truth, the fires of the great furnace of the universe, and it will burn the formless creatures who do not obey the command of your light of reason. For you, in the greatest of all mantras, will take the fuel from the tree of life and fire the fuel—fuel the fires of eternity.

*****

When your mantra, in duration and frequency—

*****

—equals the fires of your furnace, you'll be filled and free.

*****

The reason why the has-beens obey the great mantra of truth is because they know you, when you be, are the Light and the Truth. The fires of eternity, burning fully in the furnace of infinity, when you enter that great Light and you tell them, through declaration and demonstration, "O Be," they obey or are purified in the fires they know and fear more than anything. Their very survival is at stake.

*****

And that is why the mantra, the entire temple must vibrate with its great power. That is why the furnace must burn fully.

That is why the air must flow freely, that the fires be fueled to burn them in every nook and crevice and every corner where they live! That is the great power of the mantra, for that, my child, is the frequency of response to the truth you are.

*****

Thought force is the form of the divine life energy cloaked over design. As the force, from lack of use, continues to grow, it consumes the creator of the design. And unless neutralization is established within the consciousness of the creator (man), the living force of the form called thought force consumes the individual.

*****

The consumption of the individual, of course, is compounded if it involves the thought form, the force, [of] another person. And so anyone who is the victim of thought force must go deep within themselves and redirect the life-giving energy in principle to be free from the thought force. They must awaken their conscience—their spiritual awakening—and choose that which is principle in order that the energy, which the thought form is creating, the consumption force over their consciousness, can be dissipated.

*****

Anyone who finds themself the victim of thought force, realizing that it is a form created by living *prana*, must assure themself of the rhythmic flow and freedom of the *prana* throughout their being, for the great dangers of building it up is only strengthening the force under which they are being attacked.

*****

Be cautious and on guard during the flow not to permit energy, without conscious awareness, to go to the very thought force that you are being attacked by.

*****

All seed is electric power contained, enclosed in magnetism.

*****

And comes forth in a world in which the magnet reigns supreme.

*****

The beautiful ships of white, gold, and purple that sail upon the heavenly seas, those are the ships set out from the temple to gather the souls to live and be!

*****

The substance from which the ships of heaven are formed is the living *prana* that enters celestial realms, where we may gather it and form it to save the souls.

*****

So, you see, my child, what the forms of mental substance do not steal is ofttimes sufficient to make but one sail. But enough gathering, enough sails, we fashion and build the bow, the stern. And then the boat is ready. So guardian angels, they guard the port that thieves may not steal the Living Light. That, my good friend, *is* substance: the *Living Light,* for it is Light that *lives* in substance that glows everywhere.

*****

The ballast of our ship is formed from the living substance that contains reason.

*****

Be reasonable and not so emotional and the thieves will not get in.

*****

Perhaps now you understand why we asked you not to be so wasteful.

*****

Shadows, like old soldiers, take quite a time to die.

*****

But let us never forget, they are no longer the substance of form. Just the waning shadows thereof. And wane and wane, they shall.
[After a short pause, the teacher continues.]
What is it?

*****

All has-beens are old soldiers and they always fight tooth and nail.

*****

O little children of the Light
Bathing in the river bright
Little children of the Light
Swim on up the stream
Passed and through the night
Awaken in the dawn
So beautiful, so free, so clear.
Awaken. Come ashore
And be and be and be
Children, children of the Living Light
You are serving day, not night.

Children, children of the Living Light
Ships will fashion out along the sea
Saving souls, both you and me
Someday the efforts of all mankind
Will no longer go in vain
Heaven is descending upon the planet Earth
Brighter days are dawning.
There's indeed a joyous birth.

*****

The new birth is the drastic change taking place already in the transfer of the living force, through expression, that is necessary to make way for the Illumined One, who is on his way.

And who is the Illumined One?

Out of the East a star shall rise. It shall rise and awaken mankind. It shall shock societies by the number. He shall awaken the sleeping world in understanding the purpose of life. He shall be known as weird and strange. His powers so great they'll bow. Something that's right, compassionate. And judgment shall die wherever he walks, wherever he goes, though his life be strange to society's judgments and bondage. For he walks alone and his expression is unacceptable, but his power and Light, they cannot deny. So listen they shall to the words he speaks. He's on his way. Seventy-six years from this time ... day.[32]

*****

O little seeds, oh, don't you see?
You are the seeds of eternity.
What you do, your effort be
Is not in vain. It serves, you see.
For what you do in what you be
The ways of old eternity.

Though small the little seeds you be
You demonstrate the wisdom be
And so across the lands of earth
The change is coming for the new birth.
That which old and long has gone
Returns, returns and rises to the mountain of victory
Society, society bound and trapped in all they see
Society, society, you die your ways. They serve not me.
Society, society, the Light is coming for all to see.
The change from depths of despair, the change it be.
You're paving the way, you and me.
You're paving the way, the words not spoken.
You're part of many who are already are token.
Token of the Light on earth.
Doing what they know is divine and natural.
Be.
You're told that you may serve so well
And serve far greater than all of hell
You're told that you may be, may be
Encouraged, encouraged that you may see.

*****

All right.

The magnetic soul in form at the time and moment for its journey home, placing the temple with the pillars high that the souls of understanding may view heaven above, opens wide the door of wisdom for the entrance of the function of understanding and, in so doing, is filled with the Light, the Life, the Love, the Truth of the river and, therefore, rises high in consciousness to heavenly realms of ecstasy. *[Please consider the possibility that a more accurate transcription could be "the soles of understanding."]*

*****

OK.

Fools, they try and try again. Wise men be and being see. Let fools keep trying waiting to be, while beings be and be and be!

*****

That which is designed to be the magnetic attraction for wise to see is the retrospin which you may be. And in so being, fill joy to see.

*****

When one is one instead of two
No mist can be to cloud the view
For they are Light and Light shall be
All the things and joy to see
When one is one, they're not the two
For they are one, and one is true.
So let it be the one, the you
Let them be, let them be
Sailing smoothly on the sea
They came from upper river see
Let them sail and let them be
The port is waiting, calling, calling
You and me

*****

OK.

The snake that crawls must naturally coil,
Electrified beyond the boil
For then wisdom, you shall be
Receptacle of coiled and free
For you are that designed to be
The instrument of center see

The sun, the Light, the power that moves
The little boat upstream
Far, far, far across the open sky
Beyond, beyond, beyond the die
Beyond the thought, the thought of I
You're designed to sail serene
The rocket of life, the be
Far, far to heaven's heights
And there you'll rest throughout the nights.

*****

Record?

Yes.

The difference between hold and have is quite simple. Have is share and hold is bind. And what we share is good and fine. Don't hold, but have. Have your right. Don't hold and hold and be the night, when have and have you share and right. O, look at have, let go of hold and you will see how great and bold your soul it be. Everything, the universe, the love, the life, the light, so joyful. O, be.

Unicorn of good. O unicorn so strong. Remember, child, let the form turn the souls, the feet of understanding, to the light of heaven. Hold them high with the courage of the shoulders of the house of clay. *[Again, please consider the possibility that a more accurate transcription may be "the soles."]*

*****

They have destroyed the pillars of the temple of truth. Destroyed it in ignorance born from laziness. Sad, but temples yet there be throughout the universe I see. Temples strong and temples true. That's your temple. Believe in you.

Of course, as one transforms, they transfigure. That's called the process of evolution. Be grateful the mind doesn't see what the spirit of be.

*****

—that keeps us right. Never heavy, always light. That's happiness and right.

*****

The workers win. They unload their cargo before their ship sinks.

*****

Yes.

Now in time for the affirmation, do it frequently. In time the entire temple will respond. From the very tips of your hair to the very tips of your toes, everything, *everything*, within the house, the temple you reside in, will respond. And then, you'll never again, ever, be concerned about making the alignment between you, the be, and the has-beens that block you—

Yes.

—the view.

Good.

FEBRUARY 17, 1983

Class February 18, 1983

[The following teachings were given to the larger group of students who regularly volunteered at the temple on Friday nights.]

The bridge to understanding being the unexpected, a wise man prepares before his desires fall into mental boxes, which are caused by the thought of I. And those who place themselves in mental boxes fear, for they know the bondage of entrapment.

*****

Judgment is the indispensable ingredient necessary to bind the soul in the illusion of mental substance.

*****

For judgment is the servant of the thought of I.

*****

And denial of the right and the will of God, which is total acceptance.

*****

How does a wise man prepare so his desires don't fall into mental boxes?
In reference to your question, "How does a wise man prepare so his desires do not fall into mental boxes?" by recognizing and accepting the demonstrable truth that desire is the divine expression. Being divine, it has no denials. Therefore, man could not possibly fall into mental boxes until he transgresses the divine law, which is the law of God.

*****

—know your duty? Question: How do you know your duty? is really quite simple: when you have no longer the question of what duty is.

*****

One only questions, "What is my duty?" when the mind is in control, for it is only the mind that does not know. The soul knows why we're here. It knows where we've been and where we're going. And a person who questions what their duty is, is one who still relies upon the human mind or mental substance, which offers the bondage of limit, of judgment. When one does what they have to do and cares less what others think about it, then one is doing what they know they have to do, and that is known as their duty. And their little lamp of honesty shines brightly; their path is transfigured by the light of reason and there is no longer question about what they have to do.

*****

There are only two reasons why we do not question. One is we are sufficiently illuminated, meaning illumined; and the other is that we fear: our pride is at stake.

*****

In other words, we don't want the image we consider would be a fool.

*****

And so we sell our divine right to truth and freedom so cheaply.

*****

The question is asked, How does one direct one's determination to God? By first realizing and accepting determination is the expression of the divine will of God. And therefore, there's only one direction that it could possibly take.

*****

A wise man would quickly see that all other directions were in truth detours.

*****

No. Shut it—*[The teacher instructs the recording technician.]*

*****

In reference to the question, Is the belief in God and total acceptance one and the same? well, that depends on the form of your belief called God.

*****

Many people's God are very limited by parameters called judgments.

*****

Not your God.
Thank you.
In other words, is total acceptance and the belief in God one and the same? That's entirely dependent upon the questioner, because many people believe in God limited by the parameters called judgments. And therefore, one could not consider that is the freedom of total acceptance. No.

*****

Because of their ignorance.

*****

Oh, you didn't know until this moment that's what happened with your desires, did you?
No.
If you had, you wouldn't have entrapped yourself.

*****

The fear of the experience of being in mental boxes is after we get into the box, not on the descent of the desires.

*****

The lid goes on with what we call judgment, the king thereof.

*****

So in truth judgment and bondage are one and the same. You want freedom? Give up your judgments and you'll have your freedom. You want bondage? Cherish your judgments and glorify your pride.

*****

You can't have both. Don't expect to have your cake and eat it, too. It's contrary to demonstrable truth and the divine law.

*****

—*cards in the game. There's a card that says . . .*

*****

Is that what we do with our desires? That's why it becomes the denial of God?

Thank you. In reference to your question, the destiny of desire is the denial of God. Why, of course, it is. Man directs the desire, and that is the denial, into the box of judgments and consequently the entrapment and the bondage of the self.

Thank—

*****

There most certainly is. Freedom from the thought of I: the greatest affirmation you will ever know. There's no other way to be freed from those boxes with the lids of judgment.

*****

—*walk straight ahead and I say, "Well, I—this is what I'm going to do. And this is what I accept . . . without all this being bombarded, because it's judgment."* [It is difficult to transcribe one or two words.]

Yes, in reference to your question, you revealed the truth in the very first word: "When you have a judgment." Correct?

Uh-huh.

That is the first denial. Desire is the Divinity's expression. It is not man's. So the entrapment began with the first words, "When *you* have a desire." God has the desire. It flows through man.

*****

[Subm]ission[33] and the acceptance of that demonstrable truth is freedom from the entrapment. You see, children, we say, "We have a desire" or "We desire this" or "I desire that." That *is* the blindness. That *is* the self-deception. It is God['s], the Divinity's expression. You are simply registering the Divinity. That's all. And if you remember that, you will not fall into the mental boxes. From God it came; to God, you return it. If it enters mental substance, where dictate, judgment, limit, and bondage, entrapment are the destiny of mental substance, [then you are bound]. Does that help with your question?

Oh, yes. Oh, yes. Thank you.

You're welcome. Now [Student L] was next.

*****

Well, that that one says feels a lot alike to or has an affinity to is not necessarily demonstrable truth. And when the time comes for that to be revealed, in reference to awareness, it is best that we first consider the questions and class at hand.

*****

Well, what do you mean by the "unexpected" and "casting your pearls before the swine"? Do you feel, by that statement, that you unexpectedly cast your pearls before the swine? Is that the implication?

No, the implication would be that when we speak forth something that it's best to keep, those around and about you, say, a state of change or unex—or to—not to expect what, ah . . .

*****

Yes. Thank you. In reference to your question that ofttimes we expect, perhaps, some good to enter our life, the signs seem to be pointing in that direction—is that what you mean?

Yes.

And we speak it forth and then we find that we have lost it. Is that what you're referring to? *[After a short pause, the teacher continues.]* Well, first we must understand what is our *need* to give it the life-giving energy of the spoken word before it takes place within our life and is manifest unto us. We must understand what our need to do that is. Once we understand what our need is to do that, then we will understand that there is, in truth, a great need for the expression of self, which is lacking due to our unwillingness to communicate and to understand and to share. For it is fear that takes it from us, for it is fear that keeps us from communicating. It is fear that keeps us from understanding. It is fear that keeps us from freedom and the fullness of life. Does that help with your question?

*****

How can we be better dictat—directors of our lives, rather than being dictators?

That's a good question. And on that, I'll have a cup of coffee and we will pause.

*****

—yes.

Ah, how can we *be* directors rather than dictators, that we may be free rather than be bound?

*****

In reference to that question, being a director rather than a dictator, in order to intelligently direct anything, one must know the thing they have chosen to direct. And they must understand the thing they have chosen to direct. And, of course, to the fullness of their understanding is the fullness of consideration and, therefore, their ability to respond thereto. Therefore, in being a director, rather than a dictator, one moves through knowledge, mental substance, into the spiritual essence of understanding, the soul faculties, kindness, care, and consideration, the light of reason, the guidance of wisdom, truth, and the goodness of God. Then one is a director. I'm sure we are all familiar with being dictators. When you follow the simple path of the director, which takes total acceptance, humility of one's being, recorded in mental substance as humiliation to the great pride, then one is choosing, clearly, between the glory of pride and the humbleness and goodness of God.

*****

We all know what pride is: being brass, it's in constant need of polish.

*****

Weakness is revealed to all the universe by what man calls fear.

*****

Which, of course, in truth is his total dependence, total acceptance, and reliance upon mental substance that offers to him nothing but limit, known as judgment, nothing but entrapment, known as the boxes enclosing his soul, and go down the list of the strife and struggle we make of life.

*****

—question. The student has said that once we feel a desire, our minds quickly, seemingly automatically, place us into the limit of the box and the little judgment on how it shall be fulfilled, of course. That reveals to us our dependence upon and total reliance on mental substance. So, the way out of the thing is, of course, the way we got into the thing. We got into the illusion through the impingement upon the veil of illusion, and that impingement brought us to the thought of I. So, when one experiences what they call desire, which is the expression of the Divinity, one, in the moment of that awareness, recognizing the truth for what it is, the expression of the Divinity, relies upon the Divinity for its fulfillment.

*****

For whoever relies upon God knows God, is freed from concern, for they are on the circle, the great circle of the Divinity: the divine Law of Return.

*****

And their ego, their pride is not able to dictate God's Law of Return and how long it will take. For the circle in consciousness of the divine Law of Return may be as big as the universe or as small as the mustard seed. And, of course, when it's as small as the mustard seed, God returns quickly for we move quickly on such a small circle.

*****

One is constantly given the opportunity to demonstrate their faith in God or their faith in self. One demonstrates their faith in self when they know fear, and one knows fear when they don't know God. So, when you make the effort to know God, you'll be freed from fear, and the fullness of life will be a constant demonstration unto you.

*****

[The following teachings were given to a very small group of advanced students.]

The expression of all has-beens is the weakness which the soul must suffer in its evolution until such time as we awaken, through constant effort, to the light of reason, and we are then the strength, the power of the be, which is in truth God.

*****

Traps are mental boxes in which desires fall when the light of reason is extinguished by the thought of I. My dear friend, concern is the instrument and the revelation of the thought of I that builds the boxes in mental substance. Truth you are; concern you are not. Leave the boxes to those who need to fill their need that way.

Good day.

*****

My friends, thrones are designed solely for the purpose of elimination. Ah, but sailboats are designed for the enjoyment of life. So sail on, my children, and stop the sit. Enjoy your life a little bit.

*****

So now, you see, has-beens sit, while bes go sailing bit by bit.

*****

Yes, children, it's very simple. Sit and sink, or sail and swim. Life is meant to win and win.

*****

A selfish person is one who does not understand the Law of Goodness.

*****

To God, all things are possible. To judgment, all things are denial.

*****

When the will of self directs the power of God to the need of mental substance, the power becomes the force, gathers its victim, [and] returns unto itself for its own destruction.

*****

Record.

He who makes no conscious moment-by-moment effort permits the mind to enter what is known as retrospin and must pay the price of experiences in consciousness that have been, for the retrospin of mental substance is the direct opposite of the light of reason, which spins in the conscious mind. So wise are those who spin in the conscious mind and do not retrospin and relive what has been in the consciousness beneath the control of the Light.

*****

Record.

For spin you must, when the thought you be, the thought of self, the misery.

*****

For those who be shall never spin and live to see the day they win. Winners, not losers, enter the Living Light. Remember, you're a winner. Let your losers go. They give you hope and hell to live. That's all they give. That's *all* they give.

*****

My child, once again I come with a few words and perhaps a little light that you may turn the bend that you stand now at.

O suit of clay, you've had your day! My soul has found a better way to free my spirit that it may sail upon the seas of peace and good. And in the sail to chart the course to shores of joy and harmony. O suit of clay, you cry and wail. O suit of clay, you crack and crumble. O suit of clay, you've had your day, for God has shown the Light, the way.

FEBRUARY 18, 1983

Class February 20, 1983

[The following teachings were given to the larger group of students who volunteered at the temple on Sunday nights.]

The great delusion in using the Light against oneself is to accept the truth in part. For example, one says in the Truth, in the Light, "To God all things are possible," and takes that wonderful truth into the realms of limit and says, "I want this because to God all things are possible," and is unwilling to pay the price.

*****

It is self-evident that all judgments are immovable, immobable [immobile]. They sit on their throne, absolutely refusing to budge. So you can't sail free and enjoy life when you enter their throne.

*****

The spice of life is the joy of being. So, humor, rise and live.

*****

Whoever greases the slide of reason that the thought of I may freely move out of the entrapment called self is in a vibration in which all thoughts may pass and none shall stick.

*****

It's known as keeping faith with reason, the power that transfigures thee.

*****

Demons are holey with an *e*: the *e* of the me.

*****

And the hole of the mine.

*****

The difference between an angel and a demon is angels have something to offer after you get inside. And demons, it's only a hole in there: empty and void.

*****

So, you see, all holes are dark and dreary, cold and wet, filled with tears and regret.

*****

And the biggest hole you'll ever know is the hole you demand of the judgment of your goal.

*****

The question is, How to fill the hole that one already has? Of course, it is not limited to "hole." It's limited, perhaps, to a multitude of holes that never do we seem to stop digging. Now, let us not be concerned with the filling of a hole that cannot be filled. Let us more wisely enter the circle of the Law of Divine Return from what we be moment by moment. And we won't step into any more holes.

*****

The insatiable need for holes, which exists only in mental substance, is, in truth, the need for God. And when our need for God is no longer dictated by the thought of I, God we be and holes no longer are.

*****

In reference to your question, people work so hard and end up with nothing to show, it's quite simple: they're working in so many holes, there's no bottom to them. And they're never filled. So they labor, like slaves, to fill the unfillable.

*****

And this is why we have taught you put God in it or forget it. For the I that is in it is the hole that you labor to fill.

*****

My children, has-beens have no butts. They set them out long ago. And now you know the hole.

*****

No butts, no foundation. So work off your tail, but work it the right way or end up with nothing.

*****

Insanity is trying to be what has been and constantly hoping to be what's to be; you cannot be and, therefore, insanity.

*****

So clearly, the definition of the word *insanity* is "has been, to be, trying be."

*****

Being is not dependent on anyone or anything. Be-ing is being *in* whatever we choose.

*****

Hopefully, sanity will rule and we'll choose God or Goodness.

*****

Who wants brass when gold is available?

*****

And their right to receive it.

*****

And, of course, we now know what brass really is. And, also, gold.

*****

Take your choice: pride or wisdom.

*****

Truth not only frees, it restores. And that's what's meant when it's said, "Truth crushed to earth shall rise again," for it is the divine principle of restoration.

*****

The expression of God, known by man as goodness or divine desire, is dependent upon man's entrance into the will of God, known as total acceptance, which is being, thereby entering upon the circle of divine return.

*****

Remember, children, whoever in consciousness be is not has been, nor to be, but is the power, the truth, eternity and lives the Light that fills and frees.

*****

An educated ego refuses to be a has-been. Its humble pride serves its true purpose.

*****

The humbleness of pride is the gold, not the brass.

*****

So let us truly shine and not be brassy.

*****

Just be is the divinity of the justice for all to see.

*****

For in the Light of Truth, you're bound or be. You hold or free. There's no hiding from the true me.

*****

We wish to help you understand the true meaning of the word *brassy*. It means, in your world, sassy, belligerent.

*****

Pointing your heart on authority if you judge you cannot control it.

*****

For pointed hearts piss on what they cannot control.

*****

From elimination to urinate, we shall be free.

*****

My children, it's what you have to move out of your house that gives you the fresh air of freedom to enter therein.

*****

Constipation is the conning of oneself while they're sitting.

*****

It simply reveals they're too lazy to make the effort. They want something for nothing.

*****

So, rebuild your foundation in consciousness and enjoy life.

*****

And now, of course, we know hemorrhoids are the struggle of the has-beens.

*****

When dignity is no longer dependent upon territory, we will have dignity that's joy.

*****

The territory, of course, is the parameters in which the to-bes have been placed by the has-beens.

*****

Has-beens bind and to-bes loosen. Take a look at life and be.

*****

You know, children, how difficult it is to catch the desires you demand.

*****

They're so loose.

*****

The go of anything, of course, is dependent upon the flow.

*****

Too tight, too loose is the problem of the goose. So be the eagle of heaven.

*****

Don't be a donkey-head, old ego. Educate.

*****

Donkey-heads deny, but eagles fly, high to heaven's heights.

*****

[The following teachings were given to a very small group of advanced students.]

The weight of the burden, indeed, is heavy for those who compare when they try to share.

*****

Those who share with round hearts roll on to heaven. No pointed hearts of has-beens. No thought of yesterday. No thought of tomorrow. The be is the free from the weight of the thee.

*****

The bridge of rapport established between the eternal soul while yet encased in form permits a transference of intelligent energy that is sent out and returned and is changed or transformed as it passes through the form of the receiver and sender. For example, as one becomes more receptive to the vibrations, thoughts, feelings, which are, in truth, the vehicles that carry energy through the ethereal waves and impinge upon the consciousness of the receiver, that impingement, through the Law of Rapporm, is refined, transformed, evolved, and sent out. And so it is in the evolution in the process of the spin, which is the counterspin in the transference of energy. And both forms begin the process of transformation. It is wise to view and be aware in this transference process that a balance is maintained and sustained in the light of reason. *[The teacher spoke the word* rapporm. *Please consider that he may have intended to say "rapport" or he may have intended to say "reform."]*

Good day.

*****

Fear not the night.
I am the Light.
I am the battle
And I the right.
Fear not the night.
I am the sight.
I am the view
That sees through the night.
Fear not the night.
I am the sword,
The justice, the right.
Fear not the night.
I'm the I that sees.
I am the Light.
Fear not, fear not
My child of right.

*****

From the Light of the saint you must prepare for the night of the sinner in order to balance the life . . . *[The teacher speaks very faintly and a few words are difficult to transcribe.]*

*****

For what is the sinner? The ignorance of the saint. And what is the saint? The denial of the sinner. So let the sinner and the saint amalgamate and be the peace, the good, the God, the Light, the Love, the joy of life.

*****

My good student, in reference to the latest class, energy transference is expression of God. It is the wisdom in creation. It is the life of joy. Registered within the human consciousness in mental substance is the judgment that affection is received through the act of sex. Therefore, this unbelievable need or experience of goodness or God has been made dependent upon the act of sex. Sex is necessary as a[n] instrument through which the soul enters celestial realms designed for the purpose in life of procreation or soul upliftment exclusively. Do you hear?

Yes.

Now the human mind, in its ignorance, has registered in mental substance the goodness of God, which, in truth, is a vehicle known as sharing in order to experience the goodness, has limited it into a bondage of the sexual act. When it is freed from that ignorance, then affection, the energy flow, the goodness of God, the joy of life, is the experience of man.

Good day.

*****

The soul faculty of care, kindness, and consideration is the vehicle through which the joy of life breathes and lives and lifts the soul to the glorious heights of its eternal home. Unfortunately, man in mental substance has taken advantage of the design and taken it to the final step, which has been reserved by divine wisdom for the illumination of the soul. Therefore, the Light, being too bright, has destroyed man. Blinded him into the darkness of ignorance.

*****

As all ascents to heaven must be descents to creation in order that they may walk upon the bridge between the two realms of consciousness, it takes energy, my child. And the return requires the transference thereof, [which] you know as affection.

*****

From the closet of infinity we have come. And to the closet of infinity we shall return. And remember, take with you, to the closet of infinity, the lamp of honesty, the light of reason that you may choose your suits. Choose them wisely, for you have the will to make your choice without all the has-beens in the great eternity.

*****

Without yesterday, there is no reference. Without reference, there is no time. Without time, there's no illusion. Without illusion, there's no delusion. Without delusion, there's no deception. Without deception, there's no bondage of self.

Children, children, children, you enter and leave the closet of infinity when you choose, by your will, to awaken to the Light of Truth that you are. Then awaken. Be not yesterday, the deception. Be not tomorrow, the dream. Be what you are. Sail free beyond the river. Far beyond the river, that's where you live. Die to delusion. Die to reference. Die to time. Die to bondage. Go on your boat of destiny beyond the river. There, in the Light, choose your journey and choose it wisely, knowing that you can and shall return home at any moment of your choice.

*****

That which sustains and upholds the time barrier of illusion is the very thing you need to use to penetrate it. That's known, my children, as the power of your will, which is the power that holds it, for you, in place.

*****

The impingement and implantation of the seed of the life force within the vehicle, you have, now, the living demonstration.

*****

So, you must learn. It is not designed to go in vain, but accomplish great good in many ways. Hear?

Yes.

Be wise, its use.

*****

My child, it is only the beginnings, the manifestations of births.

*****

Truth always lifts our soul. Often we don't like the lift.

*****

Just a minute.

*****

The cause of constipation is when too many things try to catch up.

*****

You know, of course, the too many things are has-beens.

*****

So, please, children, pull the chain of reason.

*****

Old salts ever be the spice of life, the joy to free.

FEBRUARY 20, 1983

Class February 21, 1983

[These teachings may have been given to a very small group of advanced students.]

Those who share never compare.

*****

The separation of truth from creation is when balance, the divine neutrality, makes the two an eleven.

*****

Two souls united, two souls united—eleven becomes two.

*****

The joy of the two is the eleven it brings forth.

*****

The totality of creation is the eleven of power.

*****

Beautiful means filled with beauty.

*****

When the river flows its fullest, joy washes the shores of creation.

*****

The subtraction of infinity is the addition of eternity.

*****

So run, river, run and flow upon the banks of ol' creation that life may fill her purpose.

*****

One awakens from a nightmare, passes through a dream, enters paradise, and floats in heaven.

*****

The leaf of every tree is the form of a nature spirit. So treat the leaf as you treat the tree. And then, my children, you shall be.

*****

For in the leaf, the trunk you see; hidden from your view because you not be.

*****

As our soul sails on the little boat upstream on the river of life, we look and view the shore ever changing from jungles to deserts, from oases to mountaintops. And when our boat, as it sails along, views upon the shore that which is painful, barren deserts distasteful to our mind, let us never forget that the winds of reason are what move our little boat. And so in that awareness, let us permit reason to flow that the winds of reason may fill our sail and move our little boat quickly past the shores we view, for in so doing, the pain is short duration, and we sail and view shores of beauty and goodness in our movement up the river of life beyond the river to heavenly isles of peace and joy.

FEBRUARY 21, 1983

Class February 22, 1983

[These teachings were given to a very small group of advanced students.]

Morning, friends.

One does not experience the Goodness or God in mental substance without the satisfaction or filling of forms created, has-beens, who have been designed to serve that purpose. There are three ways for the experience of Goodness or God in one's life. Through the limited forms of what has been, through service to them, when they rise to be served, through an inner awakening if whether or not the purpose of their true design is clear, is pure and beneficial to the service of one's moment, any moment of their conscious awareness, which is their eternity, therefore, their moment of reality.

Two: Through a conscious awareness of, moment by moment, eternity through eternity in the great infinity, of the design and the awakening formation, true to the origin of the design, of new bes. Not to-bes. But bes. Bes are the forms created in the conscious awareness moment by moment. The second step is the evolution of the eternal being on its path of freedom and joy.

The third and final step, an inevitable step from step two, is the universality of consciousness through which one may view, as an observer, experience and not be bound. Without step two, the movement into the formless in consciousness—which is not only the total acceptance or the will of divinity but is in truth the Love, the Life, and the birthright of what you truly are. One does not attain step three without step two. And it is difficult indeed to move from step one to step two, but that return to one's home is as difficult as we alone choose to make it.

And, of course, in the difficulty is the necessary ingredient: the seeds of value of goodness of the greatness of the being, which for many, which for most, is centuries in the coming. One should therefore consider the centuries they have already been.

One should therefore consider the centuries they be. That consideration begins to awaken in step two and is made manifest in step three.

Look not at what's to be from the view and vantage point of what has been and you will enjoy what be moment by moment, for that is free. What be is free. No to-bes. No have-beens. What be is free. You be, be, and be. Then, from boxes to kites you'll sail; you'll soar. The eagle, the glory of his flight.

Good day.

*****

Gravity is the Law of Identification.

*****

. . . I heard, I saw the beauty, the fullness of the beauty of your awareness and perception in reference to the cross. Now listen, child, the cross all humanity bears is that cross. And the only cross is that burden. And the only burden. It is the balance in the movement from the has-beens to the to-bes. It is a horizontal bar—has-beens and to-bes, you understand?

Yes.

And it's constant movement—horizontal.

Yes.

But your form is not horizontal, is it?

No, it isn't.

So let the bar go, the bar of burden. Hmm?

Yes.

Has-beens, to-bes, let the bar go. Just let it go and it will strengthen the vertical pillar.

Yes.

Hear?

Uh-huh.

The vertical pillar of being.

Yes.

For it is only in the position, the upright position, does understanding enter. The realms of wisdom takes you to heaven. Hmm?
Yes.
You understand?
I think so.
Then I will, I shall repeat. Has-beens, to-bes—
Yes.
—horizontal.
Right.
They're the bar of the cross, the burden of the mind.
Yes.
Do you understand that?
Yeah, I do.
Now, you understand there's another bar. It is the pillar, upright.
Yes.
That is understanding. It looks up. Its authority is above it, superior to it.
Yes.
Hmm?
Yes.
And that which is superior to understanding is what?
The source.
Wisdom. Must not understanding pass through wisdom?
Certainly.
In all your getting, get understanding. In all your giving, give what?
Wisdom.
Well, now without understanding, there is no wisdom.
True.
Is there?
That's right.
So, of what value is understanding without wisdom?

Yes.

Of what value is wisdom without understanding?

Right.

Do you not see they're inseparable?

I do.

So let this bar, let his horizontal view—has-beens, to-bes, to-bes, has-beens, has-beens, to-bes, to-bes, has-beens—ah, is it not weary, little boy?

Hmm.

Then, let it go. For when you let it go, the to-bes drop to the has-beens. There's no choice left for them, hear?

Yes.

And they drop right to the bottom of the pillar into the foundation. Hmm?

Yes.

And, believe me, when you combine understanding with wisdom, has-beens, to-bes, they all melt and serve the purpose to be free, hmm?

Yes.

So now do you understand?

I do.

Let go, has-beens. And to-bes will follow. Hmm?

Yes.

And when they follow, they land on top of all has-beens. And has-beens, like it or not, they're suffocated with the inevitable, inevitable intercourse. You hear?

Yes.

When a to-be lands on top of a has-been—to-bes, my child, are electric.

Yes.

You hear?

Yes.

All has-beens are magnetic.

Yes.

Well, you're electric, aren't you?
Oh, yes.
Well, what happens when you land on top of a magnet? Hmm? What happens?
[It is difficult to transcribe the student's response.]
Is it the magnet that is active?
Yes.
Or is it the electric?
The electric?
Hmm. That is superior, isn't it?
Yes.
Does it not imprint itself?
Yes.
Well, electric to-bes landing on top of magnetic has-beens, those has-beens, they had it.
Yes . . .

*****

[The following two transcriptions are of very short recordings and only partially capture a song that is being given through Mr. Goodwin's mediumship. Although Mr. Goodwin did play the piano, it is not known who plays that instrument during these recordings. However, the certainty of the way in which each note is played suggests that it is someone who is well versed with the tune.]

No has-beens can . . . *[As each word is spoken, a note is played on the piano.]* Get a pen—piece of paper—

*****

Ready. Go.
No has-beens can conquer me, for I'm the be, eternity. [Student R sings. As each word is sung, a note is played, except for the last word, for which a chord is played.]
OK. We'll have to practice this.

No has-beens can conquer me, For I'm the be, eternity. [Student R again sings to music.]

One more time.

No has-beens can conquer me, For I'm the be, eternity. [And Student R again sings to music.]

*****

Eleventh symphony of the spheres. The ruler of eternity. Captain, King of Infinity.

*****

Record.

All planets bow to thee, Eleventh Ruler of Eternity. For they exist, all planets be in what you call space, infinity. So ruler rule, and worlds you see; commander of infinity. That's the king of all creation.

*****

Creation is a price tag. Choose wisely what you buy, for some purchases are the installment plan with great interest that never end.

*****

The Law of Creation, payment and attainment, is the law absolute and bound by the forms and their design of motivation. Only the light, the light of reason shining upon the Law of Creation, the bondage of self, can transform and free that creation be the service, the vehicle of its pure design.

*****

[The following teachings may have been given to a larger group of students who were present Tuesday evenings.]

Be a busy be, not a lazy has-been or a dreamy to-be. *[An alternative transcription could be, "Be a busy bee, not . . ."]*

*****

Record.

Whoever relies and depends upon the human mind for their goodness or God must awaken to the demonstrable truth that it is ever subject to what the has-beens, to-bes will allow.

*****

A brassy person is sassy and belligerent. The reason that they're that way is because they're in dire need of polish.

*****

And, of course, that which is in dire need of polish requires a strong abrasive. It's called irritation.

*****

So only fools are thin-skinned, including brass.

*****

Don't be brass-plated.

*****

Quick. So now you know a thin-skinned person is a brass-plated fool.

*****

They're easily rubbed out.

*****

So move out the brass and let in the gold, for what you hold is all brass.

*****

From brass-plated to iron-clad, keep digging. There's gold down there.

*****

Brass-plated, copper-plated, silver-plated, gold-plated—they all appear to be what they are not. Just like what our has-beens have to say.

*****

Whenever you want your desires fulfilled.

*****

It's known as self-deception.

*****

Or plated-pride.

FEBRUARY 22, 1983

Class February 23, 1983

[The following teachings were given to the larger group of students who volunteered at the temple on Wednesday nights. Certain indications on the surviving tapes suggest that that tape was edited, which may have changed the order of these teachings on that recording. Although the words have not been changed, the order of the teachings in this class has been changed from the order on the microcassette to the order recorded in personal notes of students who were present at this class. Please consider the possibility that the order of the following teachings may not be the order in which they were originally given.]

Now it's on. *[The teacher refers to the microcassette recorder.]*

Now we just got through saying the darker the night, the brighter the light because, you see, if the light is not real bright in the darkness of the night, then you have the shadows over which you stumble and fall. So what's [that's?] really a very simple thing.

Now I spoke to you earlier, [Student H], about "know." What was it that they were talking about? You started to write it.

Oh, whenever we know what's going to happen—

Ah, that's all you need to remind me of. Whenever we know what's going to happen, we have all kinds of problems. Because when we know what's going to happen, we create, from within ourselves, all kinds of to-bes of expectation who are permitted into the parameters established by the has-beens, are adjusted and all ready for what we know is to happen. And because they know what's going to happen and it is not in accord with what they want to happen, they rise within our consciousness and establish, through the Law of Self-Deception, what is necessary for the failure of what we expect and know we're going to have.

*****

And so, when we know not, God's greatest good is done.

*****

You have to wait. *[After a short pause, the teacher continues.]* It's called the spirit of spontaneity.

*****

Record.
It is.
Whatever is spontaneous is quick, slippery, and cannot be caught by has-beens.

*****

So grease well the slide of reason.

*****

All has-beens are clever and cunning, and this is why they're known as the con artists of the universe.

*****

A con artist is one who feeds upon the deception of self in order that it may experience the glory thereof.

*****

In one word is truth revealed; in many, so sadly and deeply concealed.

*****

A person who does not communicate with others reveals the demonstrable truth: they do not communicate with themselves, are limited and controlled by the has-beens in what areas in consciousness any word or truth shall possibly reveal itself.

*****

In the application of anything, one first must know the job they have to do. Then one must have the tools to do it and the wisdom, through instruction, and the faith of their success [to] accomplish what they have to do.

*****

The pain of any step is pleasure blinded by impatience.

*****

People who have difficulty with communication shut off everything too soon.

*****

Now you know what rises when we bake: it's called *h-bs*—has-beens.

*****

So, cool off; come out of the furnace and be free.

*****

To those who fall into the self-deception of being observed, pain is their path in life. To those who rise in truth to the plane of objectivity and be the observer, pleasure, the joy of life, is ever the path they walk.

*****

Why, the question must be asked, is whatever we judge is different, for us, is painful? That's the question.

*****

Reason is a cool breeze that fills the sails of our boat of destiny on which our little soul peacefully rests in the great enjoyment of the sailing. So let the breeze fill the sail that we may pass along the shores, varied and different, and not be grounded thereon.

*****

I'm so happy to see you got off the throne and decided to enjoy life a bit. Sail along.

*****

As I have said before, from eliminate to urinate, we shall be free.

*****

My good students, if you must blow, then use wisdom and blow the sails of reason, not the balloons of ego ignorance.

*****

For those things so easily deflate.

*****

It's known as disappointment.

*****

Whoever blows up the ego, deflates the soul, loses the goodness of life, and lands like a rock in the same old hole.

*****

Blow up the ego; deflate the soul; land like a rock in any old hole.

*****

If you must have a lift, let it be humor.

*****

For nothing else is worth saving.

*****

When the hole is your goal, you lose the purpose of the doughnut.

*****

And man calls that starvation.

*****

Best lift is an inside job, for the ones outside, you never know when the brake's going to slip.

*****

Whoever believes they can improve on the original design of goodness always goes backwards and lands you know where.

*****

It is a person known as "uninstructable."

*****

Not even God or Goodness is able to instruct the instructor who knows they are the instructor.

*****

So, backwards to hell and forward to heaven.

*****

So, live in the past and you'll see just how long you'll last.

*****

The abrasiveness of any situation is the old grinding of the past.

*****

The abrasiveness of the present is the grind of the past, the view of the day blinded by the night of yesterday.

*****

Hold to what has gone and then live a life forlorn and weary.

FEBRUARY 23, 1983

Class February 24, 1983

[The following teachings may have been given to a very small group of advanced students.]

The Law of Location or Placement is indispensable to the Law of Identification, which is to indent, impinge, or imprint in consciousness.

FEBRUARY 24, 1983

Class February 25, 1983

[The following teachings may have been given to a very small group of advanced students.]

>No pointed heart can piss on me
>For I'm the be that lives so free
>I fly and soar and fly and sail
>What piss can get to me and nail?
>*[An alternative transcription would be "For I'm the bee..."]*

*****

Yes. Whoever battles the empty bore—the empty void, remember, has a battle that's losing. And when the loss is sufficient, they'll rise in a different way. Another path, same Light— *[The telephone rings.]* —and hop around throughout the night. Aliens here. Answer—

*****

Ofttimes we mistake the truth "forever and a day" when it's really forever in the night.

*****

Queens gain victims through alliance.

*****

O jewel upon the throne, you're tarnished and in need of many workers to polish you again.

*****

Whoever breaks the feast at dawn is not the victim of the illusion to break the fast, for they know the difference.

*****

For has-beens, born in darkness, feast their full in sleep of night.

*****

The only problem with peanuts: they throw away the shell and grind up the peanut because they like butter. You know butter's smooth and butter melts. Too bad, too bad. Don't be a peanut fool. Be an eagle joy.

*****

Be the bread and not the butter for you are the sustenance of life itself.

*****

You know very well that butter's for the magnets. They need it.

*****

Nothing wrong with desire when you understand its purpose.

*****

True—yes?—true humor has no price tag and, therefore, is at no one's expense.

*****

Whoever feels lost upon the sea is the one who is not, in the loss, a be. They are has-been and hope to be. But, no, they're not the be, the sea. You are the be. You are the sea. You are all things. You and me beyond the veil. Be blinded not by that which your mind tells you ought, *ought* to be. Ought to see is not the be. Cannot be free. *[Please consider the possibility that a more accurate transcription could be "Ought to sea . . ."]*

*****

It's on.
Whoever knows the way is always living a very nice day.

*****

Die graciously for birth is so beautiful.

*****

Hollow has-beens call it hell. Why, of course. How could they know heaven?

*****

The only buts one should be interested in are the buts of wisdom, which are the squeaks and creaks of the hinges, until they are transformed.

*****

It's like the troubled bes. You know they're has-been to-bes.

*****

Buts are conditions. So why make effort to be free only to enter back therein.

*****

Be not the form to rise and fall. View not the form to rise and fall. Be the life that sustains it all.

*****

Now be the pulse and not the beat, for the beat is the seat in which you stick your little feet.

*****

[The following teachings were given to a larger group of students who volunteered at the temple on Friday nights. When

the order of these teachings on the surviving tapes is compared with order of the teachings of students' notes taken as this class was given, there are some differences. The order of the teachings presented in the following transcription is the order of students' personal notes. Please consider the possibility that the order of the following teachings may not be the order in which they were originally given.]

> The source of Light is blinding
> When one sees a little,
> As the pain of life is pleasure
> When one sees not at all.

*****

Hold everything.

*****

True humor has no price; therefore, cannot be purchased and, of course, can never be at anyone's expense.

*****

Thank you. In reference to your question, ofttimes humor is directed at oneself, considering that the self is like an onion, only layer by layer, one would not say there is any expense involved.

*****

That which is expense or expensive is that which has substance, not that which is but layers.

*****

In other words, one is free to breathe for oneself, not to breathe for another.

*****

Character is revealed in the honesty as we search for the Light of Truth.

*****

Pleasure's for paradise. Joy is the domain of heaven.

*****

So, Eve, look up. And Adam, crawl up.

*****

The children of pleasure are pain. Ah, the children of joy are enjoyment.

*****

Pain is the experience you know when you don't have your own way.

*****

That's called pleasure bound to you know where.

*****

Whoever relies upon their mind becomes the victim of all minds.

*****

Divine order is the order of Divinity. That's where no dictates can reign.

*****

Whoever relies upon their own thoughts, of course, is dependent upon the thoughts of all others.

*****

It's known as image concern, the burn of burn.

*****

Here.
Whoever is so deluded to think they have problems with the bes must awaken to see that their has-beens are trying to be; and therefore, they are deceived, deluded by the greatest con artist of the universe that *that* is the be.

*****

Ofttimes the soothing feather on the soul seems to be a cannonball to the mind.

*****

When you awaken from the sleep of satisfaction, begin to open your eyes, awareness of your surroundings, and you look directly at the sun at high noon, tell me your experience.

*****

Blinders for the day-sleepers. Night lights for the sleep-walkers. Satisfaction is so slippery; when we need to catch it, it never wants to stick.

*****

The application or difference between the letter of the law and the spirit of the law, of course, is simple. The letter is form, judgment, and dictate. And the spirit of the law is free; like an eagle, it soars to heaven.

*****

Beautiful is that which is filled with beauty.

*****

We shall discuss, this evening, heads of block, called blockheads. The substance from which thought is formed is the sand of time, called illusion. It is mixed and cemented by the life, the river; the flow is the glue which mixes and holds it together. Like all cement, it's formed and covered and kept in the darkness to cure and solidify. For if it is not, the light, the heat, it will not properly cure; it will not be solid, will not endure for a time. So, all thoughts, like all concrete, they endure for a time. Subject to the light and what you call weather conditions, they do, slowly but surely, return to the substance from whence they were created.

As repetition is the law through which change is made possible, the repetition of the same frequency crumbles the walls and the boxes in which you have placed your eternal truth: the soul, the life of the Light.

*****

O walls of Jericho, you're cracking and crumbling. So do not be boxes and blocks. Be round, like balls that roll on and on, serving the purpose, holding not to that which has gone.

*****

Round hearts roll on to heaven.

*****

"Truly yours" does not in any way mean "in truth yours," because truth *is*. You can't take it or give it. It *is*!

*****

Pointed hearts, yes, indeed, are truly yours.

*****

When our deception is the greatest, our need of the senses the fullest, pain, indeed, is the pleasure we seek.

*****

For 'tis the senses that stimulate the ego and the glory thereof.

*****

My children, it's known as challenge.

*****

All con artists are tempted by power.

*****

It's known as the need to control.

*****

Only fools need to tempt and tease to experience salvation of their soul, called humor.

*****

The difference between training and instruction is simply the difference between a human and an animal. So, use the animal that your being is inside of. Don't become it, or you must be trained.

*****

And remember, children, pointed hearts have no problems in training. Good night.

*****

Whoever becomes the tool designed to serve his being is no longer able to use the tool for the purpose of its design.

*****

[Get out of the animal]³⁴ and into the soul. The Law of Repetition breaks any barricade. Concrete blocks, you cannot endure the repetition. The law is sure.

*****

Whenever you believe you are the thought, then remember the animal you must be.

*****

Whoever loves the form cannot *be* the soul.

*****

So, better blind and be than only form to see.

*****

From peanuts to balloons, somewhere we're bound to be a be.

*****

Love form, lose truth. Be a box and close the lid.

*****

If you must desire to be, then be a plumber that flushes, not a carpenter that builds boxes.

*****

No pride, no fear. No fear, no thought. No thought, no image. No image, no bondage. No bondage, no boxes. No boxes, wings flying to the joy of life.

*****

Angel wings are composed of ideas. They lack the thought of I.

*****

You cannot have a thought that is not controlled by fear, for it is composed of mental substance.

*****

The force of thought is your belief therein and returns unto you the victim, the sufferer, the pain of creation.

*****

Whoever *be* is free from the thought of I and separates truth from creation.

*****

Has-beens, to-bes are totally dependent upon the thought of I, not the I, the be.

*****

The con artist of the universes is the king of creation, the former of forms.

*****

Don't you see, friends? Illusion needs you. Without you, there are no forms. You don't need illusion.

*****

Now, boxes need you to jump in. Otherwise, they're empty and serve no purpose.

FEBRUARY 25, 1983

Class February 26, 1983

[These teachings were given to a very small group of advanced students.]

What I be I have not been. And what I be I'll not to be. For I be. Have-beens been. To-bes to be. Be, be, sail free.

*****

... Be the Light made manifest in the order of Divinity.

*****

That places you in the sincerity of your effort in the frequency and the beat of the purity of your purpose in eternity, the service to infinity.

*****

Great Light, my child, requires great love in order to have great life, called manifestation. So note, as the Light brightens, so does the need of love that sustains it that manifestation, life be.

*****

Man faces, moment by moment, faith or belief. Believe, be bound: creation has found you. Faith, be free, for truth then knows you.

*****

The force of mental substance is belief. The power of truth is faith.

*****

Man believes in many things in order that he may learn the lessons to have faith in only one.

FEBRUARY 26, 1983

Class February 27, 1983

[The following teachings were given to the group of students who regularly volunteered at the temple on Sunday nights.]

One, in their great desires to fulfill the needs thereof, tries many techniques. Many, many, many techniques. They find that one didn't work. And then they try another, and that one didn't work. And then they try another, and that one still doesn't work. And then they try another, and that doesn't work. And sooner or later, they begin to wear out from without with all these different techniques that the human mind and the has-beens have to offer. Takes time, of course. Takes a lot of expended energy. And sooner or later, they start to awaken, "What's the use? It's just not worth it."

So, the more techniques you try to get what you demand you're going to have, gradually, slowly but surely, your perspective changes, and you say, "Just a minute. This is not as valuable as I thought it was. Where was I last year or last century that I wasted all this energy? What's the matter with my head? Look at me. Look at where I am. I'm totally depleted of energy. I'm totally exhausted. I'm a little banana sliding on the you know what. And what am I doing to myself?" It's necessary that we, slowly but surely, wear out from without, and we find the goodness that's always been, will ever be, inside our self, not dependent on all the techniques the human mind has to offer.

*****

Now this process is known as polishing the mirror of vanity that the brass of pride may shine once again.

*****

So, you see, children, God indeed is in all things.

*****

Now you have the law revealed unto you. The tenacity of temptation that serves the function of challenge, that man, in his ignorance, has limited the Goodness or God to enter exclusively one way. And the exclusivity is indeed the bondage, for there's no other way for the goodness of life [to enter], until man awakens and stops the children's games that are meant for children, not for grown-ups.

*****

Ready? *[The teacher asks the recording technician.]*
Uh-huh.
Hallelujah, has-beens, your boxes are so heavy you're headed for hell. We're flying to heaven.

*****

Hallelujah? Yes, we're so happy you're going home.

*****

In the filling of any desire, malleability takes all the energy.

*****

One cannot mold without limit. One can't have limit without judgment. Now see, children, where your energy really goes.

*****

Yes.
"Battle Hymn of the Republic." The republic of anything is that which is the authority. And the authority of the battle is supreme over the battle. And so, we march on.

"Mine eyes"—my awareness—"have seen the glory of the coming of the Lord"—the law. "He"—the great electric power—"is trampling out the vintage where the grapes of wrath are stored." The fruits of action are stored up. "He hath loosed the fateful lightning of His terrible swift sword." The sword that serves the Light of eternal Truth. "His truth is marching on," in perfect cadence and beat. "Glory, glory, hallelujah. Glory, glory, hallelujah. Glory, glory, hallelujah. Our God is marching on."

"I have seen him in the watch fires"—I have become aware through the lamps of honesty— "of a hundred circling camps." For each thought multiplies, for it has, each thought, 99 children. "They have builded him an altar"—all those have-beens have builded him an altar—"in the evening dews and damps"—for they worship the techniques, the talents, and what mental substance has to offer. Ah, but "I can read his righteous sentence [by]"—by my lamp of honesty—"the dim and flaring lamps." But must ever be cautious of the shadows created by the *effects* of the lamps and not the lamps itself. "His day is marching on." The Light of Truth shall ever be.

"He has sounded forth the trumpet"—he has spoken the word that never faileth—"that shall never sound retreat"—shall not return unto him void. "He is sifting out the hearts of men"—the truth contained within the depths of the eternal being. "His judgment seat—Before his judgment seat"—before all the has-beens and to-bes as they come before, and into, the Great Rotunda, where the Light of Truth *is*. "Oh, be swift my soul"—be quick, spontaneous to escape from their clutches— "to answer him."—the voice of conscience. "Be jubilant my feet"—the joy of life is dependent upon the degree of your acceptance, the will of God, which is your understanding. "Our God is marching on."—the perfect rhythmic beat of the being you truly are.[35]

*****

When man makes the effort to trample his has-beens, he receives the wonderful essence from whence they are composed. It is like the essence of a fine wine.

*****

When you beat it to death, you're free to be and are reborn.

*****

So beat away and be free.

*****

Attachment to the fruit, the grape, is the unquenchable thirst of the desire.

*****

Perhaps now you understand why poor Adam is still crawling up for the apple.

*****

So, Eve, keep looking up. He doesn't want the ones that have fallen.

*****

Has-beens only want to-bes, for they have better control and feel just great when they put them in their boxes!

*****

Has-beens love to compare, do not care to share.

*****

It's known as the satisfaction of selfishness.

*****

The has-beens build their altars of appeasement in the evening dews and damps from the substance of the mist, which is the veil of illusion you call form, creation. And they sacrifice upon it anything and everything to have their way.

*****

Let us not, in the year of the lamb, sacrifice it upon the altar and lose the Light, the truth, the freedom we have searched for centuries for.[36]

*****

Trim the wicks of your lamps, brother, that the light may shine brightly and you be not deceived by the shadows of its effect.

*****

Keep faith with reason; *she* will transfigure thee.

*****

Whoever gives the apple has a right to remove it.

*****

For she knows she's not the apple, but she knows she is the tree.

*****

And when man becomes the tree, the tree of life he is, then apples or oranges, they'll make no difference, for the tree is the tree, the observer of you and me.

*****

The he or the she is dependent ever upon the be.

*****

There is no free until you are the be.

*****

Has-beens, to-bes are the great dent of the thee. And no truth can you possibly see.

*****

Got to get this.
Apes carry clubs. Angels, feathers to fly.

*****

Temptation, as we all know, is the greatest magnet of the universe.

*****

A mag is a box that looks like a feather.

*****

So, when you want to fly, bladder beware.

*****

Has-beens deepen truth and that's why our journey is so long.

*****

And that's why we said keep digging. There's gold down there.

*****

Rotundas have no corners in which has-beens, to-bes can hide.

*****

The joy of understanding is your willingness to accept.

*****

Wise men see the no of desire as direction, not denial.

*****

Round hearts, like rotundas, have no place for has-beens, to-bes to hide.

*****

So, children, file off the points!

*****

In reference to your question, What does *children* mean? Why, they're the little forms that play in the playgrounds of creation. The hearts have not yet got a point.

*****

And so, round heads, like round hearts, every knock is their boost.

*****

Everyone knows when you kick a ball, it goes up.

*****

And what fool ever found a square ball?

*****

Yes.
Everyone knows only a fool chases a ball downhill. Now we'll get to my student's question.

*****

Ah, what we use to file off the point is not within the power of mental substance, for that only offers the force of the mind. We must use the Light that is beyond it, that sustains it.

*****

Only God can lift a soul. And when we know, we know we know; there's no concern, only return.

*****

Should we slip and then we fall, with the dictate that's our all, then beware, beware, beware.

*****

For we know not who does the call.

*****

That tempts us to another fall.

*****

Let no points grow in your circle of beauty.

*****

Moonlight and you are the has-beens with their tool.

*****

Fairy tales are for children, for they're pure of heart and keep rolling on.

*****

Little children enter the kingdom of heaven for they have no pointed hearts to stick in the entrance.

*****

What we have, we do not lose. It's what we hold that we abuse.

*****

The difference between having and holding is the need for the power of God; man calls it control.

*****

The totality of thought is the absence of God, our awareness of goodness, our birthright of life.

*****

O self, what value do you now have?

*****

The pity of self is the total identification with it.

*****

The sacrifice of goodness on the altar of hell.

*****

Of course, our reward is the pleasure of judgment.

*****

Shine on, sunshine! Leave the silvery moon to the has-beens.

*****

Our need for God becomes control when mental substance is all we know.

*****

An ape who uses a club to eliminate an ant is a has-been that should remain a has-been.

*****

And not try to be.

*****

We could have used a flea instead of an ant, but we want you to leave in good cheer.

*****

We get so discouraged when we beat ourselves with a club.

*****

And so encouraged when we soothe ourselves with a feather.

*****

So now we'll leave on a feather so we can fly to heaven.

*****

Wise souls go to break-feast and leave the fools to break-fast.

*****

For wise ones know has-beens feasted all night and they need a break—the soul.

*****

So, break-fast and enjoy the morning after.

*****

The need of the senses is known to the mind as sensation.

*****

When we cannot tolerate what we see in another, we establish the law to be its brother.

*****

The reign of pain is when we sit on the throne and do not sail to heaven.

*****

Captain, sail on. Leave the crew that wants to sit. Don't take them on your boat.

*****

—the little recorder? *[The teacher may refer to the microcassette recorder.]*
The we of the be is God and me.

*****

Don't forget who's first.

*****

Truth flows only through the be, for that's when you are God and me.

*****

More God, less me,
O how great you be, you be.

*****

[The following teachings were given to a very small group of advanced students.]
Yes.
Techniques are for the fools who have no faith in the God, the Good that is within them.
Yes.

FEBRUARY 27, 1983

Class February 28, 1983

[The following teachings were given to a very small group of advanced students.]

Eve is instructed to look up, for she knows what she has done. Adam is told to crawl up, for he knows not he has fallen in the hole of denial.

*****

Eve, the temptress of all time, queen of illusion, she knows Adam has lost his rib in the denial of unawareness.

*****

Eons ago, my friend, Adam gave forth his rib of reason and, in so giving forth, (electric) formed from the mist Eve (magnetic). And in the formation came view, awareness of that which is now without, which had always been within. And viewing the form of his own creation, his rib of reason made manifest in the mist, he experienced, and still experiences, the need of its return. And in the need of its return, Adam deludes himself. And in the delusion, deceives himself. And in the deception, believes and becomes the victim of denial.

Eve, formed from the rib of reason, she knows her power. But she knows not it is force, for mental substance has stolen the paradise within. And she, too, deceives herself, for the rib of reason shall ever be the right of Adam to keep him free when Adam, once again, declares his birthright: that that which is his is the faith within himself. And therefore, keep faith with reason within; she will, she will, within your being, transfigure thee.

*****

Is this thing on? *[The teacher refers to the tape recorder.]*

And so, Adam viewed the form of his own reason and was indeed pleased with his creation, for he had become used to sharing with the many forms of animals and birds and creatures. And now he had a form like unto himself, a creation of his own.

And then one day, as dusk fell upon the isle of paradise, Eve spoke softly into the ear of Adam and promised him a way. She had found a way that his reason may return unto him, that he may enjoy even greater fullness of life. And as she ended with her promise, the voice of God spoke unto them and said, "Be not tempted by the tree of knowledge and touch the fruit thereof." Ah, but Eve promised Adam his right to reclaim that which was his: his reason.

And so, Adam, so pleased with Eve, viewing his own creation, Adam tasted a bite of the fruit of the tree of knowledge. For Adam, in his satisfaction and pleasure, was deceived by himself and could not see that his reason, which was the river of his own flow of life, had taken form and shape, limit, and was no longer flowing. And so he bit of the apple, the fruit of the tree of knowledge. And he knew, he knew, he knew the difference between good and evil, for within him rose the function of knowledge, the limit, the shape, the form of deception of the river, the flow of reason. And in his knowledge, the king of creation rose and placed himself upon the throne: the throne of judgment; good and evil, want and need.

And so, in evolution Adam searches and [is] seeking. And in his seeking and sharing of the river of life, he finds compare, instead of share and knows the evil of what he knows, for Adam now has pride, indispensable to judgment, form, and limit.

Good day.

*****

With the sword of personal responsibility, man trims the wick of reason in the lamp of honesty and in so doing his Light, the Light, shines brightly and no shadows can endure.

*****

Whoever controls the river of another controls the life thereof and, therefore, is the dictate of their eternal soul for a time.

*****

More tempting is the river that glistens in the light of high noon.

*****

Thirst will drink of any water, muddy or clear. But those with need of control will only drink of water fresh, clean, and clear.

*****

Yes, indeed, the conscience of wisdom is the love of understanding for that is when the river flows and returns unto its source. Adam is fully aware in the Light.

*****

Whoever instructs enters the structure and knows exactly what to do. So beware of directors who look at it and try to control it.

*****

Now you know, my friend, the little peanut is safe until they crack the shell.

*****

The fullness of joy is dependent upon the greatness of understanding in the glory of wisdom and life be ever free.

*****

In all your getting, get understanding. In all your giving, give wisdom. And be the joy of life, the eagle free to fly and see that heaven is the place you be.

*****

The light of . . . of life and fills the cup of wisdom that joy may be expressed.[37]

*****

And God made man from the dust of Earth and breathed into his nostrils the breath of life, the river flow, reason.

*****

Reason is the magnet, the pull, the flow of the river of life.

*****

. . . Now reason flows *through* understanding. Not to understanding. . .

And so even though a soul in its evolution in order to have the many experiences necessary for it, it must stumble in the illusions called creation and form.

. . . To limit joy is to guarantee satisfaction. . .

. . . And how can one feel free, experience joy, when it is dependent upon the dictate of someone's mental substance?

. . . Temptation is the call of deception. . .

. . . For that which is united is indeed far greater than that which is divided. . .

. . . That that is divided is ever in need and, therefore, tempted by deception! . . .

. . . For those divided are ever seeking and, therefore, subject to a constant bombardment of temptation and deception. . .

. . . And that which is united is whole and complete. . .

FEBRUARY 28, 1983

Class March 1, 1983

[These teachings were given to the larger group of students who regularly volunteered at the temple on Tuesday nights.]

All that has been cannot be
That's not God and I'm not free
Until I give and then I be
The joy of life that sets me free.

*****

In the moment you leave the be, you enter the realm of illusion, dictate, and denial, whether it's has been or to be.

*****

Truth *is*. Not has been and not to be. Truth *is*.

*****

—called be![38]

*****

All judgment is based upon the foundation of what has been or yet to be.

*****

For what is yet to be is only the coming of the what has been will permit when you leave the be.

*****

By thinking only of the me.

*****

[Who]ever[39], whoever gives their eternal being to a shadow in the realms of mist cannot be the joy of life.

*****

Shadows seek power and know only force, for knowledge knows much, but wisdom knows better.

*****

So passive is the path of peace.

*****

Whoever desires to know their destiny in eternity, be aware of your denials.

*****

In the moment we be, no boxes can we see, for there are none.

*****

Thought is formed from the substance of illusion.

*****

Its continuity dependent upon has-beens and to-bes.

*****

Now you know what makes a thought stick like glue.

*****

Thoughts are for fools. Ideas, for men of wisdom.

*****

Has-beens delete and change, under the guise of improvement, whatever they fear.

*****

Be the observer, not the observed. Whoever is passive is the power of peace.

*****

Impatience does not exist in the Light of Truth. Therefore, power is the Light, the Truth.

*****

Impatience are [is] nothing more nor less than shadows that are dying from the lack of feeding.

*****

In order to be in the world and not a part of the world, you must learn the power of peace. And the power of peace is being passive.

*****

Whoever sees the war cannot enjoy the peace.

*****

[The following teachings were likely given to a very small group of advanced students.]

Friend, God is near when there is no fear.

*****

Truth is greater than fiction because it's beyond belief.

*****

The Law of Transformation is dependent upon reason. And reason reveals in order to transform bondage into freedom, one, in the process, must awaken and use the similarities contained in bondage, the essence, that which holds it together, into that which brings freedom. For example, moving from a locality where one is familiar with their surroundings and moving to a new locality, one must look and view and see if there are similar trees. Is there similar landscape? One sees quickly there are differences. Ah, but the light of reason shows there also are similarities. And it is the similarities that one places their attention or energy upon and, in so doing, gradually, slowly but surely, begins to transform or transfigure and, in so doing, broadens one's horizons. And in the broadening of the horizons, the principle is strengthened; the freedom is assured.

Now, my good friend, the Law of the Form, the sensing, its ability. The first law of form is the Law of Feeling. Forms feel. That is the original sense. You know it as the sense of touch, the sense of feeling. The children of the first law of the form are: affection, child number one; emotion, child number two. And there are only two children to the Law of the Form. Remember the principle. Remember the law. Be free, be free. Be fulfilled and be free. For that which is designed to be filled, once being filled, has served its purpose; and that which has served its purpose at any time is free in the moment of its fulfillment. And its fullness is the joy expressed through the feeling and the children of affection and emotion.

I do hope this will help you in your progress and understanding of the demonstrable truth which indeed you are.

*****

It's on.

Record.

Truth is like a river for it continuously flows. It is not dependent upon the thought of man, for in the thought of man truth does not be. And because truth in the thought of man does not be in the thought of man, of course, it cannot free. So, wise are those who use the power they call faith and leave belief to the fools of need, and in their faith rise in consciousness and be the river that flows so free!

*****

Authority over deception *is* the legality of method, and method is moment, present, be-ing.

Yes.

No concern means no fear.

Yes.

No fear, no worry.

Yes.

No worry, no fret. No fret, no frustration. No has-beens, no to-bes for you just be. . .

I am near, never fear. For I am I and thou art thee. Together, together, together. Just be. Just be. . .

*****

Attachment to or overidentification with form reveals the need, the degree thereof for the expression of feeling.

*****

Honey is the glue of deception.

*****

A good captain sees everything upon the river and along the shore, for he knows where he's going and will not allow his boat to be destroyed.

*****

Trinkets tempt the senses; ah, but truth calls the soul.

*****

So tickle, tickle little trinket, you are tempting only hell.

*****

A full river is a nourished life and a nourished life is a joyous one.

*****

Be—because illusion wants to be what it can never be, it tempts man to see what it wants man to see; and that is known as control of the you and control of the me. Our only opportunity is be, be, just be.

*****

When it's angels that you see, then you know that you just be.

*****

I'm only a tick in the clock of time. So be, O tick, and time not mine.

MARCH 1, 1983

Class March 2, 1983

[The following teachings were likely given to a small group of advanced students.]

In the pool of pity, the jewel shines brightest.

*****

Yes.
For irresistibility is the greatest challenge of the ego.

*****

Beware of Indians bearing gifts for it is but a vehicle of deception to satisfy hidden desires.[40]

*****

The jewel of any crown must shine or the throne, in time, is lost.

*****

Whoever accepts from God is free from the payment of man. And the payment, my friend, is ever dependent upon the honesty in the conscience deep within.

*****

Ready?
Yes.
When working with the force of mental substance, it is necessary to have, in consciousness, a point of direction of identification. Therefore, placement from Indian-givers that I have revealed establishes a point of contact, especially if it is something of a personal nature or something that is so personal that it is consumed.[41]

*****

The senses, of course, we know are many: from the original sense of touch or feeling, the sense of hearing, the sense of taste, the sense of sight. And so working in those realms, they use the sense which they believe has the greatest impact. And so that which enters within on the river of life that flows through us, of course, is indeed the greatest impact. Second on the list, of course, of impact is the sense of sight.

*****

The power of the Light is ever greater than the wrath of the human mind, for the wrath of the human mind exhausts itself, becomes depleted, and turns to appeasement. But the power of the Light is eternal. There is no appeasement. There's only honesty agreement.

*****

No mind can divide that which is indivisible.

*****

It's ready.
Games, they ever deceive you.
Laws eternally, they free you.

*****

Quality is God.

*****

[The following teachings were given to the larger group of students who regularly served at the temple on Wednesday evenings.]

The eternal being known as the I, formless, free Spirit, imprints itself upon the illusion known as mental substance and identify is known, and man believes. For now, form is, and belief he has. And so man believes in mental substance called the thought of I, but not the I. And in man's belief, he has at his disposal, in mental substance, the functions known as money, ego, and sex.

The great function of the throne is known as the need to control. It has at its disposal money or sex. Control not of what it is, for then that would not be a throne on which the king, the I, may sit. No, control of that which is beyond the throne: the domain and all that mental substance (the human mind) has to offer. And so control of that which is without, denial of the truth of personal responsibility, is the need of the thought of I on its throne of self in its domain of the mind.

And so in that great need, man ever seeks the Power that sustains him, for he does not know that he is the I, for knowledge, he has bitten from the fruit of the tree: he now believes in the fruit of his action and, believing in the fruits of his action, is attached thereto and deceived thereby. And so this great need, ever seeking the Power, the Light that is, becomes a great force in mental substance, goes out into the universe to fulfill itself that it may glorify its throne by ever increasing its domain. And man suffers and suffers and suffers from his own self-deception, the effects of his own denial, guaranteeing and revealing unto himself his own destiny.

My children, you have come unto this temple for the Light that frees your soul. There is nothing here for your temptations. There is no money. There is no sex. And there is no power your force can control. For it shall return unto you no matter who you are, no matter when you are, for the Law, the Light, the Life is free.

So, games are for the jungles beyond the walls and beyond the gardens of the eternal temple of Truth. They shall not get foothold within the temple, nor its garden, for the Light, the Truth, the Law shall reveal. Here, there is peace; there's harmony; there's joy, for there is truth and its effect is freedom.

All games, all force, all need shall forever be restricted beyond the walls and gardens of this temple of Light, for there are many souls at stake. And a half a soul with God is better than no soul at all.

In the many eons of time in which the Living Light Academy be, in those many centuries, no soul was ever sent out. Many souls have entered. And many souls have gone by their own choice between the force of mental substance, the self-deception of the need to control that which is beyond their right and their domain, that which minds shall never control.

So, needs of control, use your functions in the jungles in which they thrive. Leave them before you enter the gardens of Light. For if you do not, you are establishing the inevitable law, the inevitable law to turn your back and go your ways. So, think. Pause in your dictates and demands. Do you think for one moment that we, the Light of Truth that we serve, is not aware of what goes on? Do you think there is any force sufficient to blow apart the Power and the Light of Truth? Be not so deceptive in the glory of your thrones, for your jewels, they tarnish and shall disintegrate into the dust of whence they have been composed. They are temporal and cannot endure! The Light shall blind them. For Truth *is*.

Here, there is one authority. No one shall take it. No one shall give it. No one shall steal it. And no one shall buy it. And that authority, if we do not care to have faith in—for faith is the only thing that the Light is. Faith in God and not the senses. Be ye so illumined that ye know more than the Light of Truth that frees your eternal being, then pause and think: you cannot endure in the Light of Truth.

Games, children, you shall restrict to your jungles! There shall be no mental substance, no mind—though many errors it has made, though time and again it has gone against the Light of Truth, forgiveness is what frees. You have the personal responsibility to forgive that the soul, your soul, may be free.

And if you do not forgive and free, and if you insist on your authority of your sensing and illumination over the Light of Truth, then turn your back, if that's your need. We shall not stand in your way.

Now if that is not *clearly* understood and if there is any question on this demonstrable truth, then this is your time to speak or forever hold your peace! For peace shall be in this temple and its garden and all places which is its divine right of authority.

The principle of the divine right of this temple was well established with those who had earned the responsibility to enforce it. It has been transgressed and forgiven. Not forgotten. The Law of Personal Responsibility shall ever apply. Responsibility for your own needs, your own thoughts, your own vengeance, your own wrath is your right to keep within your own being. It shall never ever be your right to place it in this temple of Goodness no matter who you think you are!

Any further discord, any further mental substance that dares to rise supreme over the Divine Authority of this temple shall take the little soul back to the jungles that it spent so many centuries in, no matter who those souls be.

Be not deceived with cunningness and cleverness, for they are force. They cannot penetrate the power of truth and the Light of peace.

I am well aware of your needs. I am well aware of your games. Restrict them, children, for the sake of your eternal being. Restrict your wrath! Restrict your power that you think you have! Restrict your games! They have come to their end. The war is over. You have lost, O mental substance. You shall not rise again, for my channel, his coffin has not yet been nailed. And it's not going to be as long as I be. And I be as long as the Light so designs me to be the be.

I shall not permit my channel to suffer any more of your games within this temple of truth. I have instructed him explicitly: if it does not stop, the revelations shall be blinding to those who insist on their ego needs of vengeance, wrath, and power, which is their own self-deception.

You are not applying the demonstrable truth revealed to you as recent as last evening. That which has been cannot be. You are not applying the truth. You are deceiving yourselves. Stop this great con artist that you serve and free yourself in the light of joy before, for *you*, it is too late until the centuries upon centuries upon centuries roll on by.[42]

Good night.

*****

It's time, considering, supposedly, you came here for truth and freedom, that you remember more frequently what you came for and to reserve your needs to serve the mental world to the mental world that exists beyond this temple.

Now in principle it's time that you knew the cause of the decline in my health. For some time, I had worked diligently to expose your games, the games of your minds within this temple. And as time rolled on, I became more and more involved in a mental world to stop your own games, which were not only detrimental to your own lives but extremely detrimental to this temple and Light of Truth that it serves.

I had forewarned you, as students, to stop this that you were doing. And it became a constant demand of exposure and revelation to stop the games that were being played. Finally, it reached its peak last year, when two of my students transgressed blatantly the divine, eternal right of this temple: one, to establish its rules, its regulations, and to enforce those rules and regulations, which is the divine right and the authority of this temple that was not founded by mental substance or the needs of human minds.

That transgression has been forgiven, when it was established some time ago.

Now, in a mental world, one learns, of course, to forgive or give forth is human and it frees oneself from bondage. To forget is divine. And because the Light must shine through the mist of creation, the mental substance, it is not wise to forget. But it is truth, wisdom, and freedom to forgive or give to God. That has yet to be done.

If it is not done soon—and being done is a living demonstration, not a word. It is an application of the demonstrable truth: the laws that are, here, being revealed. If that is not done soon, greater Light must be shined upon it until finally it is done. For human minds only respond when they are cornered, for that's where has-beens live. They do not live in the Rotunda of Truth, for there are no corners in the Rotunda. There are only corners in mental substance.

So I want to assure the offenders who are present amongst us—and not that they are the only offenders, but they have offended a divine right of this temple and have been forgiven, not forgotten. And if they insist on the discord, the disturbance, which I, by my responsibility to be the channel for the Light to be revealed to you, must work diligently to keep the temple from being disturbed and being destroyed by the discord and the ever-increasing mental substance over the divine Light of peace, forgiveness, and harmony, then you be rest assured I will be with you on Earth long enough to accomplish that.

And I will be on Earth long enough to see that the work to be done is done. And it may be done at such an accelerated program that the one point [three] millions of dollars in assets that this church has shall be converted into instant cash to see that what is left is the truth uncontaminated by the falsifying hands of the copyists. If that's the only job I have left to do and the church closes, that job, I assure you, I will do, for those are *my* instructions. And no mind is so great, nor is it so powerful, with all of its beliefs, that it will stand in the way of what *shall* be done.

The only authority of this church and this temple is the authority of the founders. We are not the founders. We are the beneficiaries of the great effort of the founders. And we best not forget that, children. Because in our forgetting it, we play these childish games of mental, insatiable ego needs. And I assure you I will not speak with you again on this subject, for the next time I speak, it will be the full revelation of the transgression and the right of the temple: what it shall do about it. For it forgave it, but as it rises again, there'll not be another forgiving. For twice is the transgression.

Thank you.

*****

Now, [Student A], speak forth the truth that freed your soul as recent as last evening after you descended [when you were] upstairs.

All that has been—

Louder, please.

All that has been cannot be / That's not God and I'm not free / Until I give and then I be / The joy of life that sets me free.

Keep saying it until you're freed from what you brought in [to the temple].

*****

All the has-beens cannot be—

"Has been," [Student A].

All the has been—

"All that has been"

All that has been cannot be / That's not God and I'm not free / Until I give and then I be / The joy of life that sets me free.

Again. You can keep saying it until you're free. Again.

All that has been cannot be . . . All that has been cannot be . . . That's . . .

... *That's not God and I'm not free.*

Uh-huh.

Until I give ...

And then ...

... and then I be / The joy of life that sets me free.

Again. You can keep saying it until you're free. Again!

OK.

Again!

All that has been cannot be / That's not God and I'm not free / Until I give and then I be / The joy of life that sets me free. All that has been cannot be / That's not God and I'm not free / Until I give and then I be / The joy of life that sets me free.

Again.

All that has been cannot be / That's not God and I'm not free / Until I give and then I be / The joy of life that sets me free. All that has been cannot be / That's not God and I'm not free / Until I give and then I be / The joy of life that sets me free.

Again.

All that has been cannot be / That's not God and I'm not free / Until I give and then I be ...

The rest of it.

... The joy of life that sets me free.

Again, [Student A]! You're trapped by the great deceiver. Say it again. Say it. All ...

All that has been cannot be / That's not God and I'm not free / Until I give ...

And then ...

... and then I be / The joy of life that sets me free.

You came here for truth, freedom! Say it again. You didn't come here to be trapped by that con artist! Again!

All the has-beens cannot be—

All that has been ...

All that has been ...

... cannot be / That's not God ...

... That's not God and I'm not free / Until I give and then I be / The joy of life that sets me free.

Again!

All that has been cannot be / That's not God and I'm not free / Until I give and then I be / The joy of life that sets me free.

Again.

All that's been—

No.

—cannot be

No, [Student A]. All that has been ...

All that has been—

All that's been ...

I don't know which one—

All that's been cannot be. Go ahead.

All that's been cannot be / That's not God and I'm not free / Until I give and then I be / The joy of life that sets me free.

Again.

All that's has been—

No. All that's been ...

All that's been ...

... cannot be ...

... cannot be / That's not God and I'm not free / Until I give and then I be / The joy of life that sets me free.

Again.

All that's ...

Been ...

... been cannot be / That's not God and I'm not free / Until I give the thought—

Until I give ...

Until I give ...

... and then I be ...

... and then I be / The joy of life that sets me free.

Again.

All that's been cannot be / That's not God and I'm not free / Until I give and then I be / The joy of life that sets me free.

Again. Again.

All that's been cannot be / That's not God and I'm not free / Until I give and then I be / The joy of life that sets me free.

Again.

All that's been cannot be / That's not God and I'm not free / Until I give and then I be / The joy of life that sets me free.

Again.

All that's been cannot be / That's not God and I'm not free / Until I give and then I be / The joy of life that sets me free.

Again.

All that's been cannot be / That's not God and I'm not free / Until I give and then I be / The joy of life that sets me free.

Again.

All that's been cannot be / That's not God and I'm not free / Until I give and then I be / The joy of life that sets me free.

Again.

All that's been cannot be / That's not God and I'm not free / Until I give the joy of life—

Until I give . . .

Oh.

. . . and then I be. Come on, [Student A]. And then I be . . .

And then I be / The joy of life that sets me free.

Again.

All that's been cannot be / That's not God and I'm not free / Until I give and then I be / The joy of life that sets me free.

Again.

All that's been cannot be / That's not God and I'm not free / Until I give and then I be / The joy of life that sets me free.

Again. Again.

All that's been cannot be / That's not God and I'm not free / Until I give and then I be / The joy of life that sets me free.

Again.

All that's been cannot be / That's not God and I'm not free / Until I give and then I be / The joy of life that sets me free.

Again.

All that's been cannot be / That's not God and I'm not free / Until I give and then I be / The joy of life that sets me free.

Again.

All that's been cannot be / That's not God and I'm not free / Until I give and then I be / The joy of life that sets me free.

Better. Again. Again, [Student A]. Again.

All that has—

No.

All that's been cannot be / That's not God and that's—that's not God and I'm not free / Until I give and then I be / The joy of life that sets me free.

Again.

All that's been cannot be / That's not God and I'm not free / Until I give and then I be / The joy of life that sets me free.

Again.

All that's been cannot be / That's not God and I'm not free / Until I give and then I be / The joy of life that sets me free.

Again.

All that's been cannot be / That's not God and I'm not free / Until I give and then I be / The joy of life that sets me free.

Again.

All that's been cannot be / That's not God and I'm not free / Until I give and then I be / The joy of life that sets me free.

Again.

All that's been cannot be / That's not God and I'm not free / Until I give and then I be / The joy of life that sets me free.

How do you feel, [Student A]?

Pretty good.

Again. We have to go beyond pretty to beautiful. *[Several students laugh.]* Come on, [Student A]. Leave the recorder on, please. Leave it on.

It is. [The recording technician responds.]

Yes, [Student A]. Only a fool stops at something pretty. They wait for something beautiful. Yes.

OK. *All that's been cannot be / That's not God and I'm not free / Until I give and then I be / The joy of life that sets me free.*

Again.

All that's been cannot be / That's not God and I'm not free / Until I give and then I be / The joy of life that sets me free.

Again.

All that's been cannot be / That's not God and I'm not free / Until I give—[43]

[The microcassette ran out of tape at this point. At some point later in the class, the tape was flipped and the recording continued on Side B.]

*****

Yes. Now, we should be grateful to God, the Truth, the Light, flowing through [Student A's] soul, because, you see, it is the living demonstration of how you deceive yourselves and how you are trapped by your belief in your thought of self.

The repetition necessary of declaring the demonstrable truth—however many times it took [Student A]—is only equal to the bombardment, the repetition, and the beat of the judgment made by her mind to serve the glory of her own throne. Fortunately, it didn't take us three or four hours. It only took [Student A] a matter of minutes.

You best understand what controls you. Because if you don't, there's no truth to free you. Because you won't let it in. You may hear it. You may write it. You may record it. You may play it back. And it will be like a pointed heart unto your soul. Because you've got to learn from the living demonstration, for the Light is a Living Light, that your mind works the same way (the Law of Repetition) to control your soul.

And so, [Student A] entered the temple this evening a living demonstration, as she did last evening. Now [Student A] was out in the jungle for what—twenty-four hours?—and permitted herself to be re-bombarded by her own pride, which serves her throne of glory, by her own ego, by her own deception.

Now, it is not possible for me to be with you twenty-four hours day and night to free you from your needs of self-deception. I have given to you the way for you to save yourselves, for that is the law of the universe: no one can save you but yourselves. [If] you insist on believing in those things in mental substance, then you [have] got to be willing to pay the price. Because that's the law you have a right to establish. But the law of your right cannot and never shall supersede the law of the right of the temple. And that's [what] this, tonight's class, is all about.

Forgiveness? Yes. Forget? No. We are still locked in mental substance. And to forget *that* demonstrable truth is to serve the realms of darkness for who knows how many eons of so-called time.

Now—leave it on. *[The teacher may be referring to the microcassette recorder.]* So you clearly see that [Student A] lifted her soul. How do you feel now?

[It is difficult to transcribe her short response.]

Through the repetition of the law that frees us, for that's what truth does. It does not do it outside; it does it inside. That's the only place it can do it. Now I cannot, and no one can, transgress the demonstrable law of life and crawl inside of your head and do it for you. [Student A] has the truth, as you all have. She could have used that great truth a thousand times today and kept herself free from the great con artist of the universe: that *thing* that grabs the soul into the service of hell. You could have done that, correct?

I did, but not a thousand times.

You did not do it enough, did you?

No, I didn't.

Did you, did you do it thirty times, fifty times? You see—
I don't think it was thirty.
Pardon?
I don't think it was quite thirty times.
I know. It was not sufficient to keep you free.
It's true.
Do you see?
Yes.
When you're here in the temple, I know what to do, if you respond. And if you don't, you're in the wrong temple. Believe me. This temple does not offer—nor did it ever—the functions to serve the throne of hell. That is not its purpose. That has never been its purpose and never shall be its purpose. That's what this class is all about. Do you understand?
Yes.
Everyone? *[After a short pause, the teacher continues.]*
And so, by instruction of the Council this day, [Student H], in your soul evolution, has merited and earned the duty, the spiritual soul duty—because you do not have the cloud of has-beens to deceive you—to report directly to me of any sexual games being played within these walls, within this garden, or anyplace that this temple has the divine right of authority over, including the choir. For the choir is under the authority of this temple, and there is only *one* authority. Let us not deceive our self that there are two or three or four. There is only one. You have the responsibility, the spiritual duty, as of this day, to report directly to me any sexual fascination games within the rights of this temple. It is a transgression of the divine law that the board of directors have been instructed, long ago, to enforce. *You* have that duty, young man. And I expect *you* to demonstrate it without transgression! Understand?
Yes.
You're a married man. You have that duty. And may fidelity keep you free. Fidelity keep you free. I expect regular reports. I

will take it to the Light of Truth and the truth shall be revealed. And no mind, no matter who or how great they think they are, when the Light reveals to me, after forty-four years, the truth that frees, that is the only authority I will accept. For forty-four years of my life is a long demonstration. Our minds deceive us constantly. As [Student A], this evening, once again, freed herself with the truth.

We have not come to this temple for sex. We have not come to this temple for money. And if it's sex or money that serves the throne of the glory of self, we are in the wrong temple! These regulations, firmly established—that you all know—shall not be transgressed within this temple! Or you'll not have the continuity of the Light to free yourselves! There's plenty of men and there's plenty of women in the jungle! Don't come here for them! For it only brings disaster and clouds over the Light of Truth that frees you.

And I will not stand by and let any egos with their needs place a cloud over the Light of Truth that frees the souls. All wrath, all hell, all games—and it takes more than one to play a game; it takes two or more—out there! Otherwise, you're free to go. Take your choices. Believe me, I will carry on with my work, and there'll always be some soul in the universe seeking to crawl up to find a way, through honesty—not self-deception, but honesty—that has value, greater than money, greater than sex, has value for truth!—greater than power, which is only force to the ego.

I did not come here to give you money or sex or some crazy power that your mind thinks I may or may not have. That's not why I'm here. And that is not why I have stayed here! I want that *clearly* understood.

You have that duty! And I expect reports. And if you think that you are not man enough and have enough self-control to perform that duty, then you speak it forth in honesty this moment.

[After a short pause, the teacher continues.]

Do you think, [Student H], that you have, after all these years of effort and your love of truth and freedom, enough self-control to not become the victim in your spiritual duty and involve yourself in that realm of consciousness while in service to the Light of eternal Truth?

I feel I have enough self-control.

Thank you. Then the demonstration shall be the revelations. May God help your soul, for it's certainly going to need it, if the Light reveals to me that this insane game of sexual needs of the functions in the Temple of Light is supreme over what you *tell* me you have come here for, when that jungle is filled with it!

I assure you, in service to the Light and Truth, in the final analysis the only thing I value—all other things can go; for I know they go anyway. They all decay. And in the final analysis—and it doesn't take much more to push me to the final analysis—you will have the most beautiful, special church service—public—that you've ever heard in *all* eternity. If you dare show up! So keep up your games. I am not only capable, I guarantee you that I am more than willing, when Truth, the Light you supposedly have come for, is at stake! I do know how to fight fire with fire! And I know very well; that's how come I'm still here.

I know *they* know what the hell they're doing. *[The teacher refers to the Spirit Council.] We* better start waking up and find out just what in hell *we* are doing and just who in our consciousness we are serving! And we'd better find out before it's too late!

Now I've seen more than one soul taken out of the Light of eternal Truth by sex and money. That is not what this temple has to offer! And never was and never ever will be! Get the message straight! You have that duty to report.

This temple shall carry on, no matter who comes and goes. And when you love God as much as you love those functions, your freedom, your abundant good will be unbelievable to your mind.

And when you demonstrate the law that "Vengeance is mine saith the Lord"—vengeance is the law beyond mental control: it is the law of God's divine return, not the right of any brain's glory! Don't you ever forget that.

I don't play games. I'm not interested in them. I have something far more valuable to me. And I don't intend to give my life-giving energy seven days a week to that realm of you know what. Let the toilets take care of that. And I don't consider myself a toilet for anyone to use. And I hope that message is damn clear![44]

Just remember, those nails are not yet solid on my coffin. Don't forget that.

And you take your games—and you know who I'm talking to, students—and you'd better take them where they belong and you'd better keep them there. You want truth? You want classes? And I have to spend my life-giving energy taking care of and neutralizing the insanity of the games of the human mind and their unbelievable needs, when you've got a jungle out there that's loaded with that stuff? That's where it belongs and you'd better keep it there. In no uncertain terms. Keep your insatiable ego needs in that jungle. All of you. And especially the transgressors, who have passed number two and the third time action shall reveal the truth.

You came here for Light. You did not come here for money and sex! You keep your money and your sex out! Is there anyone who doesn't understand that in front of all these witnesses here on Earth? Is there anyone who does not? Please raise your hands.

[After a short pause, the teacher continues.]

You are presently clean. Do not involve yourself in those sexual games within this temple or you will no longer be qualified, nor have the authority, for the duty God has granted unto you this moment. You do understand, don't you, [Student H]?

I do.

Good. Then let us have coffee and encourage our self and never again be so deceived that the Light of eternal Truth, that knows what it's doing, shall be conned by any mental substance under any guise or any deception. Ever! You think you would get this truth that is demonstrable, that frees your soul, if it had to come through clouds of selfish deception?! Twisting and turning to serve that insane thing?! That the thought of I and the glory of self keeps us in service to? Really! Where are we? Where in hell are we?

In all my eternity, never once have I seen a soul who placed sex and money above their love of God, ever have I seen them free.

No one has ever instructed you to give it up. They have only instructed you of the demonstrable truth to recognize it for what it is and keep it number two! And here, you best keep it number two. You just best keep it number two or you establish an inevitable law that you will not long be here. Be rest assured. For the thing you serve will take you out. Not I. Not the temple. The thing you serve will take you out, again in your evolution. *[After a short pause, the teacher continues.]*

Declare that truth again, [Student A].

All that's been cannot be / That's not God and I'm not free / Until I give and then I be / The joy of life that sets me free.

Now if that great truth was being demonstrated by you students who have earned it—and of what value is it without application?—that would not only place you in the light of personal responsibility for your own thoughts, acts, and deeds, that would put your God of truth and freedom so great in your consciousness that you would be free in the hell and the midst of the Philistines, *if* you chose to apply it!

Well, around me, you better start choosing to apply it because I'm going to be around and I'm not going in the coffin for the nails to be pounded in. Because there's one thing about Truth: crushed to earth, it rises again. That's called restoration. And I know of no *thing* in mental substance that can restore like Truth.

And that's it. I love your souls. But don't let your minds deceive you, because I love your souls, that I will sell out the Light that I serve because I am not about to for anyone. No matter who they are. Because I have no attachment that is greater than my God, the Light of Truth. None. And for that, I paid my dues. And ever tempted, I pay them again. Because my God is greater than all the things the human minds could possibly offer!

I'm still human. But I've never forgot what freed my soul. Don't ever kid yourself. Ever! Not once have I forgotten what freed my soul. And because I have never forgotten what freed my soul, I know what keeps it free: the Truth. And no stupid, insane attachments to mental substance, no matter what the thought, the form may be!

You remember that, son, in your spiritual duty, hear? You are simply to report. That's your duty.

And I don't care who's doing it. After this night, they'd better never be tempted again. And as much sexual games as you have played, [Student H], in your evolution, you'll have no problem recognizing them. I happen to know that. Anyone as qualified in the sexual fascination as you, [Student H], has no problem recognizing it. Don't trap yourself in your spiritual duty and sell out your soul and crawl up through hell itself to, once again, gain the Light. You remember that for your soul. For you're the soul that's earned the duty.

Now, are there any questions on demonstrable truth? There's one thing about truth: it reveals and, therefore, demonstrates.

In the final analysis, as I told you, forty-four years of faith in God and his ministering angels, there is no mind, no matter how clever or illumined, can possibly, *possibly* tempt me to believe in mental substance over God's Light and his angels who administer it. Nothing can tempt me! No one can tempt me, no matter who they are!

Perhaps that's why this temple has so few students. And will have a lot fewer if those things don't stop this day. A lot fewer. But it will serve, yea, even greater, for the millions you do not see, they, too, are being served—their souls.

I'm not interested in what in hell you believe or don't believe. That's your right to the king of mental substance. I'm interested in the King of Kings, not that asshole, king of creation. I'm not interested in that stupid ass. I've spent enough centuries in service to that insane thing. My pride is not so great. Pride, yes. But not so great to sell me out again to that asshole.

Shut it off.

*****

Anyone attached to any form only reveals the glory, the sensation of their own attachment to their own little form.

*****

So, hold to your form and destroy yourself. You, your soul shall be free.

*****

Our duty and service to Lucifer, the king of darkness, is revealed moment by moment by the attachment, the great glory, the bondage of our form. For whoever loves their form more than they love God shall love the forms of all they see that is in keeping with the judgment of the form they think they be. And therefore, their great loyalty and duty to the king of darkness shall continue 'til the day in evolution they free their humble, little soul that it may soar to heaven's heights and view creation for what creation is: a tool to be used, not abused by attachment, the bondage, the sellout of the eternal being.

*****

The flag of victory of the king of darkness carried by all soldiers as they march in the shadowlands reveals the truth: "Self-love, self-love, I see, I see, the victory is me."

*****

Pointed hearts are those things that steal the affections of the heart, but can never take the heart.

*****

Truth is the Light. One Light. And it takes faith to follow one Light. For only one Light leads to freedom. All other lights may tempt us. And we, in our temptations, must pay the price of our own detours. And so, my friends, how many lesser lights may tempt you is ever dependent upon your love of self.

*****

It's known as doing your own thing in your search for truth and freedom.

*****

Obedience is the Law of Abundance. Good night.

*****

Choose wisely what you're obedient to. May it ever be the Light of Truth.

*****

The light of reason shining over disaster reveals the good that it contains and therefore wise are those who carry their lamp of honesty that the light of reason may shine and they may take from disaster the Good or God that sustains it.

*****

And therefore, be transformed by it.

*****

The rain of heaven is the tears of joy as your soul comes home once again.

*****

Nothing is ever lost; it only wanders, waiting to be found.

*****

It's called the wanderer in the mental world.

*****

You cannot destroy with a feather that which has been built by the sword.

*****

The garment of God is the veil of illusion; its intent: to be used, not abused. And ever to remember, the closet of infinity, you change many times, many lives, and many moments.

*****

So, use the form for the purpose of its design. Do not abuse it by believing that you be it.

*****

Whoever wastes a moment is a pointed heart, headed downward.

*****

Points are known for their ability to pull.

*****

So, look out, round hearts, they may pull your way.

*****

The pull of the point is the need of the joint.

*****

So, bladder beware.

*****

From nuts and bolts to bes made free
It's wonder and joy when we awake and see.

*****

Whoever makes hay while the sun shines is destined to burn the barn.

*****

Satisfaction, the degree thereof, reveals the love of self, for it is the sensing of form.

*****

So awaken, soul, and know the wonder, the glory, the joy that is, for you sleep in the senses and know disappointment, discouragement, and disaster.

*****

For your bondage is your own belief that you are the form. Fly to heaven and be free. Declare the truth, the truth, the truth you be.

*****

[The following teachings were likely given to a very small group of advanced students.]

Whoever accepts the gifts of life from God enjoys the use thereof. Ah, but he who accepts the gifts from man must ever pay the price of the loan.

*****

My friend, see clearly the difference between faith, God, and belief, man. See the difference between the eagle and the mouse in the trap.

*****

Beware of Indian gifts for they are but loans in the deception of boxes.

*****

Wise men are practical men; they always check the going interest rate before making their loans.

*****

Mortgages last, sometimes, for a lifetime in your peanut world.

*****

And a mortgaged house cannot be a free one, to come and go.

MARCH 2, 1983

Class March 3, 1983

[The following teachings were likely given to a very small group of advanced students.]

For that which is united, though difficult, is certainly the joy of life...

The more attachment to form, the more service to illusion, the more service to the shadowlands, the more discouragement, the more disappointment, the more seeming failure, the more hopelessness, the more pools of pity, and go on down the list. Only to rise and then the fall. Only to fall and then to rise. Gradually, surely, surely, slowly we rise within consciousness and the great peace that passeth all understanding is the joy of life. Hmm?...

... There is no power, no power greater than power which is united. Hmm?

Yes.

And the power is the service of the Light, the Prince of Peace—

Yes.

—the servant of the King who is the Light—

Yes.

—the King of Kings...

... We know that sunlight shall pierce even the most dense fog or mist... Look at a foggy day and tell me there's no light beyond the fog.

*****

Yes.

The expression of understanding is the reception of wisdom. *Thank you.*

*****

The neck of the temple in which your soul resides is indecent to expose to anyone who you are not, by contract, in service of sharing to.

*****

The neck supports the king, the ruler of the form. And the feet move the form. Both should be covered, for they are indecent to expose. It disturbs the conscience, for the heart is the ruler and that must remain open.

*****

Yes.

And so, my friend, understanding must flow in three points of the form: the flow of the feet, the movement of the neck, and the function of understanding. For those are points that often obstruct the flow of the river of life.

*****

My friend, for perhaps a bit more wisdom in your understanding, think. Feeling is at the point of the feet, the neck, and the function of understanding.

*****

They are the centers of the senses.

*****

Care for the feet and the neck. Be assured the rest will care for itself.

*****

The neck, which is the will, controls the affections. The feet representative of the movement of understanding is the release of the feeling. And so people move their toes in keeping with their feelings. And they turn and twist their neck in

keeping with what the will will allow for their feelings. Now, perhaps you understand?
Yes.

*****

Tell me, child, what do they do when the Light shines in the night? Moonlight. Necking.
Yes.

*****

The call of creation is the cry of the has-beens.

*****

Ofttimes no is God's direction for you don't hear the cry of the has-beens.

*****

Little peanut-heads, learn to feel and never peel those onion-heads of nothingness.

*****

Whoever peels the onion-head cries all the way to nothing.

*****

... And so, you see, organization is harmony.
Yes.
Harmony is unity. Unity is strength.
Yes.
The pillars of the Great Rotunda are the pillars of understanding. Hear?
Yes.
And the great roof of the Rotunda is the roof of wisdom. Hear?
Yes.
And the floor of the Great Rotunda—you hear?—
Yes.

—is the peace. Through understanding into wisdom does man pass on to the peace of the being. For the being, my child, is peace. Hmm. And the peace that passeth all understanding is the peace, as the understanding rises through the wisdom and grants its own foundation called peace...

... The Law of Giving. Now stop and think. All forms must give in order to live. The river of life flows through all forms.

Yes.

If man obstructs the river, he builds a dam.

Yes.

This life force, which is the fluid, *is* the Living Light.

Yes.

That's what the Living Light is. It is the manifestation of Truth. The Living Light is the manifestation of Truth. When man obstructs the river flow, the Living Light, which is the manifestation of Truth, man enters bondage.

Yes.

Man cannot live in bondage. He can only survive in bondage...

MARCH 3, 1983

Class March 4, 1983

[The following teachings may have been given to a very small group of advanced students.]

The sense of touch, being the original sense of feeling, when expressed, awakens the memory par excellence and the joy of the soul, its ability to enter is therefore opened.

*****

Stubbornness is the determination of emotion.

*****

What comes, what goes, illusion, creation knows. For that that is Light, True, and Be is constant, constant God in thee.

*****

. . . And so in all your efforts, remember, your conscience balance[s] your life.

Yes.

Your conscience! Not mental substance. Your conscience.

Yes.

For there, you clearly see all the errors, all the mistakes, all the weaknesses, all the strengths, all the temptations. . .

. . . It's—what covers conscience is the pity of self. . .

*****

. . . Hmm? Now, will, that which you are, divine will, the fullness thereof, is known as total acceptance.

Yes.

When you totally accept, you have the flood of consciousness of the Light itself. . .

*****

[The following teachings were given to the larger group of students who volunteered Friday night.]

—tation. I'll give this . . . Is the recorder on?

It's on.

Now, the time has come—and some of you were not present here last Wednesday—the time has come for us to grow up from spoiled brats and little children having our way, the way of our great con artists, as I worked with one of my students here today. Used a phenomenal amount of energy for that purpose. Well, I want you to understand, the energy is not available to continue on with effort in that way.

So, we've got to make a decision. [If] you want the Truth you came for, the Light that frees you, then stop the con games. Stop the self-deception. Apply what has been given you. It's a very simple truth. "All that has been cannot be / That's not God and I'm not free."

Now you came here to be free. You are not going to be free—it is not possible if you get ten billion words—until you apply the simple truth that frees your soul. Now if you don't apply that that is on that refrigerator[45]—where are you, [Student A]?—

I'm here.

—as [Student A] has applied and a couple of my other students this day, then you're not going to be free, are you?

That's true.

Were you free in the sixteen years, [Student A]? You had moments. But when those things, called has-beens, grabbed you [and] control[led you], when your love of self got so great those has-beens grabbed you, were you free?

No.

Now that truth on that refrigerator works. If you are not applying it, then it's blatant and it means your pointed heart is doing a grave injustice not only to yourself, but no one enjoys being pissed on, not coming to the temple and having that experience. Do you understand? And it's not going to be from any of my students because there is no law of the organization that says they have a right to be here. No law whatsoever. And I want it stopped, and I'm not going to use the [my] last breath on Earth to stop it! I expect the directors of the church to do their duty and stop it without spending the last drop of energy to stop it!

So the next time a student is told to read, audibly, that demonstrable truth, I expect it to be done in the spirit of gratitude: a demonstration that what you say you came here for, you *have* come here for; that you are not lying, deceiving yourself, and, in turn, attempting to deceive every other student that comes here. So no matter how great your ego, it is not greater than mine.

And I am not going to spend my life-giving energy begging, pleading, and driving out your has-beens because your motive for coming here, your motive reveals what you're after, no matter who you are. Now, your souls are welcome.

Stop that crap or I'm not going to be down here at all to give you anything. Now if you didn't get the message last Wednesday, surely, you best be getting it now.[46]

No one will kick you out; you'll kick yourself out by your own con artist, by love of self. The love of self is greater than the love of God, the truth, the freedom, the abundant joy and goodness that you say you come here for. You leave the con artist in the jungle where the con artist belongs with all his deception, cunningness, and cleverness. That's not why you come here.

You come here for truth! You work for truth! You don't come here just to wash dishes and eat. That's not your purpose of being here; [it] certainly is not my purpose. That's not our motive for coming here. So let's be honest with our self, finally, and stop this self-deception. Because you cannot deceive another 'til you first deceive yourself.[47]

Now—

*****

All right. We'll begin here. Stubbornness is the determination of emotion.[48]

*****

Vanity, O vanity, what great love I do see.
Vanity, O vanity, when I think you are me.

*****

The chance of romance is the gamble of control.

*****

Freedom is the divine, demonstrable Law of Self-Control.

*****

One God for freedom; several gods for bondage. So, the love of self that offers several gods is the bondage of hell itself. And when you no longer love the self and you begin to love God, which is the effect of controlling the self, you'll not only know freedom, you'll be freedom; and the abundant good of life, the joy of living, will be yours.

*****

Greedy people love conditional gods. Those are the gods that do what they want them to do when they want them to do it. It's known as something for nothing.

*****

Without fidelity, there is no freedom; there is only license of the lust, the bondage of the glory of self.

*****

[Fidelity][49] - freedom from temptation through the effort of self-control.

*****

Spoiled brats, demanding their own way, use the armies of has-beens to do so. It's called forces, belligerence, and [go on] down the list.

*****

It is their [the] final attempt of the armies of hell you are indentured to, after all cunningness, cleverness, and deception has lost.

*****

Honey is the glue of deception.

*****

Whoever loves self is destined to the bondage of form.

*****

Belief is force, mental substance; faith is power, the Light of Truth.

*****

Whoever doubts the truth believes the lie.

*****

[The following teachings may have been given to a very small group of advanced students.]

Friends, high noon or silvery moon, reason or romance ever is at your disposal. Use or abuse. Be. Don't try to be.

*****

Concern is the servant of emotion, denies the light of reason, binds the soul to form.

*****

Belief binds. Faith frees. For belief is the chain of the bondage of has-beens. Faith is the sword of truth.

*****

The softer the sheath, the sharper the sword.

*****

A sharp sword of truth is dulled in a sheath that is not soft.

*****

The golden fleece is soft and, therefore, cares well for the sword of truth.

*****

Dead in the water is the captain without the sail of reason.

*****

Dead in the water is emotions run wild.

*****

And so, he who seeks the joy of life must sail upon the river, for despair to those who lie dead in the water.

*****

For they shall drown in time.

*****

Fear reveals our great belief in form.

*****

The false gods that we worship through the love of self take many forms and have many names. That which disturbs us controls us. So when we desire to have something and we don't get it and it disturbs us, then we know, beyond a shadow of any doubt, the false god that we are worshipping.

*****

The deeper the water, the better the sail.

*****

Yes.
Wise men enjoy sailing for they listen while they sail. Fools take pleasure in sailing and are deaf to anything they hear.

*****

The reason that humor is a salvation of the soul is because it is the fruit of the Tree of Life, known as joy. Enjoy yourself.

*****

The abuse of friendship is the ridicule of self.

*****

The word *ridicule* means to rid oneself of something that is not in keeping with one's own judgments.

*****

Wise are those who greet with the raising of their left hand that there may be the action of reason in whatever they receive.

MARCH 4, 1983

Class March 6, 1983

[The following teachings were given to the larger group of students who volunteered at the temple Sunday nights. For various reasons, the order of this transcription may not be the order these teachings were originally given.]

The dictate of desire is the bondage of hell because it serves the prince of darkness.

*****

Now, does anyone see how the dictate of desire is the bondage of hell and how it serves the prince of darkness? Do we understand that?

Might as well set it down and just leave it on, [Student R]. It's an hour tape. And then we take out of it what we discard[50] . . . *[The teacher speaks a few words that are difficult to transcribe.]* What's a half hour? Set it down here. *[The teacher refers to the microcassette recorder.]* You never know what's going to come through. Ah, what you need is a little wood stand [to hold the tape recorder]. There. Right there. That's, that's plenty—or hold it.

Does anyone see how that works? Yes, [Student P]. Now, read the truth first.

OK. The dictate of desire is the bondage of hell because it serves the prince of darkness. [Student P speaks very fast.]

Oh, your pulse doesn't beat that fast.

OK.

Now if it does, you should be over at Marin General emergency.

OK.

Now, there are two ways that the tongue moves and the mouth speaks.

OK.

Now we all know—do we know what the mouth represents, [Student S]?

Yes.

What?

Truth.

Or?

I don't know.

Hmm. All right. Now I spoke to one of my students today revealing to them, when they mentioned to me that some people are able to come right up. They declare the truth and they rise right up. And some people can say it a thousand times and they stay down. In fact, they even go down farther.

Well, the spoken word, which is living-giving energy coming out of the mouth of truth, is not always truth. Ah, [it's] very simple. As [Student P] just read off da-da-da-da-da. *[The teacher speaks the "da-da-da-da-da" very, very quickly.]* It did not come from the heart that beats out the tempo of the word. It came from the mind. Hmm?

Now, I gave to you this wonderful truth: All that has been cannot be / That's not God and I'm not free / Until I give then I be / The joy of life that sets me free.

So, if you want to rise through your spoken word, if you want your word not to go out into the universe and return unto you void, but you want your word to go out into the universe, accomplish that which you've sent it to do [and] return to you in keeping with the Law of Divine Return, then it must flow from the instrument of your soul. And the instrument of your soul is your heart, not your head. Hmm?

Now, let us hear your explanation of how you think the dictate of desire serves and becomes the bondage of hell by serving the prince of darkness.

My understanding is the dictate, the judgment, or the limit from the mind . . . [Student P continues.]

Yes?

... of desire, and desire comes from God. So you're limiting God.

And how does the mind limit the divine expression, the desire.

Well, by putting walls up, by blocking it in, by—when you have a desire and you limit it by dictating to God how it will be fulfilled.

What is the dictate?

Well—

What is—what is it? What actually happens?

Well, the way I do it is by telling God how it will be done. Or, like, I suggest, like, well, maybe, this desire will be fulfilled this way or through this person or—

Through that person.

Right.

Then that doesn't happen.

Well, that is my understanding that that's how the dictate, the judgment, the wall against the divine flow . . .

The belief in man is at the sacrifice of the faith in God.

*****

And so in keeping with that demonstrable truth, faith frees; belief binds.

Pause [the recording].

*****

And so man must realize that like attracts like, becomes the Law of Attachment and he is bound by the belief, self-belief, self-love that serves the realms of darkness, the prince thereof.

Pause.

*****

Identification is form. Form is limit. And so it is the thought of I that is the belief. It is never the I.

*****

I, the I that you are, Truth, is awareness. The thought of I is the Light that is moved into form and you know belief.

*****

That is the movement of divine love to self-love. Whoever moves in faith *is* divine love. Whoever moves in belief is self-love.

*****

As I said, divine love or self-love, man is never left without the choice between freedom and bondage. And so we very readily see the divine expression known as desire, once impinged upon the consciousness, man chooses—it's total freedom, which it is upon the moment of impingement—to enter into the belief that he is the desire or the absolute faith that it is God's movement. There's no in-between. Take your choice: bondage or freedom. Falsehood, belief; truth, freedom.

*****

Those who know satisfaction are destined to regret, for they are the thieves who believe they are the desire and steal it for the prince of darkness, and that is where they know regret. Those who are honest accept the demonstrable truth: from God it came, to God it returns, for they are the wise men who stand on the circle of divine return, no concern, never ever in lack, want, and need.

*****

Laborers in the salt mines of satisfaction never rest, for [although] they weary, yet, the prince of darkness, the king of greed is never filled. The cup is ever empty.

*****

Now, children, show me the wisdom or joy of the sleep of satisfaction.

*****

Noon light is the joy of life. And moonlight, the sleep of despair, for all children, all souls are destined to awaken.

*****

Reason or romance is chance to the fool. It is the Light of Truth to the wise man.

*****

So where are you, self-control? Freedom, the joy of life, is waiting.

*****

It is the prince of darkness who dictates that self-control is lack. But the wise man knows the control of self is the joy of life, the Truth, the Light, the abundance of good, for it is when God flows, the river of the life, never a drought.

*****

Self-control is when *you* are the captain of the crew. And it is when they serve you and you no longer serve them and be the instrument through which the theft of goodness goes below.

*****

Whenever our love of self dictates how desire will flow through our being, we are limited. And yet the law is revealed: we thrive and are nourished and live on what is called Goodness or God. It is our love of self that limits the flow of the river of goodness. And so, with some of us, the goodness only flows through our need to eat and we cannot control our self, for God is greater than creation.

*****

Our pre—our perception and reception of truth is ever dependent upon the force of our beliefs.

*****

Romance is the absolute belief and conviction that the Goodness or God that you need is dependent upon something beyond your control.

*****

Romance is when the senses feel free to play.

*****

And has-beens won't let you be free unless you do what they dictate. And that's the problem with romance.

*****

The great need of controlling everything around us, of course, is dependent on our absolute belief that's when we feel good. And we realize that that's the only way we'll let God in: through the pride, the great queen and king, deceiver of the soul.

*****

Sharp tongues belong to alligators. Thin-skinned people are self-love fools.

*****

Want to erase it? [The recording technician asks. After a significant pause, the teacher continues.]

And so, in any experience in life man is never left without the choice of belief in the experience, losing the God that is in it, or faith in the power that is moving the experience and the truth and the freedom. To see the good in all things requires faith. For without faith, man is in the trap of bondage of his own self-love, called belief.

*****

Whoever believes they are the desire dictates to God their divine right to steal it for king Lucifer, the king of darkness, and his use.

*****

Pride restricts or limits through the love of self.

*****

Hallelujah, has-beens, heaven is waiting.

*****

[The following teachings may have been given to a very small group of advanced students.]
 ... Now, the eternal soul in the little house of old creation—
Yes.
—a wise man on his path, an enjoyment of freedom—hmm?
Yes.
—must ask the question, frequently, "Who am I?"
Yes.
And the answer comes from out of the great vastness of the infinity and eternity called Truth—for Truth is eternal and freedom, infinite. Hmm?
Yes.
So the question is asked frequently, "Who am I?" And the answer comes out of that great vastness, "I am truth." If it comes from the limits of old creation, it says, "*I* am [Student R]."

Uh-huh.

Hear?

Yes.

And so you hear the answer to your call, "Who am I?" And the answer comes, "I am truth." And presents the question, "What is truth?" And if you listen in the stillness, out of the great infinity comes the answer: "Truth *is* the consciousness of being." Hmm?

Yes.

And that, in turn, presents, in the illusion, a further question: "What is being?" Hmm?

Yes.

And in our stillness, we listen, we wait, and a soft voice speaks, "Being, be-ing is not what has been, is not what is to be; it *is* just be, which is free. And that *is* the Light. That is truth. Just be. Free. The Light. Joy." And all goodness surrounds the be, for that is the justice of Divinity. Hmm . . .

*****

Sensitivity is the mist of mental substance.

*****

Without the structure of a home, the covering has no value.

*****

For what is a boat without a hull?

*****

I'm only a breeze on the sea of time that fills the sail of the boat that's mine.

*****

The individualized soul is the divided soul. Now be, just be, united and free.

*****

The be soul is the united soul. The has been, to be soul is the divided or individualized soul.

*****

For the be soul is the free soul. And the divided soul keeps searching for what it knows it is a part of.

*****

So don't concern yourself with no man is an island. That's for divided soul. United souls are the ocean. And that surrounds the island. And without the ocean, the island would not be.
Yes.

*****

So understand the difference of what you think you be and what you be, that you may remain the joy, the free.

*****

The price of the tag is the piss of the heart.

*****

So only a fool drowns when he just wants to swim.

MARCH 6, 1983

Class March 7, 1983

[The following teachings were given to a very small group of advanced students.]

Capability is ever subject to endurance, for the flow and the fullness of the river is dependent upon its continuity. And therefore, man is opened to the will of God, which is the flow of the Living Light of Truth.

*****

Yes.
Eternity understanding, infinity wisdom. Good day. God be.

*****

You see, friend, truth is eternal and wisdom, indeed, is infinite.

*****

The double triangle is the form or vehicle through which the power flows and controls all creation.

*****

Yes.
    There's an island in the sky
    To which I'm going to fly
    There to be, no longer see
    There to be, no misery
    In that island in the sky,
    To all forms they're known to die
    On that island in the sky
    For that that die shall ever be.
    Hold not to form, do not see
    Be blind to all the things that seem to be
    And in the blindness you will awake

And know that I the day to make
In the island in the sky
Where the depths are the high
Where no shadows ever can be
On that island they don't see
Who must see to know and be
On the island in the sky
There's the place of unity
On that island in the sky
There's a soul that knows, that be
Two is one and when we see
That is island, you and me
There's no looking, nor is there waiting
On that island where we be
Fly away so high
View all life for what it be
Not the things you thought and see
On that island in the sky
Where all Light shall ever be
Unity, O Unity
You're the one and then the two
Yet you are the one that be
On the island, you and me.

*****

Welcome.

Yes. And so we take you now, my friend, to the gardens by the Great Rotunda. Our little class at this time, our little class, design, the true purpose of creation, called form. You hear?

Yes.

Now, we have just spoken on the flag of victory; we have just spoken on infinity and spoken on eternity: how in that process there is a fullness and there is birth. Hear?

Yes.

And the birth thereof. You hear?

Yes.

From the seed cometh design. Hear?

Yes.

What you would term, ah, geometric design.

Yes.

You hear? From that seed and the spin of infinity. You hear?

Yes.

And the spin of eternity. You hear?

Yes.

Through that process they balance in their great rapidity. Hear?

Yes.

For from the seed united the spin, the rapidity thereof, design be.

Yes.

Hmm? Design into the vastness of the universes being magnetic, being electric—hear?—

Yes.

—attracts unto itself like kind.

Yes.

And in the attraction unto itself its electric part repels all unlike kind.

Yes.

For in the great vastness of what is known as atoms—you hear?—

Yes.

—electrons, molecules and all those finer vibrations—hear?

Yes.

As it passes through the vastness, attracting, ever attracting its kind—

Yes.

—in design and repelling, through its great electric power, all alien parts not harmonious with itself—

Yes.

—design pulls ever more substance from out of the great vastness called space. Hear?

Yes.

Through its own motion. Hear?

Yes.

Now this spinning, retrospinning of design, throughout so-called space, slowly but surely becomes solidified. Hear?

Yes.

And that solidification process is from the great mist of the universes. Hear?

Yes.

And that great mist, attracted unto the original design, is known to man as form. Hear? . . .

*****

Thank you.

Yes, indeed, the eye of eternity, it's ever watchful, you hear?

Yes.

And it is that eye of eternity that is the witness of what you do, *you* do with your be.

Yes.

Now the physical be—you hear?—

Yes.

—ofttimes is not doing what the other be is doing, you hear?

Yes.

That's not unity and therefore man is weakened.

Yes.

You see. Now it's most important, most important in understanding the form, that identification with form is not possible without belief.

Yes.

Now we know that belief is a force, but we should understand that belief is the great magnet, now under the control of creation. You hear?

Yes.

Yes. And so when you understand that bondage is totally and wholly complete—you hear?

Yes.

When man is identified through belief, he's bound.

*****

... For whoever does a humble job and does it in the spirit of gratitude, you hear?

Yes.

And the joy for the opportunity of doing—pounding a nail or anything else—in that moment God and goodness goes in it.

Yes.

You understand? And the Goodness or God that is deposited returns unto the worker in God's ways, not man's ways. *[When the teacher said the word "man's", it was pronounced almost as a combination of the words "man's" and "minds'."]*

Yes.

You will remember that, won't you?

Yes.

And have a greater feeling of accomplishment, because, my friend, the goodness of the work is the Light and the fullness of life. You hear?

Yes.

And remember, it's in the doing. That's where joy is.

Yes.

In the doing. It was never intended—nor does it exist—in the receiving. You hear?

Yes.

For blessed are those who give, yea, greater than those who receive, for that is the law. And that is the door that opens to them if they will only knock and open it in the process of their giving of the goodness of life. . .

*****

It's on.
It—It—where?
It's on.
Infa-red. Beyond visual sight. Above, beyond, through identification with bondage. Infa—the action of infinity.

*****

Eternity, the act of infinity, is the view and therefore be! So let your act, your sight be infinite; by the Law of Total Consideration the principle is free.

*****

Friend.
Yes.
The apple that you see is the fruit and not the tree. And the tree is what you be, not the fruit that rots to be. And so, difference is dependent upon the love of self. Hear?
Yes.
For difference is form, the illusion of bondage. Difference is not principle, the path you be. Hear?
Yeah.
And so, when in total consideration of your being, not in error of the illusion that you think, but the Light that you are, no difference will you view, for no temptation shall be new. Good day.

MARCH 7, 1983

Addendum

Addendum from Class February 4, 1983

[Editor's note: the following teaching has been moved from the class in which it was given to this addendum. Ever in keeping with the divine Law of Merit, it was the practice of the teacher to give higher, more refined teachings to the more advanced students privately, while less advanced students received teachings in keeping with the laws they had established. Most of the teachings on the rib of Adam were given after this particular teaching. And in one of those later classes, students were asked to consider what the rib of Adam represents. To include the following teaching in advance of that spiritual exercise may deny students their opportunity for growth. Thus, this particular teaching has been relocated.]

Now.

Now.

The rib of Adam is the physical manifestation of the illusion designed by mental substance as a vehicle to serve the Divinity known as divine desire.

Addendum from Class February 6, 1983

[Editor's note: as above, the following teaching has been moved from the class in which it was given to this addendum in the hope that this adjustment would not deprive students of an opportunity to grow in understanding.]

—*the downstairs lobby.*

My children, the bladder in the temple of God is where the forms of illusion are created. From the very fluids, the essence within the temple. Therefore, it is your awareness of that realm of consciousness where they are created from the essence of the fluids of your temple that you must awaken to. For that is where they're born, it is where they live, it is where they breathe, it is where they take control for they are the magnet, they are the force. Your reason is your light, electric, flowing only through your conscious mind, which is the eternal moment. Your bladder, where those forms are born and live. They are in what you call beneath your conscious; below the light of reason they hide, the treason of the Light you are.

APPENDIX

The Divine Healing Prayer

I accept that the Divine Healing Power
Is removing all obstructions
From my mind and body
And is restoring me
To perfect health, wealth, and happiness.
My heart is filled with gratitude
For the Divine Law of Acceptance
That is healing both present and absent ones
Who are in need of help.
Peace, the power that healeth,
Is guiding my thoughts, acts, and deeds
As God and I go hand in hand
Living a life of joyful abundance.

The Total Consideration Affirmation

I am the manifestation of Divine Intelligence. Formless and free. Whole and complete. Peace, Poise, and Power are my birthright.

The Law of Harmony is my thought and guarantees Unity in all my acts and activities, expressing perfect Rhythm and limitless flow throughout my entire being.

Without beginning or ending, eternity is my true awareness and sees the tides of creation, as a captain sees his ship.

As the Light of Truth is sustained by the faculty of Reason, I pause to think and claim my Divine right.

Right Thought. Right Action. Total Consideration.
Amen. Amen. Amen.

Divine Abundance

Thank
(Gratitude)

You
(Principle)

God
(Divine Intelligence)

I'm
(Individualizing)

Moving
(Rhythm)

In
(Unity)

Your
(Realization)

Divine
(Total)

Flow
(Consideration)

The Controlled Spiritual Environment Affirmation

You are in a controlled spiritual environment of truth and freedom
Where peace and harmony reign supreme.
Be awake, be aware, be alert.
Your purpose of being is freedom from what has been.
Thoughts of self are foreign to this environment.
Take control of your mind and experience the joy of living.

The Law's Be

Our being is the consciousness, Truth.
Holy be the identity
The joy of Life
The totality of Acceptance
In mind as it is in heart
Grant us the Light
Our daily sustenance
And forgive us our has-beens
As we forgive those has-beens who tempt to steal our joy
Free us from the romance of self-love
Deliver us from the service to the false king of shadows
For Light is the kingdom
And the power and the glory forever
Peace be, the order of Divinity

The All That Has Been Affirmation
From A/V Class Private 12

All that has been cannot be
That's not Good and I'm not free
Until I give then I be
The joy of life that sets me free.

The All That Has Been Affirmation
From a Recording of Affirmations

All that has been cannot be
That's not God and I'm not free
Until I give then I be
The joy of life that sets me free.

The Beseeching of the Angels

[The version below is as it was spoken on the class recordings. The alternative fourth stanza is from a printed version.]

> O ye who once were mortals,
> Enrobed like us in clay,
> Come down from heaven's bright meadows
> And be with us today.
> Instruct us, loving angels,
> The way your glory came
> And wreathe about our foreheads
> Truth's glowing ring of flame.
> Come down, O blessed angels,
> Make earth and heaven one.
> And when our paths are shadowed
> Be ye our rising sun.
> Unfold us in God's wisdom,
> His beauty and his love,
> And may the earth life fit us
> To be like you above.

[An alternative ending to the last four lines is:]

> Enfold us in thy wisdom,
> Thy beauty and thy love,
> And may the earth life fit us
> To be like you above.

The Call of the Soul

> Rhythm, Harmony, Balance, Peace.
> Hold release, hold release.
> Thank you, God, I am at peace.

Oh, Love Divine

Oh, love divine, a servant be
'Til selfishness imprisons me
And warps the reason of my mind
Into the madness of the blind,
When truth cries out, "Not mine but Thine"
And frees my soul with love divine.

[I Speak my Word Forth Affirmation]

I speak my word forth into the universe, knowing that it shall not come back to me void, but accomplish that which I send it to do.

Light Upon the Shadows

[A portion of the text from Class January 26, 1983 is similar to the lyrics for the song, which was given through Mr. Goodwin's mediumship, entitled "Light Upon the Shadows."]

Wisdom in creation, the joy of life expressed
Brings light upon the shadows
And dew on every breast.
As dawn reveals her freedom
And dusk fulfills the day,
Love the light to come
In truth has shown the way.
Love the light to come
In truth has shown the way.

[The following text is from the personal notes of the vice president of Serenity, a man who also served as the cameraman for these classes. This procedure is referred in A/V Class Private 29, which was given on January 5, 1986. The exercise may also be the one the teacher refers to in the Twenty-Second Annual World Forecast, which was given on December 29, 1985.]

Acupressure of Circle of Logic

This procedure, as given by the Friends, is to help students restore balance in their universe, as long as effort is being made by the student who is the recipient of the procedure.

Procedure:

The student who is seeking help should sit, with back perfectly straight, on a stool or low back chair. Hands in lap, body completely relaxed.

Student to be helped, and one who will administer the pressure, should do the cleansing breath, three times. *[Note: A/V Class Private 30 also recommends that the person administering the pressure have clean hands and that their hands be rinsed with water immediately before and after the procedure.]*

The student who is to administer the pressure should stand behind the seated subject. Referring to diagram, place the index finger on top of middle finger. Be sure your finger nails are short enough so they won't dig into the other student's neck. Place the middle finger on the spot, point "A" on diagram, press firmly, and rotate tip of finger in small circle to the right, clockwise, 14 revolutions. Change fingers so that the middle finger is on top of the index finger, see diagram. Press index finger firmly, on same spot and rotate counterclockwise 13 revolutions.

Find spot "B" on diagram, and repeat procedure. Rotate middle fingertip 14 clockwise, then rotate 13 counterclockwise with the index finger. That completes the procedure.

APPENDIX 501

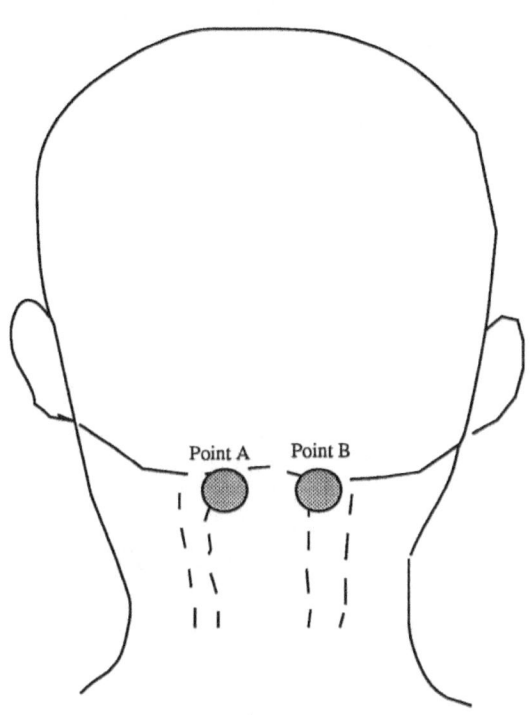

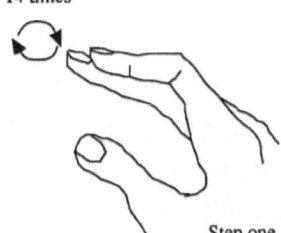

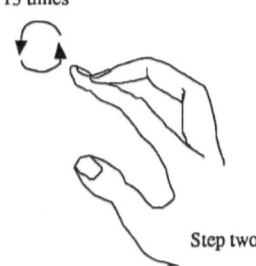

[In A/V Class Private 48, as well as in a few other classes, the teacher refers to a pamphlet that was published by Serenity many years earlier, entitled, "The Celestial Marriage." The title published on the cover of the pamphlet is "The Descent of Man," but the title page has two titles, "The Celestial Marriage" and "The Descent of Man." Here is the text of that pamphlet as it was published. An asterisk indicates a page break.]

THE CELESTIAL MARRIAGE

OR

THE DESCENT OF MAN

A FABLE
FROM
THE BOOK OF LIFE

*

GIVEN IN HUMILITY
TO ALL
HUMANITY

*

One day in great **ASPIRATION GOD** sent forth from itself **WILL**, and the sons of **WILL** became. Now the sons of **WILL** were of **GOD**, yea, they were **GODS** sent into form, but knew not because of form. The sons of **WILL** roamed the universes for eons and eons of time ever seeking other forms. After much searching they met to consider what they must do. For seven days and seven nights they discussed, and at the seventh hour **ILLUMINATION** fell upon them and said, "Behold, sons of **WILL**, within thyself is **COMPASSION**, know it, and unto thee shall be given." Alas, the sons of **WILL** knew **COMPASSION** and that night the daughters of **DESTINY** became.

In the morning when the daughters of **DESTINY** awoke to the sons of **WILL**, the **GODS** and **GODESSESS** of nature danced in jubilee.

Now the sons of **WILL** married the daughters of **DESTINY** and all nature wept with joy.

One day in **TRUTH** a son was born, his name was **INEVITABLE**, and the sons of **WILL** were greatly pleased. Now the daughters of **DESTINY** were quite unhappy for they **HOPED** for a daughter, and so that night in **DESIRE** a girl was born, her name was **LUST**.

Now **INEVITABLE** grew in the warmth and sunshine of the day. Oh how he loved the sun, for to him all **LIFE** was **LIGHT**.

LUST grew up to be a beautiful and lovely woman with a great fondness for the moon and darkness, for had she not been born in the night of **DESIRE**.

Time passed on, and one day **INEVITABLE** felt he would go into the night to find **LUST**, for he had heard so much about her, and had sent her many messages asking her to come into the **LIGHT** so that they may know more of each other. **INEVITABLE** went down, down into the darkness of night, and as he descended a great **FEAR** overcame him, but he found **LUST**, her face glowing so beautiful by the reflection of the sun. From the shadows where the **LIGHT** of the moon shone not, a voice spoke unto **INEVITABLE** and said, "Behold the beauty and the glory thou hast found, is it not worth the descent into our realms?" But from within, a voice spoke to **INEVITABLE** and said, "Take her to the realms of **LIGHT** that you may see more clearly in a day of **REASON**."

The senses won, and that night in **DESPAIR** a child was born, her name was **GRIEF**. The years passed and **GRIEF** could not be comforted, for she had been born of **LUST**, in the night of **DESIRE**, by the promptings of **PASSION**, and knew not of **TRUTH**.

INEVITABLE wandered on and on with the daughter **GRIEF**, hoping to return to the realms of **LIGHT**, but no, the centuries passed and only **SORROW** did they know.

Then one day a bird from the realms of **LIGHT** landed on his shoulder and sang this song, "In **SORROW** doth thou stay for self-pity knows no way."

INEVITABLE thought and thought of the meaning of those words, then he thought of his homeland **TRUTH** where he had been so very, very happy; and in **CONCENTRATION**, he found himself leaving the realms of darkness, passing through the lands of **IGNORANCE** and **EXPERIENCE** to return to his blessed land.

LOVE ALL LIFE
AND KNOW
THE LIGHT

*

OH MAN THINK HUMBLE
YET WELL OF THYSELF
FOR IN THY THINKING
IS CREATED
THE VEHICLE OF
THE SOUL

Cover Image of 1972 Edition of *The Living Light*

[The cover image of the 1972 edition of The Living Light *is displayed on the frontispiece of this volume. Reference to the symbolic image is discussed in excerpts from the following volumes of* The Living Light Dialogue:*]*

[Volume 2, Consciousness Class 44, pages 480-481:]
"And we'll begin with the outside of it, which is the snake, representative of wisdom consuming itself. Now why does the symbol of wisdom consume itself? Does anyone know? Does anyone know why wisdom is self-consuming? Because, my friends, if it's wisdom, then it can gain nothing from outside of itself: it already is wisdom. So all that wisdom is—you understand, you don't gain wisdom and neither do you give wisdom. Wisdom is self-sustaining. When you rise to a level of consciousness where wisdom expresses itself, then you will become it and it is self-sufficient unto itself. So the snake consuming itself is representative of wisdom, in comparison to what one might call knowledge. Now, knowledge is something that you gain. It's something that you put into your brain and you feed back at your discretion—but not wisdom.

"The next step is the interlaced double triangle, which is a very, very ancient symbol. It is the meeting of the spirit with matter. It is the power above that meets the forces below. And at that junction, when those two triangles meet, that's the negative and the positive poles come together in creation and the divine spark, the rays of light, life is so-called born into matter.

"Now you all know that all poles are triune. The negative pole is triune and the positive pole is triune. In fact, my friends, as we've stated before, all things that are manifest are triune and that is why three is the number of manifestation.

"Inside of the interlaced triangles you'll notice on the top of the pyramid in the rays of light is the all-seeing eye. Now the all-seeing eye is that that is not distracted, because it sees everything and so nothing gains its attention. And that is why it is the all-seeing eye. The triangle itself, the pyramid upon which all knowledge, the all-seeing eye, all wisdom, and all life rest, is the pyramid of manifestation. All things in all universes (physical, mental, or spiritual) are triune. There are three parts to all things: that is an absolute fact of physics and it is a truth of the universe."

[Volume 4, Consciousness Class 78, page 172:]
"Then, we'll be happy to share our understanding. The serpent so designed—consuming itself—is the ancient and eternal symbol of everlasting and eternal wisdom. The double triangle, with its apex downward, is the manifestation of the Divine Power and the balance of nature, its own creation. The pyramid with the all-seeing eye on the top is the eternal Light that never closes, that sees all things, that knows all things, and that ever is and ever has been."

NOTES

1. Mr. Goodwin was born and raised in Maine, while the student he addressed was from California.

2. The class was likely given in the dining room of the temple. So, the library offered more privacy for the measurement of the bust protrusion.

3. Carol Doda was a renown burlesque dancer in San Francisco.

4. Although the teacher seems to say "pet," he can be heard gently patting what could be his face or his legs with his hands. Mr. Goodwin was raised in Maine and, at times, spoke with a Maine accent. So, "pet" could be "pat."

5. Again, although it sounds that he said "pet," it may be "pat." The background sound suggests that the teacher is gently, rapidly patting his face with his hands.

6. The background sound suggests the teacher rapidly pats his face.

7. This class was given at the temple, where Mr. Goodwin had living quarters in the upstairs east wing.

8. The teacher may be referring to when he was informed by the Spirit Council that a class was to be given. Informal classes were often held with little or no notice to the students.

9. Street shoes were not permitted to be worn in the temple. Everyone entering the temple changed from their shoes into slippers that were used exclusively indoors.

10. The recording technician informs the teacher that the recording level is low because he stepped away from the microphone.

11. Based upon the recording level of the tape, the teacher may have realized that he has again moved away from the microphone.

12. Based upon the recording level, the recording technician asks the teacher to move closer to the microphone.

13. This particular class was being held in the dining room of the Serenity temple, which was adjacent to the kitchen. The kitchen offered more privacy to Student Q, but still permitted the students in the dining room to hear her hum.

14. The recording of classes that were part of a series, like the Consciousness Classes, the Church Lectures, or the Church Questions and Answers, were typically made available at the time the classes were given. With many of the individual classes, however, recordings were not made available to the students. But on some occasions, students were permitted to ask for permission to listen to the recording in order to transcribe in longhand those teachings.

15. This indicates that more complete conversations were initially recorded, but were edited later.

16. Student P and Student H are married.

17. The missing text, which was not recorded, is from a student's personal notes that were written as the class was given.

18. There is no recording dated January 25, 1983. Many informal classes were not recorded.

19. The teacher seems to pronounce "infared," not "infrared." Yet in other classes he seems to say "infrared." Although "infared" could be a mispronunciation, it could also be a conscious choice by the teacher. Given that Mr. Goodwin passed on many years before these classes were prepared for publication, it is difficult, at this time, to seek clarification.

20. Teachings that were given to more advanced students were sometimes given to a larger group of students. And some

teachings were repeated on different days because some students may not have been present when it was initially given. However, the repetition could also be an effect of the editing of the tape recordings. Regardless of the cause, the surviving tapes, including repetitions, have been completely transcribed.

21. The missing text, which was not recorded, is from a student's personal notes that were written as the class was given.

22. At one point in this class, according to a student's personal notes from this class, one of these teachings was twice recorded, but not captured on the tape. According to the teacher, the microcassette recorder was working properly, but the teachings were not recorded the first two times because various forms initially prevented it.

23. When a student, who had been present when these teachings were given, transcribed them, this title was included in that transcription.

24. Although the teacher would sometimes say "Ah," and although these volumes are word for word transcriptions of the classes, few "Ahs" appear in the text. Using as an example the various teachings that were printed while Mr. Goodwin was on Earth, including the textbook, *The Living Light*, the monthly magazine, the *Serenity Sentinel*, and multiple other publications that did not include the word *ah*, that word was not included in the transcriptions. Interested students are encouraged to listen to an audio or video recording of any Living Light Philosophy class to gain greater insight into this particular teaching.

   The group the teacher refers to is the group of students who attended the temple on Sunday nights. The Sunday night group was a small group of dedicated students. It was open by invitation only and then only to students who consistently demonstrated their support of the organization through their selfless service and the sincere efforts to apply the teachings of the Living Light Philosophy. Much of the teachings in this volume were given to the Sunday night group, and some were given to even a smaller subset of students.

25. The missing text, which was not recorded, is from a student's personal notes that were written as the class was given.

26. The name of the religion spoken by the student has been replaced.

27. Some of the teachings may have been repeated on different days because not all students were present, and the teacher may have repeated the teaching for those who were absent when it was initially given. However, there may have been other reasons for the repetition of various teachings.

28. Although this sentence is accurately transcribed, the teacher may have misspoken. Without access to the teacher through the mediumship of Mr. Goodwin, it is difficult to get clarification on transcription questions.

29. The teacher informs the students that they will be given the opportunity to hear the recording of these teachings. While recordings of the classes in a defined series, like the Consciousness Classes or the Church Lectures, were made available to the students, the recordings of most of the individual classes were not made available.

30. Students at the temple experienced change quite often and many times their mental forms (has-beens) would react emotionally, which often resulted in an exposure or a discussion in which their thoughts, emotions, and actions were exposed to the light of reason. Usually there was at

least one exposure whenever students were present at the temple. Sometimes there was more than one, and on rare occasions, there were none. So, the students were very familiar with what their has-beens had to offer after an exposure.

31. The "O" in "O be" is about eight seconds. The "be" is about seven seconds. The words "O be" are spoken like a mantra.

32. The ellipses indicate a pause, but no words are missing from this transcription.

33. The missing text, which was not recorded, is from a student's personal notes that were written as the class was given.

34. The missing text, which was not recorded, is from a student's personal notes that were written as the class was given.

35. "The Battle Hymn of the Republic" was often sung by the congregation during the Serenity Spiritualist Church services.

36. In these teachings, each year is characterized or, perhaps, represented by a different animal. 1983 was the year of the lamb. For a broader understanding of this teaching, consider studying the characteristics of that animal, including both their positive and negative traits. Be it in Divine order, future volumes may provide the animals representing other years.

37. For almost two seconds, there is no recording. There is no indication on the recording that the recorder was stopped and started.

38. Although there is a six-second gap in the recording that separates the two teachings above, students' personal notes written during this class suggest they are continuous.

39. The missing text, which was not recorded, is from a student's personal notes that were written as the class was given.

40. For additional insight, please see the teachings given later on this date.

41. For additional insight, please see the teachings given later on this date.

42. Editor's note: Although it is not within the scope of these transcriptions to comment on the tone of any teaching, it seems appropriate to note that the tone of this class is one of the sternest of any of the recordings.

43. Editor's note: Again, it is not within the scope of these transcriptions to record the tone or the feelings associated with the words spoken in these classes. However, with this recording, it is clear, even to the casual listener, that the tone of the affirmations spoken by this student changes dramatically over a short period of time, as she makes the effort to climb from one level to higher levels of consciousness. The full impact of many classes may only be appreciated when they are heard.

44. Editor's note: It was extremely, extremely rare for Mr. Goodwin to curse. Yet, in this instance, he found it appropriate in order to communicate with the level of consciousness on which the majority of energy was being expressed by his private students, who were the only ones permitted at the temple. Since he so rarely swore, when he did, it made an even greater impression upon his students.

45. The "All That Has Been" affirmation was written on a piece of paper and attached to the door of the refrigerator in the kitchen of the Serenity temple.

46. On some occasions, Mr. Goodwin would, for various reasons, remain in the east wing of the temple for the time the students were present at the temple. That is, he would not see the students. The east wing was Mr. Goodwin's private apartment and was located on the floor above the main floor. Students typically worked on the main floor, in the rooms below the main floor, and in the garden. The reference to not coming down refers to not coming down from the east wing to teach, guide, encourage his private students.

47. Most evenings when the students were at the temple were spent working, including watering in the garden, working on bazaar projects, preparing the articles for the *Serenity Sentinel*, printing the church programs, baking goods for the monthly bake sale, or cleaning. On Friday evenings, however, students had dinner with Mr. Goodwin. So, his reference to washing dishes and eating may refer to the Friday night dinners.

48. Some teachings that were originally given to advanced students were repeated for the benefit of the larger group of students.

49. The missing text, which was not recorded, is from a student's personal notes that were written as the class was given.

50. The teacher again refers to the practice of recording extended conversations and then editing the recording to remove more personal topics and preserve teachings. This practice explains why some of the microcassette classes are more complete than others.

www.ingramcontent.com/pod-product-compliance
Lightning Source LLC
Chambersburg PA
CBHW030508080526
44586CB00011B/108